PITT LATIN AMERICAN SERIES

D1599906

To Hell with

PARADISE

A History of the
Jamaican Tourist Industry

FRANK FONDA TAYLOR

UNIVERSITY OF PITTSBURGH PRESS
Pittsburgh and London

For My Mother
Olga Herminia Taylor

Published by the University of Pittsburgh Press, Pittsburgh, Pa. 15260
Copyright © 1993, University of Pittsburgh Press
All rights reserved
Manufactured in the United States of America
Printed on acid-free paper

Library of Congress Cataloging-in-Publication Data

Taylor, Frank.
  To hell with paradise : history of the Jamaican tourist industry /
Frank Fonda Taylor.
    p. cm. — (Pitt Latin American series)
  Includes bibliographical references and index.
  ISBN 0-8229-3754-9 (acid-free)
  1. Tourist trade—Jamaica—History. I. Title. II. Series.
G155.J25T4 1993   93-1004
338.4'7917292—dc20   CIP

A CIP catalogue record for this book is available from the British Library.

Eurospan, London

Contents

Acknowledgments

THIS BOOK has been long in gestation—perhaps too long. The main body of the research was done between 1969 and 1971, in connection with my University of the West Indies (UWI) Master's thesis in history, entitled "The Foundation of the Jamaica Tourist Industry, 1890–1914." Immediately on completion of this dissertation in 1971, the time period focused on in my initial research became extended, when I undertook a project on behalf of the University's Institute of Social and Economic Research (ISER) to study the Jamaica tourist industry between 1919 and 1939. I owe a profound debt of gratitude to my mentor, Dr. Alister McIntyre, at present vice chancellor of the University of the West Indies, for the opportunity to engage in that extended study in 1971–1972, when he served as director of the ISER. I am indebted likewise to Professor Douglas Hall, now retired from the UWI's Department of History. It was on Professor Hall's advice that I ventured into this hitherto unexplored area of Jamaica's past, and with his skillful guidance as my thesis director, brought the work to a conclusion. However, foremost among the original contingent of persons who inspired this work is my former wife, Ms. Regina Dumas. Her understanding, forbearance, and invaluable comments are cherished memories, and her friendship a lasting treasure.

Unquestionably it would not have been possible to have done research of this nature without the assistance of the very kind and helpful library staff at the Institute of Jamaica, in particular, and at the main library of the University of the West Indies. I am especially grateful to Miss Dunn, then at the Institute of Jamaica, for the assistance she rendered to me in obtaining some of the information. On a more recent quest for data a few years ago, I received some very useful assistance from Mrs. Pauline Kerr at the Library of the University of the West Indies; for this I wish to record my deepest appreciation. Likewise I wish to record my appreciation to Miss Marie Bailey of the National Library of Jamaica, for assistance extended to me during my January 1992 visit, and to Miss June Vernon of the same institution, for assistance given over the years of data collection.

Regarding the financing of this research, thanks are due to the University of the West Indies for the award of a postgraduate scholarship that enabled me to undertake the work in the first place. Later, after I joined the faculty as a teacher, I received sundry other forms of assistance that permitted me to extend my investigation of the subject in question. Lastly, I owe a deep debt of gratitude to the Hamilton College administration, and to Dean Eugene Tobin in particular, for a generous grant that enabled me to pursue research in Jamaica in January 1992 and thus to complete this study on the Jamaica tourist industry.

Over the years, many of the chapters of this book have appeared in some fashion or the other. I am grateful to the editors of these publications for the permission to reproduce them here, bringing the work together in print under one cover. The chapters that appeared earlier in print whether in whole or in part are listed here. Chapter 2 originally appeared as "From Hellshire to Healthshire: The Genesis of the Tourist Industry in Jamaica," in *Trade, Government and Society in Caribbean History 1700–1920: Essays Presented to Douglas Hall*, ed. B. W. Higman (Jamaica: Heinemann Books [Caribbean], 1983). Chapter 4 appeared as "The Resurrection of Jamaica: The International Exhibition of 1891," *Revista/Review Interamericana* 14 (1984). Chapter 5 appeared as "The Ordeal of the Infant Hotel Industry in Jamaica, 1890–1914," *Journal of Imperial and Commonwealth History* 16 (January 1988). Part of chapter 6 appeared in my analysis *Jamaica—The Welcoming Society: Myth and Reality* ((Jamaica: Institute of Social and Economic Research, 1975), *Working Paper No. 8*. Chapter 7 was produced earlier as "The Burial of the Past. The Promotion of the early Jamaica Tourist Industry," *Boletin de Estudios Latinoamericanos y del Caribe* 40. Some of the material on the Jamaica Tourist Association presented in chapter 7 appeared as "The Birth and Growth of the Jamaica Tourist Association 1900–1914," *Jamaica Journal* 20 (November 1987–January 1988). Finally, chapter 8 appeared earlier as "The Tourist Industry in Jamaica 1919–1939," *Social and Economic Studies* 22 (June 1973).

Many people associated with the enterprise unfortunately cannot be mentioned; to all I owe heartfelt thanks. Special mention, however, must be made of Ms. Marlene Saunders-Sobers, administrative assistant at the UWI, Trinidad, for the encouragement she offered when I began to put the material together for publication in book form and for her work in typing some of the earlier draft chapters. I am also indebted to Mrs. Janice Edwards, secretary at the Department of History, UWI, Trinidad, who typed the first draft of this work, and to Ms. Rita Ordiway, secretary at James Madison College (Michigan State University) who at short notice but with patience and good humor prepared a penultimate version of this work. Last but not least my wife, Belinda Anastasia Taylor, typed the final chapters of the book and inspired me to bring the work to a successful conclusion. For that I am deeply grateful.

As the title of the work I have chosen the famous phrase "to hell with paradise," first uttered by James Mitchell of St. Vincent. The occasion on which Mitchell is said to have coined this expression was the Caribbean Travel Association's 1972 Haiti meeting, where he insisted that the paradise marketed by regional tourist boards has never existed. This historical conflict between myths and reality is uncovered in these pages on the Jamaican experience.

To Hell with Paradise

Chapter 1

Introduction

JAMAICA IS a small island situated off the southern tip of the Florida peninsula in North America. Located at 17° to 18° north latitude and 76° to 78° west longitude, it is about 4,000 nautical miles from London but just 1,500 miles from New York and 1,100 from New Orleans. Because of its proximity to the United States a strong pull has long been felt in Jamaica from its continental neighbor; and indeed, though the political, economic, and cultural predilections of the ruling classes in Jamaica were riveted upon Britain during the colonial past, the countervailing influence of the United States was always seductive. By 1900 the island found itself at the very epicenter of the geographical sphere of U.S. interests in the Caribbean. Given its locus among Caribbean Basin territories, Jamaica holds a place of especial significance in the study of regional problems. As one author remarked with perspicacity in an 1898 publication, in this island the most typical Caribbean Basin questions can be viewed in microcosm by the research analyst.

The island is almost at the exact centre of the great American Mediterranean. It lies just half-way between Galveston and the mouth of the Orinoco, the southern point of Florida and the northern part of South America, the eastern end of the Antilles (St. Thomas) and the western indentations of the Gulf of Honduras, and the most northern of the Bahamas and the Gulf of Atrato. *This position is important from political, geographic, biologic, and geologic points of view, and makes the island a typical base of study for one interested in Antillean problems.*[1]

Physically, Jamaica is a most beautiful place, and today it is an internationally renowned tourist resort. But it was not always

3

recognized as such. At one time diseases were so rampant in the Antilles and the mortality rate so high that travel to (or residence in) the region was thought by whites to be quite unwholesome.[2] Yet, whatever the historical reputation of the Caribbean with regard to salubrity, by the turn of the twentieth century the image of the area had undergone so drastic a transformation that these shores were instead lauded as eminently desirable places to visit. So much, for instance, had Barbados become a vacation resort by 1911–1912 that the colonial secretary was obliged to note in his report, "the colony owes much of its increasing prosperity to the visitors who stay in the island."[3] These came not only from North America and the United Kingdom but from South America as well, particularly from Brazil.[4]

The Bahamas likewise had been emerging as a rich man's paradise as far back as 1873, when it had recorded its largest tally so far of visitors, with nearly five hundred arrivals.[5] The takeoff of Bahamian tourism occurred, however, in the 1890s, when Henry Flagler, who had brought the Florida East Coast Railway to Miami, turned his attention to Nassau, where he not only purchased but built hotels.[6] Still another boost for Bahamian tourism came in 1895 when the second independence war broke out in Cuba, diverting to these nearby isles the hundreds of Americans who had been in the habit of visiting Havana. As for Cuba itself, one American tour organizer alone, Colonel H. B. Plant, brought some 20,000 visitors to the island each winter season prior to the outbreak of the 1895 rebellion.[7] In short, from Barbados to the Bahamas, Cuba to Bermuda, by the early twentieth century these islands began to be transformed into playgrounds for itinerant Caucasians in search of health and enjoyment.[8] Once tropical plantations, purportedly unfit for white residence, these islands were being touted as veritable gardens of Eden.

Placed in historical perspective, the growth of tropical island tourism was but the spillover into these parts of the passenger traffic until then confined to a holiday circuit in the North Atlantic. Modern tourism owed its gestation to the industrial revolution and the need it engendered for periodic relief from the psychological stresses and strains of the factory system and urbanism.[9] Facilitating this imperative for the occasional holiday in quieter and healthier surroundings was the growth of mechanized transport, which was making substantial strides forward at that time. Perhaps the greatest revolution in transportation since the inventions of the wheel and the sail was the creation of the steam engine, and through it the railway and steamshipping. Steam, which had played such a dynamic role in the industrial revolution, on being applied to transport in the nineteenth century made it possible for far more people to travel, and travel far more cheaply, than before. As the demand for travel grew the tour operator made his appearance, a reflection in itself of the quickening pace of life.[10]

The earliest and most renowned of these agents was Thomas Cook. In 1841 he embarked upon his career as a tour organizer and arranged an excursion by train from Leicester to Loughborough for 570 trippers at a return fare of one shilling per person.[11] A decade later Cook was arranging travel and accommodation for 165,000 visitors to the Great Exhibition in London. Following that, he initiated trips to the Continent, beginning with the Paris Exhibition of 1855. Such was his success that 20,000 people participated in Cook's tour to the Paris Exhibition of 1867 and over 75,000 to the exhibition of 1878. By 1866, Cook ventured into transatlantic tours with the organization of his first trip to the United States. It was from this developing holiday enterprise, therefore, that some individuals in the 1860s felt Jamaica could gainfully benefit, by promotion abroad as a health spa.[12]

That tourism as a phenomenon first materialized with the industrial revolution is demonstrated by the fact that the word itself had not existed in the English language before then.[13] In the manufacturing centers of the U.S. northeast, around 1800, where Puritanism held sway, a lust for recreational travel (i.e., tourism) was considered something morally reprehensible—as sinful as alcohol and as aberrant as sexual fantasy.[14] But a quarter of a century later, change had commenced with the inception of tourism in the Catskill Mountains, for example, and the erection there of a huge hotel on the crest of a ridge with a majestic view of the Hudson Valley.[15] The clientele for this hotel were the social elite of New York and Philadelphia, who voyaged for eight hours up the Hudson River by steamboat and then rode a rugged twelve miles by stagecoach to experience the hospitality of this first-rate establishment and bask in its splendid setting.

As time passed, the taboos against tourism steadily faded, and by the post–Civil War years, the holiday traffic was no longer just domestic but international. Already some 40,000 U.S. citizens and alien residents were traveling annually to foreign countries in the 1860s and 1870s, and 100,000 traveled abroad in the 1890s.[16] Scarce wonder that some in Jamaica tried to capitalize on this burgeoning enterprise. Though tourism was a novel form of traffic between Jamaica and its republican neighbor, trade per se was nothing new for the two. Commercial intercourse between them dated back to over a century before U.S. independence.[17]

Money also was becoming more mobile in the United States toward the end of the nineteenth century. By 1900, it was evident that throughout the British West Indies in general the United States was displacing the United Kingdom as the dominant trade partner, taking, for example, over two-thirds of these territories' traditional export, sugar.[18] Jamaica itself by 1900 was the target of one of the most intensive U.S. economic penetrations hitherto in the Caribbean Basin. Its railway, for one thing, was in the hands of an American syndicate named the West India Improvement Company. That firm also possessed 74,443 acres of the best Crown lands locally, having acquired these under the terms of an agreement made with the colonial government wherein it received one square mile of land for each mile of rail laid down.[19] Hundreds of acres of land in Jamaica had been bought up by American agribusinesses like the Boston Fruit Company. By the 1880s the banana had become Jamaica's largest export crop and was shipped exclusively to U.S. markets. As for the island's import trade, U.S. goods (footwear, glassware, hardware, iron, agricultural tools, furniture, etc.) had begun to supplant British brands.[20] In all, perched on the geographical periphery of the United States, by the close of the nineteenth century Jamaica seemed ready to succumb to the status of an economic appendage.

In spite of the fact that the economic bonds between Jamaica and the United States tightened, the social relationship between the two became more strained. The nadir was reached by 1912 when the relationship had so deteriorated that one Jamaican described the United States as a "social enemy but commercial friend."[21] Paramount in this perception was the color question, which nowhere else in the North Atlantic was manifested with as much vehemence as in the American republic.[22] Although Jamaica itself was not free from the problem of caste (a legacy of slavery), it was not under a regime of lynch law, as was a large part of the United States, where approximately 1,700 blacks were lynched from 1885 through 1894. There also, this "blind, wicked unreasonable race prejudice" (to use Reverend C. A. Wilson's term) further took the lives of some 1,100 black victims between 1900 and 1917.[23]

The Southern way of thinking was fast threatening to engulf the nation in general. Following the United States' adoption of a policy of imperialist expansion into the Pacific and the Caribbean in 1898, the spread of belief in the so-called inferiority of tropical peoples served to bolster the existing justifications and myths of Southern states regarding race.[24] Amid this background of mounting chauvinism, as the United States assumed the "white man's burden," a new aspect in the relations between Yankees and Caribbean Creoles came with the inception of tourist travel to these islands. Jamaica was center stage in this development, as it was among the earliest of the West Indian islands to host the moneyed leisure classes from Europe and North America.

While in most export businesses producers and consumers are

separated and seldom interact face-to-face, the unique feature
of tourism as an export staple is that the tourist must come in
person to the spot to partake of the product. According to one
Jamaican analyst, feelings of race hatred generally accompanied
Americans abroad.[25] Back in 1860, well before the Jamaica tourist industry began, William Sewell had complained of this. In
response to the naked racism exhibited during visits by American sea captains, for example, Sewell remonstrated that "the
feeling here [in Jamaica], and in all the British West Indies,
against America and Americans owing to just such bad taste and
brutality, is bitter in the extreme."[26] Jamaican blacks, however,
barely differentiated between Americans and other Caucasian
passersby. Facing the universal racism of whites of that time,
they responded with a general indifference and a perceptible
disdain for the occasional foreigner. Another visitor to the colony
in 1861–1862 was snubbed time and again in his encounters with
local blacks:

"Can you tell me, my good man, where I can buy some tobacco?" was
the query I addressed to a large black, who was busily employed in
eating a piece of sugar-cane.
"Tobacco," he drawled out.
"Yes, tobacco; for smoking."
"Why, dere's some to be got up dere," he said, in a tone which pretty
clearly showed that he disliked being questioned—(certainly it was very
hot, lazy weather, but that does not affect a negro)—pointing with his
hand up the street, but in such an indefinite way that "up dere" might
mean the church steeple or the blue mountains in the distance.
"Well, where? Up this Street? This side of the way?"
He looked at me with a sort of sleepy stare, grunted out "Yes; 'spose
so," and resumed his attentions to the sugar-cane.
I had similar good fortune with two others I addressed. After that I
did not dare ask any more questions. It is disagreeable to be snubbed,
even by a black man.[27]

When the tourist industry emerged a generation later in
Jamaica, one hurdle in its path to success was the manifest
xenophobia of the typical black islander. Compounding this di-

lemma, the years after 1870 witnessed a new imperialist movement and the partitioning of the African continent, alongside
which a new pseudoscientific racism developed to rationalize
white hegemony over the tropical world at large. The "damned
niggers" with whom the Caucasian tourists had to deal were no
less sensitive about their freedom in 1900 than they had been
two generations earlier when Sewell, for example, had visited
the area.[28] What these black sensibilities meant for the burgeoning tourist industry constitutes one of the major preoccupations
of this study.

There were numerous complications inherent in any attempt
to found a tourist trade in Jamaica. To begin with, the island had
to transform its feared reputation as a white man's graveyard
into a new renown as a vibrant health resort. It was also necessary to breach the traditional anti-Americanism of black Jamaicans if the island was to emerge as a playground for visitors from
the mainland. What was the character of the interplay between
Jamaican society, with its much vaunted absence of Jim Crow
regulations, and the American tourists, cultural vectors of a society steeped in racial segregation? What was the role of the
tourist industry in the economic history of the colony, and how
did this relate to questions of economic transformation and development? What, finally, was the legacy of the infant holiday
trade? It is with such questions that this work is concerned.

The study presented in the following chapters is a historical
exposé of tourism in its various economic, social, and political
manifestations. Though primarily focused upon the past, its op-
tic is not narrowly historical, for many of the dilemmas this book
delineates are today still unresolved. The backside of the contemporary tourism in the Caribbean continues to function as "a
bastion of last resistance to social change."[29] One author por-
trays some of the issues in question today in these terms:

Tourism has become a trap for the Caribbean people. It has deepened
the economic dependency of the region, chiefly on the United States,
and has caused deep psychological and cultural damage. . . . Tourism
has grown to become the largest single industry in the Caribbean. But it

is an industry out of control, where the costs often outweigh the benefits and where the benefits often go to foreign firms. Being somebody else's playground has meant that the Caribbean's fishermen have become beach boys, its farmers have turned into waiters, and the TNC hotels are defining the local culture.[30]

How that all began is discussed in part one of this study. Part two discusses the legacy bequeathed to subsequent generations of Jamaicans.

Part One

THE FOUNDATION PERIOD

Chapter 2

The Deliverance from Hellshire

Insects are the curse of tropical climates. . . . In a moment
you are covered with ticks. Chigoes bury themselves in your
flesh. . . . Flies get entry into your mouth, into your eyes,
into your nose; you eat flies, drink flies, and breathe flies.
Lizards, cockroaches and snakes get into your bed; ants eat
up the books; scorpions sting you on the foot. Everything
bites, stings or bruises. . . . Such are the tropics!

—Sydney Smith

I N T H E southwestern corner of the parish of St. Catherine
in Jamaica stands a range of hills once called the Hellshire
Hills because of their proximity to extensive malarial
swamps. By the close of the nineteenth century, however,
these hills had acquired the new name of Healthshire Hills—a
change symbolic of the radical alteration that had transpired in
informed thinking about the climate of the island and its natural
environment in general.[1] Whereas Jamaica's erstwhile reputation had been as a graveyard for white folks, by 1900 it had
cultivated renown as a white man's sanatorium. In fact, one
promoter proudly boomed it abroad as "the new Riviera."[2] In
the past the holiday history of the island had been in the reverse,
as it had been the fashion for residents to flee their so-called
fever-inducing environs and seek temporary refuge abroad in
cooler climes from time to time.[3] By 1900, though, it had become "the patriotic duty" of these same elites to wipe away the
attitude that Jamaica was nothing other than a final resting place
for any foreigner hapless enough to go there.[4]

In spite of its scenic charm, Jamaica indeed was once among the most insalubrious spots under the sun. Such actually was the death toll of whites in the colony at one point that Leslie, writing in 1740, observed that numerical estimates purported that the entire white populace perished once every seven years. "No doubt the multitude that dies would soon leave this place a Desart," he bewailed, "did not daily Recruits come over from Great Britain."[5] Everywhere in the Antilles, a shortened life expectancy was the norm up to the late nineteenth century. Though the archipelago as a whole could lay claim to being the sugar bowl of the world, it also endured infamy as "the cradle of fevers" and was little else besides "a demographic disaster area."[6] "Everyone seemed caught up in a race between quick wealth and quick death." Dunn remarked, "The spectre of death helps to explain the frenetic tempo and mirage-like quality of West Indian life—gorgeously opulent today, gone tomorrow."[7]

Each new arrival had to run a virtual gauntlet of fever, by dint of which he who survived was considered seasoned or acclimatized. Epidemic was endemic. Besides malaria, yellow fever, and other strains of distemper, the familiar disorders included dropsy, dysentery, leprosy, mal rouge, cholera, typhoid, and yaws. Despite this state of affairs, little was undertaken in the field of hygiene to fortify the health defenses of the colonists.[8] Contaminated drinking water was common. As for sanitation, there was an almost complete disregard for the fundamentals. The roads in each island port were littered with refuse. No regulations existed to enforce the safe disposal of sewage. Under cover of darkness the contents of chamber pots were simply strewn in the streets.[9] Decaying animal carcasses cluttered the ditches and lay strewn along the principal highways. Were it not for scavengers like the vulture, the pig, and the pariah dog, West Indian towns would in those times have been hardly habitable.[10] A decided lifesaver was the sunshine, which is so powerful a bactericide that (to paraphrase a later governor of Jamaica) its purifying efficiency controlled what would otherwise have been an even more stupendous death toll.[11]

High as the mortality was among civilians, it was even higher among military troops. In their lodgings, men garrisoned in the region were "huddled together as an intelligent farmer would never crowd his pigs."[12] Atop the roofs of their dwellings were tanks that stored drinking water throughout the long dry season for continued consumption even after it had become foul. Open cesspits were also in service on these premises and were seldom cleaned or emptied. Rancid bread, rotten meat, a scant supply of vegetables, and a surfeit of rum formed their daily diet. All in all, conditions in camp did not befit human habitation. But when soldiers fell ill, as was inevitable, the hospital provided no health haven; it was just marginally better than the barracks.[13] In the circumstances, the high average death rate among the troops— 121.3 per thousand between 1817 and 1836, for example—is not surprising.[14]

The fevers were inescapable. Everyone had an encounter with them, and none more than the newcomers. In their case the very first fever contracted was commonly called acclimatization fever. It was among these novitiates that the mortality was highest, as the statistics attest.[15] John Hunter, an eighteenth-century medical practitioner who studied the diseases of the army in Jamaica, writes that the Eighty-eighth Regiment, for instance, lost about one-third of its men during its first year in the colony (1780) and nearly one-fifth in the second. The regiment remained for four months on the island after the end of the second year, till it was drafted, and in that time one-eleventh of the men were lost to disease. Altogether, within two years and four months about 44 percent of the regiment's complement had died.[16] The lot of— the Eighty-fifth Regiment was worse: 42 percent of the men died—in 1780, their first year in the colony. Within the next eleven months rather more than 7 percent passed away. The Ninety-third Regiment landed with a great number of its troops sick after the long and exhausting voyage. Within six months of their disembarkation over 50 percent died, and of the remainder only 71 soldiers were fit for service. The Ninety-fourth Regiment was also very sickly on board the transports, and some of the men even died during the voyage. They landed 531 men, but by the end of the first year over 50 percent were dead. In the second year 14 percent of the remainder died. At the end of two years and four months only 14 percent altogether were fit for service.[17] One factor behind this tale of woe was thought to be "the great and sudden heat, which renders the body feeble and languid." Hunter believed, however, with regard to these illnesses, "it is chiefly to be ascribed to this circumstance, that the human frame acquires by habit a power of resisting noxious causes. . . . Hence Europeans, after remaining some time in the West Indies, are less liable to be affected by the causes of fevers than on their first arrival."[18]

It was this degree of mortality among the military that cemented on these territories their reputation as graveyards for Europeans.[19] Fever was an invisible assailant that lay in wait for prey among Caribbean combatants, influencing the outcome of the military missions in the region. For instance, in 1741 the British government ordered Admiral Edward Vernon to take Cartagena, the Spanish stronghold on the Main. On that expedition some 13,000 troops were dispatched but of this number 8,431 men expired from fever, thus causing the assignment to be abandoned.[20] Even the successful accomplishment of a mission was little cause for celebration, as the real challenge confronting troops was not in the might of their antagonists but in the seemingly invincible fevers and fluxes. The story is told that, in the course of the American War of Independence, 5,000 of the bravest troops in the world took possession of the island of St. Lucia. In their clashes with adversaries the losses in killed and wounded were small, yet at the end of a year hardly a man was alive from that original number.[21] One soldier expressed great joy, in a letter from Cuba dated October 1762, that with the grace of providence he was still alive.

I think myself extremely happy in being among the number of the living, considering the deplorable condition we are now in. You will hardly believe me, when I tell you, that I have only 33 men of my company now alive, out of 100 when I landed. Our regiment has lost 8 officers, and 500 men. They mostly died of the fluxes and intermitting fevers, the general diseases here. The other regiments have lost in proportion. We are now very sickly, as you may imagine, when out of 17 batallions here, we cannot muster 600 men for duty. The appearance of this country is most beautiful, and its natural advantages are many; yet a man's life is extremely uncertain, as many are in health one morning, and dead before the next.[22]

High as the mortality rate was in these islands, it was felt there was very little that could be done to reduce it. The popular conception was that the fevers were the necessary evil of tropical countries. In these regions the warm, wet climate gives rise to extensive, luxuriant vegetation, and there is always a considerable amount of fermenting organic matter. The thinking of the time held that the fever was generated by a certain malignity in the tropical atmosphere.[23] The very designation *malaria,* or bad air, attests to the old assumed association between the fever and the atmosphere. The disease was not considered contagious in the ordinary use of the term; that is to say, it was not believed to be transmitted from person to person by contact. Contraction was presumed to be through inhalation of foul emanations from the earth, water, or air in the victim's vicinity. In the tropics the white man thus considered his health menaced by miasmas and was unaware that the mosquito is the real pathogenic vector.

Given this nightmare theory about envelopes of bad air or miasmata, the logical prescription for the restoration of health to the afflicted lay clearly in their removal from the fever-inducing environs. Dr. George Bone, for instance, was not unique in advising that "it is the removal from foul air, whether stagnant or rushing with great force, which prevents yellow fever."[24] Transfer of the troops to the surrounding mountains was accordingly recommended in Jamaica. The hills, it was felt, were healthier due to an absence there of heat and water in the right combination necessary for generating noxious exhalations.[25] In the hills, too, when rain fell it tended to run off through gullies and valleys toward the foothills, washing away any decayed vegetable and animal matter and thus purifying the atmosphere. On the plains, by contrast, everything was foul. Rainwater collected there and formed stagnant pools; rivers became slow, sluggish, and sometimes even stationary; above all, it was there that the marshes were located. It was believed that placing troops in the hills would elevate them beyond the perpendicular range of the lowland miasma.

If the hills seemed a more salubrious site for the military, they were no less so for the plantocracy. The settler-planter-historian Edward Long was quite emphatic on that score. At his insistence, gentlemen who could afford a horse or carriage would be well advised to erect residences in the hills, whereto they could retire at nightfall when their business in the lowlands was done. "Throughout this island, wherever we turn our eyes, it appears crowded with hills and rising grounds ventilated always with a free and salubrious air, that we cannot but condemn those persons who choose low, damp, and sultry hollows, for their constant residence; and who often suffer from the ill effects caused by such situations, without discerning the real source of their bad health."[26]

On sea as on land fever stalked man, since it was just as prone to be propagated there as ashore. So habitual was the distemper aboard every ship, warship or merchantman, that yellow fever under one of its many aliases was called "ships' fever" and the tropical latitudes as a whole "the yellow fever zone."[27] Ships' fever took the lives of some 11 percent of the troopers who embarked for the West Indies between October 1776 and February 1780. According to the findings of one modern study, of the 8,437 men who composed the twelve regiments dispatched to the West Indies during that period, 931 persons perished in passage.[28] The learned Edward Long suggested that such transit losses were perhaps owing to "noxious exhalations, raised during long continued calms, when the water, not being agitated as usual by the trade winds is subject to become corrupt near the surface, where it is less charged with salt, to preserve it from stinking."[29] Fever nonetheless was only the most frequent complaint at sea. Another affliction that spread rapidly was the plague, given the high density of rats aboard seagoing vessels. Scurvy was also common—the scourge of the mercantile marine and navy.

Whereas the distemper on land was considered the result of natural forces, the consensus among the medical faculty was that at sea it was due in the main to artificial causes. In his *Inaugural Dissertation on Yellow Fever* of 1846 Dr. Bone, for example, pointed out that due to technological defects there was a tendency for miasmas to be mechanically generated upon ships in the tropics. In these regions, he explained, the small steamers became hot ovens, not scientifically ventilated. In consequence, as bilge water and the oozing from the boilers collected with the filth, sulphur, slush, and tar in the hold, it gave rise to "a poisonous and suffocating air."[30]

For those on land the removal from foul air was prescribed; for seafarers the remedy was to remove the foul air itself. No substantial difference of principle marked these two prescriptions. Rather, "the same principle applies to a foul ship; the crew should be removed from herto a healthy situation, and the vessel should be thoroughly cleaned."[31] Learned works were therefore produced in which the types of cargo most likely to stimulate a deadly miasma were specified. It was not uncommon either for entire cargoes on an infected ship to be dumped into the deep or for freighters on which there had been frequent outbreaks of fever to be scuttled and sunk.[32]

Civilians had come to the Caribbean before the late nineteenth century in quest of El Dorado, not Elysium. Each year the fevers claimed numerous lives; many of those intrepid enough to set sail for these parts perished in passage. High as the death toll was from fever, it was augmented by random epidemics like smallpox or cholera. In Jamaica alone, as late as 1851, an epidemic of cholera claimed the lives of possibly 30,000 on the island.[33] And yet, despite this situation, a view in contrast to the traditional belief that the island was just a graveyard for Euro-

peans had begun to manifest itself beginning in the mid nineteenth century. Robert Baird remarked, for example, on his
return to England from Jamaica and the West Indies:

> I have, since my return from the voyage of which these volumes contain
> a brief record, observed a growing tendency in the public mind in this
> country to regard Jamaica as a place of sanitary resort and as likely, if
> not to supersede, at least greatly to interfere with the island of Madeira
> in that respect, and certainly truth compels me to admit that there are
> few places to which an invalid from Europe could go with better hope
> of benefit than to the salubrious island of Jamaica.[34]

The attempt made in the second part of the nineteenth century to promote Jamaica as a health spa was, in the circumstances, a revolutionary departure, as it sought to overthrow the
old conception of the colony's climate and replace it with a radi-
cally different orthodoxy. Charles Plummer's *Concise Cathechism*
of 1862 enshrined the doctrine of this new creed. According to
this early apostle of tourism, the island's climate was "generally
healthy," its atmosphere invigorating rather than fever inducing, and if the malarial lowlands were avoided, a sojourn in the
hills of Jamaica would provide relief and cure for sundry ailments. From then on, this depiction of Jamaica as Healthshire
was to become the creed of a growing band of converts. In fact,
in the long run it was to dispel the old view of the island as
Hellshire:

Q. Is Jamaica unhealthy on account of its Heat?
A. Certainly not.
Q. What then occasions unhealthiness in the Island?
A. The miasma which is generated in low-lying, swampy and marshy
   districts, from decayed animal and vegetable matter in a state of
   decomposition.
Q. Is Jamaica generally healthy?
A. It is; and in some particular localities such as the Santa Cruz
   Mountain districts, the climate is said to be the healthiest in the
   world. The Northside is generally healthier than the Southside.
Q. Is the climate of Jamaica efficacious to the sufferer from certain
   diseases?

A. Yes: and Jamaica offers a welcome home to persons in whom, from hereditary or other causes, there exists a tendency to scrofulous disease or pulmonary consumption. To the sufferer from rheumatism and gout the prospects of relief are most cheering.[35]

While historically there had always been some criticism of the state of public health in Jamaica, this in general had been to little avail. The island's assembly government regarded issues of public health to be a private rather than a public sector matter. Throughout the urban areas, for instance, mountains of refuse accumulated in the yards of householders and yet were subject to removal only at the option of these individuals and at their personal expense. Such cost considerations must have conduced to these premises remaining as health menaces.[36] Public facilities for disposal of the dead were woefully wanting. In Kingston, for example, a major health hazard was the overcrowding of city graveyards; from want of space, bodies were piled one upon the other, to the extent that sometimes many corpses rested too near the surface.[37] It was only in the years after the Morant Bay Rebellion (1865) and the constitutional change that ensued from government by local assembly to direct crown rule, that substantive efforts were made to address these problems. Beginning with the administration of Sir John Peter Grant metamorphosis occurred. First governor under the new constitution, Grant in 1868 founded the public medical service on the island and launched a new era in the colony's health history.[38]

First off (though until almost the last decade of the nineteenth century the miasmatic or telluric theory continued to hold sway) the new government launched a crusade against garbage and filth—albeit with the wrong premise of presumed health gains through reduction of stench. A sanitation revolution, ushered in by Grant, occurred in Jamaica from about 1870 onward. The showpiece of achievement was the city of Kingston, long the dirtiest and most malodorous town on the island. By the early 1870s Kingston was engaged in a massive cleanup campaign and in institutionalizing mechanisms for sustaining the momentum

that had been initiated.[39] Besides tackling the garbage problem
and the clearance of drains, another forward step for Kingston
was the conversion of the May Pen Estate into a cemetery (1874).
The other burial grounds were closed, and the traditional practice of intramural internments was terminated.

From its inception the watchword of the new era in Jamaican
health was prevention. Early efforts were made to establish general vaccinations among the population and institute and enforce more effective quarantine laws.[40] City officials founded
a potable water system and addressed the disposal of human
waste. Historically, Jamaicans drew water from rivers and wells,
most of which were probably saturated with decayed excreta. In
1871, however, the Kingston and Liguanea Waterworks were
purchased by the government, remodeled, and outfitted to provide filtered water of fairly good standard. By the end of the
century nine other parishes had also come into possession of
waterworks, while Kingstonians received an additional supply of
piped water from the Constant Spring reservoir. By 1895 Kingston was equipped with a street sewage system, and the task of
linkage with private residences had begun.[41]

Summing up the practical significance of these developments,
Rupert Boyce in his 1910 publication *Health Progress and Administration in the West Indies* noted that it was thanks to them that
cholera and dysentery had been arrested and yellow fever cur-
tailed. The result was that, though the normal death rate itself
did not appear to fall below a figure of 23–24 per 1,000, it
nonetheless did not rise much above that, as was so common-
place previously when killer diseases had rampaged.[42] The
Antilles began to undergo the transition to a region of healthy
tropical resorts so alluringly depicted by Charles Kingsley, Sir
Frederic Treves, and others.

In the ranks of the military, as among the civilian population,
there were striking improvements in health prospects.[43] By
the first quarter of the nineteenth century the West Indies had
ceased to be the war theater and the darlings of empire they had
once been.[44] Throughout the nineteenth century there were

continuous reductions in the numbers of troops stationed in Jamaica. This initially occasioned some improvement in the health of the army, since overcrowding, for example, ceased to pose a problem. Equally significant, the reductions in strength led to the abandonment of the more unhealthy military stations in the vicinity of swamps. But despite that initially promising outlook, things continued to stagnate up to the last third of the nineteenth century. Effective measures to promote health among the troops were not in fact set in motion until around the same time as those among the civilian population.

Under the supposition that yellow fever was unknown at a height of 2,500 feet above sea level, in 1841 the white troops had been moved to Newcastle, a newly constructed barrack on the hills of the parish of St. Andrew. The troops relocated to this site trusted blindly in the theory of elevation limit, as though that in itself could guarantee protection against tropical ailments. "The distinction had not been clearly made between Malaria, i.e. 'Marsh Miasm' . . . and 'Civic Miasm'—the Miasm of people, their habitations and surroundings," Maunsell contended.[45] In their ignorance the troops took with them to Newcastle primitive standards of hygiene and sanitation. Around their quarters unwholesome cesspits abounded, into which liquid and solid excrement were ejected. There were few arrangements for removal of surface refuse, and the system of drainage was most deficient. But it was not until 1868 that redress began, despite the ruling of a royal commission a decade earlier that the duties of army medical staff included not simply curative but preventive measures as well.

The commission urged the periodic inspection of hygenic conditions in camp, but in Newcastle no concrete steps were taken until 1867, when a further outbreak of fever (this time at Cuzco, 11,000 feet high in the Andes) finally shattered the myth of the elevation limit. In 1869 the dry earth system of conservancy was established at both Up Park Camp and Newcastle.[46] In 1874 a "camp of isolation" was erected at Papine, where infected troops could be placed under quarantine. Improved

nutritional standards, provision of better barrack room accommodation, and attention to the physical and psychological needs
of the men all contributed to a drastic diminution in the death
rate among troops. From an average of 121.3 per thousand
between 1817 and 1836, mortality declined to an average of
11.36 per thousand between 1880 and 1889. These statistics in-
dicate the deaths from all causes, but in the first period the
deaths attributed to fever were 101.9 per thousand, and in the
last a mere 4.3 per thousand.[47]

Although people remained unaware of the real causes of the
fevers, the second half of the nineteenth century saw a remarkable (though slow) advance in scientific knowledge regarding the
etiology of these diseases.[48] In 1848, for the first time, Joseph
Clark Nott of Alabama forwarded the hypothesis that the mosquito was in some way connected with the transmission of fever.
Nott was ignorant about exactly how the insect transmitted
fever, however. The French scientist Louis Daniel Beauperthy
was another early proponent of the view that the mosquito is in
fact the vector of malaria.[49] Beauperthy, though suspecting the
means of transmission, mistakenly believed that the poison was
extracted from extraneous decomposing substances, and like
Nott, the thought that humans themselves might be the source
of infection did not occur to him. No further progress was to be
made for a generation.

The first genuine breakthrough in human knowledge regarding the etiology of fevers was made by Charles Louis Alphonse
Laveran. In 1881, Dr. Laveran, while serving with French troops
in Algeria, discovered a tiny protoplasmic body in human blood,
which having attacked the red cells became larger, acquired a
black pigment, and underwent certain changes that bore a remarkable similarity to the various stages in an attack of malarial
fever.[50] Subsequent inquiry following on Laveran's disclosure
revealed that this parasite could be transmitted from person to
person through injections of blood. But while Carlos Finlay of
Cuba (like Beauperthy previously) contended that it is the mosquito that is the vector of this parasite, Finlay was regarded as a

mere theorizer, if not a crank. Belief in the old miasmatic conception persisted—many held to the view that the protozoal organism was bred in swamps, that it was capable of aerial transmission, and that it entered the human body through inhalation. It was left to Professor Ronald Ross in 1895 to conclusively demonstrate that it is a special type of mosquito, a member of the subgroup *anophelinae,* that is the sole vector of the parasite that causes malaria.[51]

The sequel to this advance was an unprecedented spate of investigations into the possible role of the mosquito in sundry other tropical ailments. Following Ross's findings it was proven, for instance, that *Filaria* (a blood worm said to be the cause of elephantiasis) entered the human body via the proboscis of the culex mosquito. But of special significance was the breakthrough in the etiology of yellow fever (1900) by a team of U.S. scientists working in Cuba. The *stegomyia* (*Aedes*) mosquitoes were at last discovered to carry that disease, and thereafter measures were assiduously employed to exterminate the species. As a result of this growth in knowledge, humanity acquired a greater power over the tropical environments of the world and, indeed, in a number of these places virtually erased yellow fever and malaria. The locus classicus of achievement in this regard is perhaps the instance of the Panama Canal Zone, where in the 1880s several thousand men died of malaria and yellow fever during the abortive De Lesseps endeavor to construct a transisthmian canal. Yet, thirty years later the construction of modern hotels had begun, Panama suddenly having been transformed into a tourists' asylum.[52]

The Panama *Star and Herald* tells the story as it had unfolded by the winter months of 1911–1912:

We think it is safe to refer to the tourist incursion now as a rush. Five years ago they came in twos and threes; three years ago they mounted to scores; within the past two years they came in hundreds. Although the city of Panama has made no bid for visitors, the name Panama has been advertised abroad probably more than any other. The canal construction and the extraordinary progress in sanitation and hygiene accomplished on the Isthmus have been instrumental in awakening interest in the place and an increasing stream of visitors is the natural result.[53]

This occupation of Panama by throngs of tourists just before the First World War was made possible only by advances in the theory and practice of tropical medicine and by the offensives these permitted against diseases throughout the Caribbean Basin. Thanks in particular to the advent of piped water supply systems, the population no longer needed to use barrels, drums, and other open containers, favored breeding grounds of the yellow fever transmitter *stegomyia*.

While on land the development of piped water supplies had dealt a deathblow to the *Aedes aegypti* mosquito, at sea this scourge was suppressed through advances in nautical technology.[54] In the old days, before the invention of the steam condensing plant, the custom had been to carry fresh water in casks that were often leaky and frequently contained *stegomyia* larvae, which developed during the voyage into the winged creature. All that was necessary for an outbreak of yellow fever on board was for an infected laborer or someone else from shore to come aboard, or alternatively for some member of the ship's crew to contract the disease while on shore leave. By feeding on the blood of the infected individual, every mosquito on the ship would soon become infected, and within a short time most of the crew would be down with the fever. Development of the steam condensing plant, however, eliminated the need for water storage on board ship and thus reduced the likelihood of outbreaks of fever at sea.[55]

In voyages to the Caribbean islands so considerable a decline occurred in the incidence of maritime illness in the late nineteenth cetury that transoceanic travel was transformed from a hazardous affair into something even glamorous. With the reduction of the length of ocean voyages through the growth of steamshipping, scurvy, for example, ceased to be a problem.[56] By 1880 the wooden schooners plying to Caribbean shores increasingly began to be displaced by steam vessels of iron and steel. Lighter, stouter, secure against leaks in the keel, and less liable to becoming infested with insects, the iron or steel ship was in every way a more healthy unit.[57] Compared to wooden vessels, which were limited in length to about three hundred feet, steel permitted almost any length of keel. Sturdier, safer, and swifter ships meant that travel by sea was comfortable and pleasurable for the weak and the strong, the old and the young. For the first time, the voyage to the Caribbean assumed a therapeutic dimension, and passenger cruise tours to the region began.[58]

At the onset of Jamaican tourist traffic it was the cool, bracing air of the mountains, rather than the island's white sand beaches, that was advertised abroad as the key attraction for the visitor. In part this was the logical extension of the practice of all sane people up to the turn of the twentieth century to avoid the noxious miasmas of the coastal areas. It was also due to the belief that Jamaica's mountain regions promoted health, especially for sufferers of a variety of ailments. Earlier in the nineteenth century the hills had merely been considered healthier than the plains; by the close of that era, they were purported to be healthful in themselves.

Among the earliest to eulogize Jamaica as a health spa were an English visitor, the Reverend David King, and a former assemblyman for the parish of Portland, William Anderson.[59] It was inconceivable at the time of emancipation that any sane person could have considered Jamaica a health spa. According to one itinerant around that time: "I have heard it [Jamaica] recommended as a resort for invalids, but, on the contrary almost everyone, in general terms, pronounces it unhealthy."[60] By 1850, however, an apparent volte-face had begun. People like Anderson, seized with a sudden appreciation of the physical attributes of the island, were prepared to recommend it to Americans, for example, as a place close to home with a "genial climate" where they could sojourn during the winter months. Jamaica, Anderson felt, was the perfect retreat to which the mainland could send invalids for asylum in the winter: "Its proximity must be of peculiar interest to that class in the United

Elder, Dempster & Co.'s

WINTER ∴ TOURS ∴ FOR HEALTH AND PLEASURE.

To Jamaica—the New Riviera.

By the Magnificently Appointed Steamers of the

Imperial Direct West India Mail Service Co., Ltd.

Regular Fortnightly Sailings between **BRISTOL** and **JAMAICA.**

These Steamers have been specially built for the service, and have magnificent accommodation for First and Second Class Passengers at Moderate Fares.

Sea Passage 10 to 12 Days.

Imperial Direct West India Mail ss. "Port Kingston."

A voyage to JAMAICA offers exceptional attractions to TOURISTS and those seeking health. The island possesses great natural beauty, and its warm, healthy climate is recommended by the medical faculty. Polo-playing, yachting, golf, tennis, riding and driving are particularly good. Excellent shooting and fishing.

THE LARGE MODERN HOTELS, "CONSTANT SPRING" AND "MYRTLE BANK" PROVIDE ACCOMMODATION AT REASONABLE RATES.

Apply—

ELDER, DEMPSTER & CO.,

Colonial House, **LIVERPOOL.**   4, St. Mary Axe, **LONDON.**   Baldwin Street, **BRISTOL.**   30, Mosley Street, **MANCHESTER.**

This advertisement by Elder, Dempster and Company shows how Jamaica had changed by the end of the nineteenth century from a white man's graveyard to a health resort. Courtesy of National Library of Jamaica.

States whose constitutions are unable to endure a severe winter climate. Pulmonary patients who go sufficiently early to Jamaica, almost invariably obtain relief and restoration to perfect health and ability for every kind of exertion."[61]

Anderson was following in the path of Reverend David King, who a year earlier, having passed the winter in Jamaica, had written in more or less the same vein. In his publication King condemned both the classification of the colony among the unhealthy regions of the earth as well as the exaction by insurance companies of a large premium from any client who visited it.[62] The impression abroad that Jamaica was a white man's grave was in King's view a gross distortion. As to what he had witnessed there himself or had learned from conversations with physicians, many diseases fatal in Britain were unknown in the island or found only in modified and gentle forms. If mortality due to fevers was high, King contended, it was driven up through imprudence, fast living, and intemperance. In any case, the fevers followed a seasonal pattern, and the winter months in the northern hemisphere coincided with the healthiest time of year in Jamaica. In all, "I could not learn of an instance where an invalid or any of his friends coming to Jamaica to spend a single winter there had died of fever."[63]

The historical paradox is that, in spite of the traditional consensus of opinion about the unhealthiness of the islands, as far back as the seventeenth and eighteenth centuries there had actually been some measure of tourism to these parts. In his *Yankees and Creoles*, Richard Pares says that, in the eighteenth century, the sickly of North America and the sickly of the West Indian colonies of Great Britain had visited each other's homes in search of relief. For instance, Barbados had sent to Philadelphia its hard drinkers, with their "carbuncled faces, slender legs and thighs and large, prominent bellies," and young Major George Washington had accompanied his sick brother in 1751–1752 to that island.[64] By 1740 the Bahamas enjoyed a rather premature reputation as a health resort for invalids from the mainland. In North America, where the ailing sometimes found the winter months debilitating, the Bahamas seemed a sort of sanctuary.[65] Neither the magnitude nor regularity of this early tourist traffic was enough, however, to institutionalize it as an industry at that period of Antillean history. If there was any prerequisite for the conversion of that fortuitous trickle of visitors into a sustained torrent, it was the transformation of the epidemiological environment.

But while it was one necessary factor in the institutionalization of tourism in Jamaica, epidemiological change alone was not sufficient. Tourism develops as an industry only when there is a strong economic incentive to do so, as the history of Barbados discloses. Tourism there, as in Jamaica, was first organized in any economically meaningful way only as a consequence of the changing local economic conditions in the last half of the nineteenth century. When sugar from Barbados lost its preferential treatment on the British market in the middle to late nineteenth century (ostensibly because the sugar islands could no longer compete with cheaper and higher quality producers elsewhere), the Barbadian product experienced a precipitous decline in value. As sugar earnings fell, estate land went down in appraisal, and several properties were transferred to Chancery or otherwise went out of business. Given the epidemiological transition and the economic decline, it is little wonder that some planters and merchants soon seized upon tourism as a logical alternative (or supplement) to sugar. Thenceforth, the long-standing reputation for hospitality that the island had acquired since the midseventeenth century was renovated and converted into something that the elite could cash in on.[66]

Well before Barbados, Jamaica had taken the lead as the scene of pioneering efforts by private individuals to peddle the island abroad as a rendezvous for vacationers To understand how it was possible for this development to predate any substantial change in the island's health situation, it is instructive to look at the objectives of those early protagonists of tourism, focusing in particular on Anderson's 1851 pamphlet entitled *Jamaica and the*

Americans. Anderson's real intent in writing was to attract men
and money from the United States to aid in the postemancipation reconstruction of the economy of the island. To attract
these factors of production, not only promises of high investment returns were necessary but also assurances regarding the
entrepreneurs' health and physical well-being—hence Anderson's transparent emphasis on Jamaica's "genial climate." One
recurrent rationale for promoting tourism lay in the expectations expressed by Anderson, and others like him, that tourism
might serve as an indirect developmental mechanism pumping
fresh capital into the island and perhaps infusing it with fresh
supplies of white blood. Basic to the encyclical of these acolytes
of tourism was the view that the visitor, exposed firsthand to the
colony's potential, might be induced not only to invest but perhaps to settle there.[67]

Thus, in the second half of the nineteenth century a new
propaganda about Jamaica as tropical spa was spread abroad for
the first time, in the hopes of attracting a stream of visitors (and
potential investors) to the island. The sick in the North Atlantic
population were urged to pursue their prospects of recovery in
Jamaica's highlands. There one would find dry mountain re-
treats pleasing in panorama and invigorating in atmosphere,
ideal for the hypochondriac and dyspeptic. Alternatively, there
were moist localities, such as Newcastle, suitable for the nervous
and for those who suffered from a parched and irritable condition in the lungs.[68] Jamaica felt it had a product to offer
unrivaled by any other spa. "The clear, rare atmosphere of
our higher elevations, I venture to affirm will do more for the
individual than Egypt, Mentone, Nice, or the Riviera for Europeans, and California, Nassau, Bermuda, or Florida for the
American."[69]

It was not the salt waters of the Caribbean Sea that were first
extolled in the infant days of the Jamaica tourist industry but the
flow from the island's springs—chalybeate waters for the feeble
and mineral baths for persons afflicted with gout or rheumatism. Abroad, the winter months meant for invalids "confine-

ment, imprisonment and death." With its perpetual summer
Jamaica offered a haven, boasting few days in the year when
some form of outdoor exercise cannot be taken. The winter
season was advertised as the best time to visit the island, because
the nightmare theory of the miasma had not yet been abandoned. The danger period for the fevers was commonly held to
be the rainy season, when numerous foul-smelling pools of stagnant water formed. The winter months in the northern hemisphere coincide with the dry spell in the Caribbean, which was
perceptibly the healthiest time of year. Advocacy of the northern winter as the season for tourists was thus in part a reflection
of the current thinking on matters relating to health in the
region.[70]

To develop tourism there was, in addition to the epidemiological hurdles, a host of entomological obstacles to grapple
with. In the popular stereotype, the tropics were home to
myriad winged or crawling insects, loathsome if not noxious and
inclined to bite, bruise, or sting their human victims. "Every
second of your existence you are wounded by some piece of
animal life that nobody has ever seen before," Sydney Smith
mused. These insects swarmed everywhere. "All this reconciles
us to our dens, bogs, vapours, and drizzle . . . to our old British
constitutional coughs, sore throats and swelled faces," Smith
added.[71] It hardly seemed an inspired locale for health spas,
and yet Jamaica by the closing decades of the nineteenth century
was eager to dispel the stigma and miasma that had been its
historical lot and launch a novel future as the new Riviera.

The advent in 1895 of the first English cricket team to tour the
Caribbean was a decided windfall. Considering the immense
popularity of the sport at that time, the tour gave tremendous
impetus to the efforts to portray the region as a resort for health
and pleasure. According to the manager of the team, their decision to visit the Caribbean had been credited with a courage
associated only with youth and recklessness, and when team
members were leaving, their friends had generally bade farewell
as if they never expected to be reunited.[72] In their schoolbooks

the players had read that these islands harbored all kinds of horror. They were led to expect to be rendered listless by the thousands of insects that fed upon the blood of Englishmen. They were warned that the climate would kill them within a few days of their arrival; that the hot sun would give them sunstroke; and, if the sun spared them, that they would die of yellow fever. Instead, the cricket team discovered that the longer they stayed in Jamaica the better they were physically.

In point of fact, their manager said, while the team had been luxuriating in these climates, the metropole back in England had been gripped by an epidemic of influenza and rheumatic sickness. The sole thing that might have killed the cricketers on tour was not the sun, the mosquitoes, or the yellow fever, but the excessive and indulgent welcome the team had received everywhere. One Jamaican journal, reflecting on the words of rapture that came from the manager, described the tour of 1895 as a "missionary cricket campaign."[73] Alongside the reports on these matches in the English dailies many were startled to read of the salubrious and scenic character of the colonies. The belief in Jamaica was that the cricket tour would go far in projecting the Caribbean area as a fashionable winter spa.

The lesson of the cricket tour was that other sporting pastimes could as readily be pursued by the vacationer in Jamaica for health or pleasure. The golfer, for example, need only bring along his driver, putter, and mashie; Jamaica would supply the caddie. But sports aside, there was little diversion to ease the tedium of a stay on the island. "Some people might be bored here—possibly," Olivier wrote.[74] "There is no Casino: no music: no drama: not much to be done in the evenings: no antiques or architecture, no work of human art worth looking at . . . except the ornamental Gardens of Hope, King's House and Castleton." Still a trip was well worth it, it was claimed. Jamaica was the model retreat for rest, if not recreation.

However plentiful the postulates about the island's attributes as a health spa, these must be scrutinized in any inquiry into the subject and their worth determined. A series of articles penned by an anonymous visitor and published in the *Lancet* every three weeks, from 5 October to 28 December 1907, examines the colony's claims to recognition as a resort. Central to Jamaica's resort aspirations were its mineral baths. Yet, if the Milk River bath was representative, the facilities provided were "entirely inadequate to the needs of anyone acutely ill."[75] To begin with, the springs were located in a low-lying malarial district, which was terrorized by sandflies and where "the mosquitoes came up in thousands at sunset." No soda water was obtainable at the site, and to quench their thirst, guests relied upon water from the river, unboiled and passed through an ancient drip stone. The sanitary arrangements were ill-ventilated earth closets under a house in a sort of dark cloister. As for the bathhouses, these were gloomy and ill-ventilated. "The redeeming feature of the whole place was the bath itself."[76]

Bad as things were at Milk River, at Malvern in the Santa Cruz Hills they were no better. Owing to its dry climate, suitable for sufferers from rheumatism and pulmonary complaints, Malvern had the potential of becoming the chief health resort of the

Bathhouse and lodging house at the famous Milk River Mineral Spring. About thirty visitors could be accommodated at a time. Courtesy of National Library of Jamaica.

Jamaican highlands. As at Milk River, however, the facilities offered were totally unfit for delicate patients.[77] At one hotel, the drinking water was supplied from a large uncovered tank that stored rainwater collected from the roof of the house. Inside it floated a thick coat of duckweed that, it was believed, kept the contents of the tank cool. Nor was the water boiled before being drunk but simply passed through a drip stone. The diet offered at the house was "monotonous" and the sanitation was "distinctly unsatisfactory." All this notwithstanding, it seemed "a fair sample" of the public accommodation in the district.[78]

More useful in evaluating the validity of Jamaica's claim as a health resort is the evidence offered by Dr. W. T. Prout in his survey on malaria in Jamaica at the turn of the twentieth century.[79] Dr. Prout noted in his study that, despite the breakthrough in the etiology of tropical fevers, the population in Jamaica continued to demonstrate a gross ignorance about the life history and habits of the mosquito. Nor did the scientifically informed do enough to translate knowledge into action. According to his estimate, the death rate from malaria from 1898 to 1907 had been lowered to 4.4 per 1,000 of the population. However, the average percentage of malarial deaths to total deaths was 19.7 percent—approximately one-fifth of the deaths in the island were still caused by malaria. In absolute terms, 4,094 deaths in the colony were attributable to malaria in 1907, while the combined mortality for the preceding ten years was 34,695.[80] Jamaica, in fact, was by no stretch of the imagination a health spa, despite the claims of tourism protagonists. Inadequate antimosquito measures and the seeming scarcity of clean, comfortable lodgings in most of the Jamaican countryside were apparently in 1907 still a brake upon the evolution of the island into an authentic health resort.

The first flush in the history of the Jamaican tourist industry came to an end in 1914. That year saw the termination of the foundation phase, in part because of the outbreak of World War I. The year also marked the opening of the Panama Canal, an event that seemed to augur entirely new and unprecedented dimensions for tourism in the years to come.[81] While an undisputed rise in health, hygiene, and science was in motion, socially an accelerated process of putrefaction threatened to engulf the island with the rise of tourism.[82] This encompassed more than an accentuation of the color question in the colony, though perhaps that seemed the most prominent of the myriad aspects of the social question. The *Jamaica Times* felt constrained to warn in one of its issues:

Of two things there can be no doubt, first, that with the entrance of wealthy American tourists here we must look for attempts to introduce into Jamaica the colour discrimination on ships, in hotels and even in churches that disgraces the United States. That is one fact. The other fact is that at any cost, whether it means the loss of money, the hampering of trade, having to dare and curb powerful business interests and corporations or whether it costs even more than this, we must keep out of this country this colour line policy. We must keep it out as we are struggling to keep out the Plague.[83]

Chapter 3

God's Agents in Paradise

I am sure that the Boston Fruit Company is one of God's agents to right some of the ills of that beautiful island.
— N. S. Hopkins

GIVEN the local traditions of easy hospitality, the Jamaican tourist industry, when it emerged in the late nineteenth century, encountered a warm reception among local men of capital, who welcomed the wealthy white transients from abroad by making the colony as much a home away from home as possible. These local entrepreneurs, however, were not the parents of the infant enterprise. Tourism was sired by American banana traders, who had made the island a major base of operations. It was on the banana boats that the first vacationers from North America were brought to Jamaica. Near the end of the nineteenth century the Boston Fruit Company alone, for instance, counted in its service sixteen steamers plying the sea-lanes between Jamaica and the ports of Boston, New York, Philadelphia, and Baltimore.[1] With vessels departing almost daily for the United States, no other West Indian island enjoyed as frequent communication with the mainland as Jamaica.[2] In addition to ferrying visitors to and fro, banana companies were pioneers in providing modern hotel accommodations for these guests.

It was due to the banana that paradise was rediscovered in the form of Jamaica. Here, according to the brochures, was Eden resurrected: an island world devoid of blizzards or snow, of worry or hurry; here was a province of pleasure, leisure, laughter, and love everywhere.[3] Because the saga of the banana is cardinal in any chronicle on early Jamaican tourism, it is discussed in this chapter along with the unfolding tourism.

Throughout the colonial history of Jamaica there was a marked difference in the role of the hills and that of the plains in shaping the economic, social, political, and cultural destiny of the island. Before the complete manumission of the slaves in 1838, the lowlands had been the indisputable base of Jamaica's wealth. With Emancipation, however, many of the properties there sank into ruins, while in the hills progress was soon in evidence.[4] A large number of freedmen retreated there and were able to acquire land easily since it had not been preempted by the sugar plantations, thanks to topography. One salient feature of the slave system was that it inhibited the development of a native peasant class. This evolved in the post-Emancipation period. At best, before freedom slaves had been a protopeasantry.[5] It was manumission that, like a midwife, delivered this fledgling socioeconomic form from the womb of a plantation system wracked with the acute labor pains that followed the collapse of slave-driven production.

The most mountainous part of Jamaica is in the east. There too is the heaviest rainfall, owing to the influence of the prevailing northeast trade winds. The eastern parishes of Jamaica are noted for their fertility, and provided that proper drainage is created and correct cultivation methods followed, conditions there are ideal for banana production. This part of the island was the cradle of the banana business. That peasants were producing this staple for export little over a generation after Emancipation indicated the extent to which they had consolidated themselves in the intervening years.[6] It was also proof of the tremendous physical and economic suitability of the banana to that form of agrarian organization.

As a crop the banana is most amenable to peasant production. It not only matures quickly and is relatively easy on the soil, but the waste from the plant is itself a good manure. Bananas are not as labor- and capital-intensive as sugar, nor do they require semiprocessing before export; a general simplicity typifies their cultivation. Before Emancipation, the crop had been used as food for the slaves; after Emancipation, to plant it was in Sydney Olivier's words, "a backwood's 'nigger business.'" A former governor of Jamaica, Olivier pointed out that the old planter class could never have accomplished the feat of fathering the banana industry in Jamaica because it was, in essence, impotent.[7]

Sewell, in like manner, had earlier revealed the economic debility and entrepreneurial lethargy of the local planter regime:

They cry out at the high price of labor, and pretend they can not grow corn, when corn is grown at five times the cost in the United States and exported to Jamaica at a handsome profit. They import beef, and tongues, and butter, though this very parish of Manchester offers advantages for raising stock that no portion of America possesses. They import mackerel, and salmon, and herrings, and codfish, though Jamaica waters abound in the most splendid kind of fish. They import woods, though Jamaica forests are unrivaled for the variety and beauty and usefulness of their timber. They import tobacco, though their soil in many districts is most excellent for its growth. *The negroes, who have never been taught these things, are learning them slowly by experience, and a gradual decline in certain articles of import demonstrates that they now raise on their own properties a very large proportion of their own provisions.*[8]

Because of that constitutional inability of the planter class to acquire what Kindleberger has termed a "capacity to transform," the banana industry in Jamaica was piloted by the freedmen—people whose energies had been liberated from the inhibiting mentality of the sugar sector. In the years after 1870, what until then had been mere "nigger business" underwent a transformation into big business. Behind this metamorphosis lay the growth of the North American market for the fruit.

During the second half of the nineteenth century, the densely populated U.S. eastern seaboard provided a rich and growing market for agricultural produce. For some time prior to 1868 this market had become familiar with the small red Cavendish banana from Cuba. The Gros Michel had also appeared in New York since 1866, when Carl Augustus Franc, a steward on a Pacific mail steamer, successfully took a few stems from Panama (then a part of Colombia) to New York.[9] Encouraged by the profits he made, Franc soon set up a firm to engage in a regular trade in bananas, apparently the first venture of the kind.[10] When in 1868 the Jamaican banana made its debut in the export trade via Captain L. D. Baker, it thus encountered an embryonic market in the United States that appeared open to further development.

That the early banana trade concentrated exclusively on the U.S. market derived to a large extent from the nature of the fruit itself. Bananas are highly perishable, and cargoes could not be shipped the long distances to the United Kingdom and the European markets until steam power reduced the time spent on the voyage and refrigeration prolonged the life of the fruit. The product required a market within fairly easy reach, both geographically and in terms of the current trade policy of its government. Such as outlet was found in the northeastern cities of the United States. In addition, many of the sea captains in the early trade were Americans. Considering this, and given the lack of British metropolitan restraints on colonial commerce with foreign nations, the U.S. market was the natural target of the Jamaican staple.[11]

Many problems accompanied the establishment of this early enterprise. For instance, without proper roads the fruit cannot reach the wharves in prime condition. Careful handling was necessary during the loading and off-loading of the transports, given that bruised fruit degenerates rapidly. Furthermore, at the time that the trade started most of the bottoms employed in West Indian–North American trafficking were sailing ships,[12] subject to adverse winds and often unpunctual and unreliable. It was impossible to coordinate the other operations in the industry—the cutting and carriage to the ports—with the irregular arrival of these vessels. The early industry was unpredictable, particularly in the sprint to the overseas market, as the cargo could be spoiled before it reached its destination if the winds were unfavorable and the carrier becalmed. It was always a race against time. "Quantity, quality, despatch" was thus the maxim of the fortune seeker in this commercial endeavor.[13]

Time brought technological advances that facilitated the further development of the trade. The growth of steamshipping after the mideighties brought both regularity and rapidity in transport. As the sailing schedules of steam ships were more predictable, ground operations could be better timed to the arrival of the vessels, thereby shortening the time previously spent in connection with the turnover of the freighters. The cable and radio telegraph systems aided the process by allowing greater speed in transmitting directions and market information. The telephone further accelerated business operations.[14] Finally, by 1900, the introduction of controlled ship refrigeration preserved the fruit and enabled its shipment farther afield.

There was a lot of money to be made in the early export trade and the enterprise was quite competitive at its beginning. The essence of the contest, however, was to destroy competition, as the stronger vied to eliminate their weaker trade opponents by crushing attempts at rivalry. In the struggle for control of the banana trade only the fittest could survive, and two methods in particular were employed.[15] One was to outbid the rival buyer of fruit from the local growers and deprive him of supplies. The best counter to this was to possess lands of one's own and thus be assured of an independent supply source. The second tactic was to undersell the other contenders in the U.S. market. The logic of the competition in all instances was to eliminate trading opponents and establish a monopoly.

Bananas are heavy, bulky, and perishable. Importing the fruit therefore demanded not only a substantial capital investment in shipping but also large reserves of capital to cushion against the risks inherent in the commerce. The form of competition that characterized the trade was thus from the outset oligopolistic. Though there had been a few local merchant enterprisers involved, these were handicapped from the start because they lacked the command of enough capital to meet the trade's requirements and the strenuous competition. To a large extent this stemmed from their inability to draw upon local private capital for support in their ventures. Sydney Olivier has explained why: "When I first knew Jamaica, banana-growing was still despised as a backwood's 'nigger business,' which any old-time sugar planter would have disdained to handle, or, if tempted by undeniable prospects of profit, would have thought an apology was required."[16]

The Jamaican merchant enterprisers in the banana business had to contend with profound prejudices as well as that peculiar economic lethargy that Sewell had noted. It was owing to this, in addition to the bitter struggle for the trade, that these merchants finally failed. Foreigners in contrast faced no such constraints, and so were able to amass financial fortunes while local conservatism kept their Jamaican competitors in the traditional economic groove.

In the competition for dominance in the Jamaican banana business, Lorenzo D. Baker, a Massachusetts sea captain, proved the fittest. Captain Baker was without doubt the most outstanding enterpriser in the early banana traffic. Conditioned by his boyhood upbringing in the fishing industry, his outlook was very much that of a gambler. But Baker was also adroit in choosing good men to work for him and organizing their talents in the most efficient manner.[17] His energy was indefatigable, his personality compelling, and he possessed sterling business acumen. Because he was non-Jamaican, Baker was less subject to the influence of the plantation culture and its censure. To top it all, he was able to draw with assurance upon the funds of friends and associates overseas for the capital reserves that conduct of the trade necessitated.[18]

From the outset it was Baker's ambition to dominate, develop, and control the banana business. To do so he had to be strategically established in the successive stages of the enterprise—in production, transportation, and distribution. To acquire a reliable source of supply and better equip himself competitively, he purchased extensive lands in Jamaica, settled there, and became a banana producer. In the sphere of transportation Baker was also able to gain supremacy. By his formation of the Standard Steam Navigation Company (1884), he obtained an organization to transport the fruit. As for the marketing end, he was able to develop a highly efficient system of distribution in the United States and thus gain a competitive advantage.[19] It was to the credit of his entrepreneurial spirit, sagacity, foresight, and limitless energy that Baker accomplished all that he did. A veritable Cortez of his time, Baker had landed on a strange shore, sensed treasure there, and succeeded in carrying off the golden cargoes in his holds.

Baker's culminating feat was the formation of the United Fruit Company in 1899. This was a giant combination of the major firms in the banana business, and it dominated every aspect of the enterprise internationally. A mammoth corporation of continental proportion, the United Fruit Company was consolidated with a capitalization of $20 million.[20] Not only did it own large plantations for growing fruit in Jamaica and Central America, it had over sixty steamers to carry its produce to U.S. markets. Thenceforth oligopolistic competition was crushed. The history of the banana trade in Jamaica during the next three decades was to be in the main a record of attempts to break the monopoly of the United Fruit Company.[21]

For a time prior to the development of the banana trade, communication links between Jamaica and the United States had been waning. This, however, was remedied by the growth of the banana market, for that intercourse brought more regular and rapid transport to connect both island and mainland. Thanks to steamshipping, less than five days separated Boston or Philadelphia from the land of perpetual summer. With a return fare for travelers from Boston to Port Antonio costing about £12 ($60) per person in 1892, it was not surprising that the tourist traffic blossomed.[22] With the building of larger, better, and more comfortable steel boats in the late nineteenth century, the tourist trade thus became a valid economic adjunct to the banana business.

In the extreme northeast of Jamaica lies the parish of Portland—the foremost banana land in the island. It rises from the seacoast to the highest peak of the Blue Mountains and is known for its fertility and beautiful scenery. Port Antonio, the chief town of the parish, possessed two of the finest and most secure harbors in the island, with accommodation for large seagoing vessels. By 1889–1890, Port Antonio was also in possession of a reservoir "with very good water" and a piped water supply.[23] It was here at Port Antonio that the first resort area of any significance developed in Jamaica, and for many years it dominated the island's infant tourist traffic. The close connection between Port Antonio's banana business and its early prominence in the holiday trade is clear from the oral testimony given by an informant some years ago. According to his recollection, "in the early days of the Jamaican fruit trade the weekly sailings out of Port Antonio exceeded the weekly sailings out of Liverpool."[24] The extent of traffic in those days is corroborated by *Who's Who in Jamaica*, which wrote of Lorenzo Baker in 1916, the first year of its issue: "He materially assisted in bringing tourists to the island. About 30 steamers with a total average tonnage of 20,000, each capable of carrying upwards of 50 passengers, reach Port Antonio every week from Boston, Philadelphia, Baltimore or New York."[25]

Captain Baker was, characteristically, among the first to discern the potential for tourism that Port Antonio, his headquarters, possessed. As he and his associates expanded local operations, they required greater accommodation for their growing management staff. Tourists soon began to make the trip on Baker's banana boats. He resolved to build a hotel,

Modern sea transport made holiday cruises to the Caribbean feasible by 1900.
Illustrations courtesy of National Library of Jamaica.

choosing as its site the crest of Titchfield Hill with a delightful
view of both sea and land. Having made up his mind to construct his hotel there, Baker refused to let anything or anyone
stand in his way, including a local resident who had erected a
house there and who bluntly refused to sell.[26]

Baker resorted to different tactics to persuade the gentleman.
A boat was being built for the owner of the house by the same
person who constructed most of Baker's cutters. Baker connived
with the boat builder to make the terms for payment on the
vessel so difficult that the owner was obliged to surrender the
house in part payment for the schooner. Thus Baker was able to
acquire the site he desired and erect the first Hotel Titchfield on
the spot. This was little more than a boardinghouse and was
demolished a few years later, to be replaced by an impressive
building of 150 rooms and elaborate dining facilities.[27] When in
1909 this was destroyed by fire, an even finer edifice was erected.
Only the first construct was the captain's private venture; the
others were company projects.[28]

Just as he had sought supremacy in the early banana industry,
so Baker by his calculated entry into the hotel enterprise sought
to control, mold, and dominate it from its infancy. He integrated
all aspects of the business—bringing tourists to Jamaica as well
as lodging them and catering to them there. An analogous act in
the banana enterprise had been Baker's expansion from shipping and distribution into cultivation of the fruit. He bought
land of his own to grow bananas partly because he lacked assurance that the peasantry would always provide a ready supply
of the fruit for his freighters. In like manner, it was because he
could not guarantee visitors first-class accommodation in existing lodges that he entered the hotel business. Baker stood to lose
the budding passenger traffic in which his boats were engaged if
there were no improvements in the quality of the accommodation offered the overseas visitor, as the standard in most public
places was poor.[29] It was through his anxiety to maintain and
increase the number of visitors to the island that Baker embarked upon hotel keeping.

(Top) *The first Hotel Titchfield (c. 1897). Built by Captain L. D. Baker, a strict teetotaller, no liquor was served on the premises. Liquor was also prohibited on Baker's boats that brought tourists to and from Jamaica.*

The second Hotel Titchfield (bottom) *was in operation by 1904. It had some one hundred fifty rooms and continued a policy of temperance.*

Illustrations courtesy of National Library of Jamaica.

A 1904 advertisement for the Hotel Titchfield and for its subsidiary, the Peak View Hotel Cottages, located on the other side of the island. Courtesy of National Library of Jamaica.

Baker's sally into tourism was not restricted to Jamaica but extended into the United States. Just as he had placed himself in the vanguard of the early Jamaican tourist industry, Baker also pioneered the holiday trade of his Massachusetts hometown, Wellfleet. The sixty-two-room Chequesset Inn that he built there was operated in summer alone, with the same staff that ran the Titchfield Hotel in winter.[30] It was a tribute to Baker's entrepreneurial foresight that he predicted that summer residents and vacationers would bring a new source of prosperity to Wellfleet. Faith in a resort future of his hometown impelled him to acquire summer cottages there as well as a large expanse of undeveloped shorefront totaling some 4,000 acres.[31] Raised among fishermen, Baker had become another type of fisherman: his catches were tourists and his bait a holiday idyll.

The captain and his associates were not the only persons in the banana business to enter the hotel enterprise. In 1896 a small group of Jamaicans, by their successes in shipping bananas in refrigerated storage to England, demonstrated the economic feasibility of such an undertaking. In a sequel to this, Sir Alfred Jones, head of Elder, Dempster and Company, inaugurated in 1901 the Imperial Direct Line to bring the fruit to England. The United Kingdom had acquired a taste for the banana, as Elder, Dempster and Company had for some time been trading fruit in the Canary Islands.[32] The firm had its ships fitted up for the conveyance of not only bananas but passengers and had built fine hotels in the Canaries, pioneering these islands as health resorts. In Jamaica, therefore, Sir Alfred's interests readily ranged beyond banana trading. In 1901 he obtained by lease the two principal guest houses in Kingston, spent some £30,000 refurbishing them, and advertised extensively to persuade Englishmen to winter on the island.[33] Like Baker, Jones integrated both the transportation and the accommodations of the tourist traffic. Unlike Baker, however, Jones did not have much success in either endeavor.

Jones's venture into the hotel business in Jamaica was a big

(Top) *Afternoon on the piazza of the Hotel Titchfield (1908).*
(Bottom) *Bathing at the Hotel Titchfield bathhouses (1908).*
Illustrations courtesy of National Library of Jamaica.

failure, although his advertising did for a while develop among
the English an interest in the island as a resort. One of the chief
factors that baffled such efforts was the distance between Jamaica and the United Kingdom.[34] The voyage from England
took too much time out of a winter vacation. By contrast, the trip
from New York for a winter holiday, with a fortnight's stay, was
so comfortable and easy that by 1915 a number of Americans
had even erected winter villas in the colony.[35] Distance aside, the
failure of Jones's hotel caper in Jamaica might have been due to
the possibility that he had overextended himself. In the opinion
of the directors of the Royal Mail Steamship Company, Jones, in
attempting to run hotels in Jamaica as well as buy and sell fruit
rather than just carry it, had taken on far more responsibility
than he was capable of handling.[36]

As for the prime object of the Imperial Direct Line—the banana traffic—Jones's intervention was equally uneventful. Despite widespread expectations that he would be successful in this
enterprise, Sir Alfred's banana business was ill-starred from the
start. Supplies of the fruit from the big estates were largely
controlled by the United Fruit Company. The men commissioned to buy the fruit and load the ships were more or less new
to the banana business.[37] Further, the first shipments of the
fruit were spoiled en route. Through competition and other
setbacks, Sir Alfred was soon forced to enter into a partnership
with the United Fruit Company in order to rescue his business from bankruptcy. Within a mere two years of the launch-
ing of Jones's transatlantic trading, the initially independent
market in England was thus subverted by the United Fruit Company's acquisition of nearly half of the shares in Jones's banana operations. At a later date the United Fruit Company
acquired even more shares in the firm and thereby seized control. The Elder, Dempster line became a mere tool of the United
Fruit Company's hegemonic hold over the island's banana
industry.[38]

If monopoly was a prevailing feature of the youthful banana
business, so also was seasonality. Northern buyers of Jamaican

fruit had little demand for it in the summer months when their own strawberries, raspberries, cranberries, summer apples, pears, and plums were plentiful. Shipped at any time other than the months of November to April, bananas were a drag on the market and fundamentally uneconomic. The banana trade and, by extension, the tourist traffic (since the banana boats conveyed the visitors) were both essentially winter operations. Since these months were also the busiest time on the sugar estates, the Jamaican economy as a whole now found itself hyperactive during the first part of the year and rather inert thereafter. To the dead season in sugar production was now added the off-season in tourism. It was, in fact, Baker who initiated the practice in some areas of closing hotels during the summer months.

In surveying the gestation of the banana and tourist industries in Jamaica, close attention must be accorded to the obvious interconnection between both businesses and the domestic growth of the U.S. economy in the second half of the nineteenth century. Between 1870 and 1910 the U.S. population more than doubled, growing from forty to ninety-two million,[39] and the disposable income of families rose as the nation mastered the intricacies of technical civilization, thereby enabling the economy to take off. Outputs in agriculture and industry increased phenomenally in the last decades of the nineteenth century as the economic giant awakened. Among industrial countries, for example, the United States ranked fifth in the world in production in 1850 and fourth in 1860, but by 1894 it had taken the lead globally, producing twice as much as Great Britain and half the combined amount of all Europe.[40] It was the opportunities that this economic growth generated that Baker was alert enough to seize; the thriving economy enhanced the effective demand for both trade and travel. Regarding the volume and value of the latter, "it was estimated by shipping companies that before the First World War 150,000 Americans crossed the Atlantic annually to Europe where their expenditure was reported to be gratifyingly extravagant."[41]

Jamaicans were not unimpressed with the American enterprise that fostered such tremendous advances. The *Jamaica Post* sounded infatuated: "to us all such growth in our neighbour-hood means a better future."[42] It was to American enterprise, after all, that the rekindling of the economic life of Jamaica was attributed, thanks largely to Captain Baker, whom many viewed as the personification of the genius of U.S. capitalism. In the beginning, Baker had been just passing through Jamaica, but because he was impressed with its potential he had returned, developed it to both his and the country's benefit, and settled there. Perhaps other American visitors might be enticed to do the same. Perhaps the tourist industry might prove to be an instrument of providence to advance the economic lot of the colony. Having mused on such possibilities, the *Jamaica Post* was unequivocal about its sentiment.

The object we have principally in view, we will frankly state, is the introduction into this country of the American element. . . . the leaven-ing of our mass with the energy and spirit of "go" found in Americans and found in an equal degree in no other people. They were the pi-oneers in the regeneration of the island of which the Parish of Portland gave the earliest signs . . . and we have great faith in seeing this coun-try, through American enterprise and skill in agriculture, a Florida with far greater fertility and greater beauty.[43]

Jamaica was thus offered as a paradise, not only for health seekers and winter tourists but for foreign capital as well.

But while the trend was to surrender the task and the benefits of developing the island's resources to foreigners, a minority opinion hoped for a revolution in local attitudes regarding Ja-maica's economic development. The remedy for Jamaica's afflic-tion, it held, was for the local people to take up their beds and walk. An 1891 letter to the *Jamaica Post* was a clear example of this different sentiment. Why, it asked, does Jamaica import furniture? Why does the island not instead export to the rest of the world furniture of exquisite construction, made from the beautiful woods that grow abundantly in it? Why does Jamaica depend so much upon foreigners to give impetus to local pro-

duction and upon foreign lands for almost everything that
is consumed, whether of food or clothing? Where does loaf
sugar, for example, come from? Why is it not made in Jamaica?
Does not Jamaica say to all the world: "Come! Make use of and
grow on my wealth, for I am too stupid and too indolent to use it
myself?" Why should Jamaica sigh for second editions of Captain Baker? Why should Americans be implored to come and
develop the island's resources, so as to take out of it fortunes,
which but for an unaccountable lack of energy and determina-
tion could be made and kept by locals? Awake! Awake!, Jamaica!, for indeed, thou art heavy with baneful sleep.[44]

Chapter 4

Jamaica Awakens

The night of Jamaica's adversity has passed away; A brighter and a happier day has dawned upon the land.

—*Jamaica Post,* 24 December 1890

The Jamaica International Exhibition will be a landmark in West Indian History . . . not only because it is a plucky effort to march abreast of the times, but because it is decided proof that the "dead West Indies" are not so dead after all.

—*Jamaica Exhibition Bulletin*

ALTHOUGH since 1850 there had been isolated individual initiatives to promote Jamaica as a holiday resort, in 1890 Jamaica was still terra incognita to the traveling public of Europe and the United States. It was not until then that the first concerted campaign was initiated to establish the tourist industry on the island. In 1870, for example, many of the parishioners of Kingston, intent on increasing the volume of trade between Jamaica and the North American mainland, submitted a petition to the governor requesting that a subsidy be granted to shippers for the purpose of establishing regular steamship communications with New York.[1] This "memorial" was signed by some six or seven hundred merchants, shopkeepers, and other residents of the capital. In part, it urged that "direct steamers would induce the many wealthy Americans, who previously visited Cuba during the severe winter to seek Jamaica and open a cheap and ready road for ourselves and families to visit America for a change." However the memorial itself did not intend any new promotion of Jamaica as a winter resort for northerners.

The petitioners doubtlessly desired to develop trade but not especially the tourist trade. Though there were some economic advantages from a greater movement of persons between the island and North American ports, the prospective returns did not seem attractive enough to appeal to these parishioners. They were more preoccupied with the gains from general trade between both places than with tourism specifically. It was not until the gestation and growth of the banana business that this desire for more contact with the United States was actualized.[2]

The decision to hold an international exhibition in Jamaica in 1891 heralded the first intensive effort to promote tourism in the island. Although A. C. St. Clair, a Jamaican, was the first to suggest it, the idea of holding a local exhibition began to take shape only when W. Fawcett, the director of public gardens, recommended it to Sir Henry Blake as a means of developing, among the peasantry, an interest in the economic potential of the colony.[3] Both Fawcett and Governor Blake discussed the feasibility of the idea and elaborated upon its original conception. The governor felt that a display limited just to small-scale West Indian cultivation would be undesirable, since the planter class needed to be stirred up as much as the local peasants. It was decided, therefore, to put on display the most improved type of machinery suitable for use on the sugar estates. Consideration was also given to the idea of enlarging the scale of the fair by involving the other British West Indian islands in this unprecedented venture.

In the words of the governor, Sir Henry Blake, who became the moving force behind the exhibition, its principal purpose was to educate the people, awaken them from their economic stupor, and "stir them up and arouse their interest in the possibilities of the country."[4] Besides exhibits of the most up-to-date sugar technology, the exhibition commissioners were determined to display demonstration models depicting the most recent improvements in the production of minor Jamaican staples. For instance, they planned to display the newest procedures in extracting coconut and other oils by compression, the most modern methods in preparing coconut coir or fiber, and the latest processes in extracting fibers from plants.[5] Suitable for exhibit were gadgets for curing and preparing ginger, spices, coffee, cocoa, and anatto, as well as fruit-drying devices, small windmills, turbines, and other time- and labor-saving contrivances.[6]

Popular support was a prerequisite for the exhibition's success. Speaking platforms were set up throughout the island to inform the public of the exercise and gain general endorsement for it. In the exhibition schema a special role was reserved for the herbs and plants in the local pharmacopoeia. W. Fawcett, for example, planned to display a collection of such plants, many of which, he claimed, possessed valuable medicinal properties.[7] At an exhibition meeting in May Pen, Fawcett explained that the substance that certain peoples of Africa use to poison the tips of their arrows, had recently been ascertained, and when this substance was sent to England for analysis it was found to be a very valuable drug for coronary ailments. Fawcett believed that many of the native herbs, barks, roots, and medicinal plants in Jamaica were similarly of great value and that people used these items in one way or another without knowing the full range of their potential. A further interest of his was to exhibit a specimen of banana and plantain meal, for an old woman had recently visited the exhibition office with a sample of bread made from the breadfruit, and it was truly excellent. At the time, the process of obtaining flour from the breadfruit, banana, and plantain was unknown to the white population. But, Fawcett submitted, these would yield a worthy substitute for imported wheat flour that was just as nutritious. On another note, he encouraged exhibits of samples of starches or dyes.[8]

At that same meeting, a Reverend Henderson observed that, ever since his arrival in Jamaica, he had been astounded at the amount of marketable material wasted simply because the people were not cognizant of its worth. He has seen valuable berries permitted to fall from the trees and decay, while in the same district the people were complaining of hard times and unemployment. In this Garden of Eden, poverty was a paradox.[9] The exhibition, he felt, would enlighten the folk about the unexploited value of many of their resources.[10]

Beyond stimulating the existing enterprises, the exhibition's principal objective was to generate new and promising economic undertakings. For example, possibilities existed for making paper stock from bamboo and *megass,* but these had heretofore been ignored.[11] There were plants in Jamaica yielding oils and perfumes reputed to be rich with potential profit for both the chemist and the florist. In sum, plans for the exhibition expressed hope that there would emerge in Jamaica a new kind of person, who would appreciate the economic opportunities in the island. Such people, through the application of English technology to native raw materials, would create in the colony a new industrial dynamism and propel it along a more rapid economic growth path.[12]

One of the island's unexploited resources was its climate. The tourist trade was one of the foremost of the new industries that the Jamaica International Exhibition was expected to foster. As the *Handbook of Jamaica for 1891–92* explained, "the Exhibition would bring many to Jamaica for the first time, who would make known the advantages of Jamaica as a winter resort to others and thus lay the foundation for a steady and increasing flow of tourists to the Island."[13] The promoters of the venture believed that the International Exhibition would herald the takeoff of Jamaica's tourist traffic, until then a conspicuously insignificant element in the domestic economy. Through the International Exhibition, the hope was, the populace would see the light and realize that prodigious wealth was to be garnered if Jamaica could be sold as a winter paradise to northerners.

The real value of tourism, however, as conceptualized by even the promoters of the exhibition, lay not so much in its income-producing potential as in its capacity to indirectly encourage foreign investment in the island.[14] Tourism, it was anticipated, would bring the captains of foreign industry to the colony and expose its investment possibilities to them. If there was a general ignorance of the island's prospects at home, considerably more existed in the world at large.

A premier objective of the exhibition, then, was to introduce the colony's potential to the world outside. In an interview with a foreign correspondent of the *New York Herald,* Governor Blake made this feature of the exercise clear. At a time when U.S. capital had begun to migrate abroad, the exhibition's function was to publicize Jamaica's investment attractions: "The idea we have at present is to invite everybody and to exhibit to them all that we can produce on the island. We believe that there may be some products very little considered just now, which may turn out to be of great value when examined by experts.."[15] In this manner might be laid "the foundation of exports as valuable even as the exports of sugar or bananas."[16]

But in order to open up the Jamaican countryside to foreign investors, proper accommodation should be made available to the overseas visitors traveling in rural areas.[17] It was alleged that, in the past, foreigners who might have been interested in investing in the island had been compelled to depart without "half seeing" it, due to the difficulty of getting about in the countryside.[18] By 1890, roads in the rural districts were much improved and continually being extended. It was, therefore, the lack of comfortable accommodation that apparently continued to hinder the growth of the investment potential of the island.[19] Hotels were regarded as a panacea for the depressed economic condition of Jamaica. As one journal observed,

Effective hotel accommodation once established with us, there is no calculating the marked change for the better which will take place in the future of Jamaica. At present, we are constantly retrogressing from positive inanition. A new, intelligent, active and increasing population will inspirit us afresh, and indulge us despite ourselves to cast off much, if not all of our present lethargy. Jamaica is full of resources; they wait only on the energy of men for their development. Hotels will prove the first step to the attainment of this end.[20]

Because hotels were deemed crucial to the long-run economic development of the island and because they were required at once to house the large numbers of visitors expected at the exhibition, the colonial legislature enacted a law to promote hotel building. The Jamaica Hotels Law of 1890 empowered the colonial secretary to contract, on behalf of the government, agreements for erecting, extending, completing, and maintaining hotels in the island, on such terms and conditions as the governor in privy council might approve. Before the colonial secretary could enter into an agreement with any company under this law, the plans, specifications, and estimates of the firm first had to be ratified by the governor in privy council. Work on every hotel contracted to be built, extended, or completed under this law must also be fully finished and the building equipped within nine months if it were one mile from the limits of Kingston and if outside that perimeter within twelve months of the law's passage. The reason for allotting a shorter time span for hotel construction in and around Kingston was the need to ensure that accommodation was available in time for the opening of the International Exhibition in January 1891.

One of the most prominent features of the Jamaica Hotels Law was the prodigal character of its provisions. It exempted from import duties all building materials, furniture, and fittings imported into the island in connection with building and equipping these hotels. The government pledged the general revenues and assets of the colony as a guarantee on the principal and interest of any debentures and certificates that companies might issue to cover the estimated cost of their undertakings. The aggregate amount of the debentures and certificates to be issued under this law was not to exceed £150 thousand in value. Despite a fair amount of foreboding in some quarters over the largesse and even the advisability of the Hotels Law, the "paternal" government, in its wisdom, chose to ignore such criticisms.[21] In the end, however, the hotels scheme failed. Ultimately it saddled the taxpayers with what came to be termed "the hotels loan incubus."[22]

Still, what was obvious when the Hotels Law was passed was the fervent optimism of the time and the heady anticipation of the gains from hosting the International Exhibition. The Jamaica Hotels Law merely attested to these extravagant sentiments. It was because the visitor was a putative investor that he was wooed to Jamaica. One possible area for investment from overseas was, of course, the hotel industry itself. According to a letter that Eugene Baker, a member of the parochial board of Portland, wrote to the editor of one daily newspaper, an abnormally high profit margin could be forecast for the hotel industry.

Sir,

Kindly publish the following five reasons why Jamaica would make a better winter resort than Florida and attract more visitors:—

1. (a) Florida being a semi-tropical country has an uneven climate and is subject to frost during winter months.
   (b) Jamaica being tropical has an even climate and no frost.
   (c) A country with an even climate and no frost ought to make a better winter resort than a country with an uneven climate and frost.
2. (a) Florida is subject to yellow fever and dengue fever.
   (b) Jamaica is not subject to yellow fever and dengue fever.
   (c) Therefore, Jamaica is more healthy.
3. (a) Florida is a low, flat country; highest elevation about 400 ft. with rivers running slow and sluggish.
   (b) Jamaica is a hilly country, highest elevation 7,360 ft. Rivers run quiet, pure and healthy.
   (c) A hilly country with quick flowing rivers ought to be more healthy than a flat country with slow flowing rivers.
4. (a) Scenery in Florida has a great deal of sameness about it and is very tame.
   (b) Scenery in Jamaica is diversified, picturesque, beautiful and wild.
   (c) Jamaica being a country with diversified, picturesque and beautiful scenery ought to attract more visitors than a low, flat country with a tame same scenery.
5. (a) Jamaica has better roads, more valuable mineral springs and more natural curiosities than Florida.
   (b) Jamaica with the best roads, mineral springs and curiosities ought to attract the most visitors.
   I am, etc. Eugene B. Baker[23]

Although the acolytes of the exhibition idea, like T. H. Sharpe,[24] had been urging the people to prepare exhibits and compile investment data on the natural resources of their districts, an exhibition mania never quite gripped the public. Among the common people there were many rumors that the exhibition's purpose was much different than that officially alleged. For instance, it was held that the venture was a mere pretext to show the government what the people could do so that extra taxes could be imposed upon them.[25] Another insinuation was that Sir Henry Blake, the governor, had been commissioned by the Queen to set up the exhibition in order to find out what the land was good for, so that she might sell it to the Americans. A third rumor was that the governor had been sent to the island to make the people slaves again, and the exhibition building was a huge barracoon to which they were to be lured and held captive.

Confronted with this widespread suspicion and disaffection vis-à-vis the exhibition idea, the event's promoters intensified their campaign to publicize the real nature of the undertaking and its considered value. It was also necessary to assure the people that its benefits would be shared by all. According to Governor Blake, import substitution was a prime objective of the exercise: "We hope to find that you can make many things that we now import, so that the money we send away to pay for these things shall be paid to you instead for your labour."[26] From the platform, the classroom, and the pulpit, the promoters propagandized the masses and painstakingly instructed them on the parts they were to play. Even the simplest of things, they stressed, could be submitted for display at the exhibition. For example: "Suitable saplings for walking sticks and umbrella handles may be exhibited and a considerable trade established."[27]

The role of the masses was not restricted to compiling exhibits but also included keeping their huts and yards clean and tidy to avoid possible pestilence. Nothing would be more injurious to the infant tourist industry or to the success of the exhibition than an outbreak of disease. Archdeacon Farrar of Jamaica thus sermonized his flock, "set thine house in order."[28] Cleanliness was related not just to godliness but to the secular advancement of the colony's macroeconomic interests. In a like crusading spirit, the governor personally offered cash prizes to the people of Kingston for the best-kept and best-arranged premises under the assessed annual value of £8.[29] No one responded, as the secretary of the exhibition reluctantly admitted.[30]

Under the existing system of assessing house property, the people had little inclination to improve their premises. The house tax militated against the development of better and nicer homes because, as Robert Craig submitted to the legislature, when the assessors in Kingston went on their rounds they usually assessed at a higher rate any house that was cleaned, painted, and had a garden in good order.[31] In contrast, a better property that was less tidily kept would be assessed at a lower rate. No wonder the governor's scheme was a failure: nobody contended for the prize because nobody wished to be assessed at a higher rate. While the government offered incentives to provide better accommodation for foreigners, insofar as the question of better housing for locals was concerned, its fiscal practice was a distinct disincentive.

Although the exhibition had been designed to show the world Jamaica's capabilities and products, from the beginning an implied admission of the inferiority of Jamaicans permeated the thinking of the planners as they prepared for the event. Among the initial errors of the exhibition commissioners was their unwillingness to permit native contractors even the chance to compete with foreign firms for the contract to erect the exhibition building. Instead, James Richmond, engineer of the central district, was instructed by the governor to go to the United States to enter into a contract with some responsible firm there to construct the Jamaica Exhibition building.[32] In the end, however, though Richmond received many U.S. tenders to erect and furnish material for the building, these were all in excess of the amount appropriated. At the final reckoning, therefore, the native builders rejected at the outset were the ones to whom the exhibition commissioners were compelled to resort. As one of the local tabloids put it, "the stone which the builders rejected has become the head of the corner."³³

Jamaica's International Exhibition opened at last on Tuesday, 27 January 1891. An address was delivered to the Prince of Wales, and after His Royal Highness's reply, a choir sang the Hundredth Psalm to the accompaniment of the West India Regiment band.³⁴ The bishop offered up a prayer of consecration. The governor presented the Prince of Wales with a golden key to the building, and His Royal Highness formally declared the exhibition open, amid tumultuous applause. A fanfare of trumpets and salute of artillery signaled the fact of the opening. When the ceremony was over the royal party toured the exhibition buildings and grounds. The day's proceedings climaxed in a grand ball at King's House.

The exhibition building was an elegant structure in a Moorish design, situated to the north of the Kingston racecourse on a portion of the Quebec Lodge lands and the waterworks land at Cavaliers Pen. "The general external aspect of the main building," we are told, "was graceful, light and imposing and the beauty of the scene was greatly enhanced by the background of magnificent hills which formed as it were, the setting of the structure." Within the building itself, "the light and airy character of the structure with its subdued and harmonious colouring, the rich, and in many cases, brilliant hues of the exhibits, the glitter of bright metal and glass, the waving fronds of palms and other tropical plants, and the ever moving, many coloured dresses of the visitors, formed a scene never before witnessed in Jamaica and which could not fail to impress."³⁵

Exhibits were on display from many parts of the world, including the sister colonies of the West Indies. Jamaica itself showed samples of the island's chief products: sugar, rums, coffee, cocoa, oils and essences, roots, starches, fibers, preserves and pickles, cabinetwork, fancy woods, gums, resins, native wines, liqueurs, cigars, and cigarettes. The West Indian island of St. Vincent exhibited six Caribs, who displayed their skills in weaving baskets and other handicraft in one of the huts of the

The Jamaica Exhibition building. Courtesy of National Library of Jamaica.

model village set up on the exhibition grounds.[36] The Scottish court sent out a piper for the exhibition, who filled the halls of the building with sweet strains from his bagpipe.

On the evening of 2 May, the Jamaica International Exhibition came to a close, a little more than three months after it had been opened by Prince George of Wales. In financial terms the exhibition was a failure, but according to the *Jamaica Post*, it had been "a foregone conclusion," in any case, that there would be a deficit.[37] That, indeed, was the alleged norm in English or colonial exhibitions. Rather, the Jamaica Exhibition was conceived by its protagonists as a means of accelerating the economic growth of the island, and in that light was to be regarded not as a financial flop but as a form of investment. Moreover, in terms of the number of locals it had attracted, the exhibition was an unqualified success. "It has been estimated that, in proportion to the number of inhabitants in the immediate neighbourhood and the city of Kingston, the Jamaica Exhibition was more largely attended than any preceding one in Europe or America."[38] Given exhibits like the model dairy and the model industrial village, many applauded the exposition as "a splendid object lesson" from which the Jamaican masses would benefit.

So it was misleading to judge the outcome of the Jamaica International Exhibition by its immediate results in terms of pounds, shillings, and pence. The only meaningful measure for assessing its financial denouement was on the basis of its long-run returns. From an educational point of view the Exhibition could only be voted a success, as it had shown the people of Jamaica what articles they needed to develop their resources and where these items could best be bought. The *Jamaica Post* advised:

In view of the fact . . . that Jamaica is being talked of throughout the world and more especially in the U.S.A. and Canada, as it has never been before—that the beauty of its scenery, the salubrity of its climate and the fertility of its soil are now known . . . and that this knowledge will undoubtedly lead to a great influx of tourists into the island every year, we think that the inhabitants of Jamaica, or rather the Exhibition guarantors, have made a very profitable investment of their money.[39]

Though the exhibition itself had come to an end, the objectives it had been designed to achieve had not disappeared. In fact, Jamaica was said to be henceforth "on perpetual exhibition."[40]

Chapter 5

"Ho-tel Me Not"

PRIOR TO 1891, when Jamaica hosted the International Exhibition, there was no such thing as a hotel industry in that colony. The flow of visitors to Jamaica was meager, and the accommodations were, by and large, squalid, consisting primarily of taverns in the towns and inns in the rural areas.[1] Taverns were public houses where one could secure food, drink, and shelter. Travelers in the countryside took refuge in inns, which offered a lower level of accommodation than taverns. The reason for this difference in quality was that few people spent more than one night at any of these inns, located at more or less convenient spots along the main roads. The inn was a mere refreshment place for man and horse, and in general its facilities were quite elemental. The taverns were not much better for their part. "Much cannot be said for the West Indian hotels in general," Trollope commented in his travelogue of 1860.[2] According to Capper over a quarter of a century later, in some cases the inn was "a mere hovel."[3]

To start with, the typical sitting room in these places was almost always in "a sorry state." At nightfall, the room was lit by a kerosene lamp, the glare of which attracted "myriads" of winged ants, moths, and other creatures. As for the bedrooms, moth-eaten pillows and mattresses and a coverlet of dubious cleanliness was the common offering. At nine, with candle in hand, the guest normally repaired to his bedroom. There, hopes for a fair night's rest were contingent upon the unlikely good fortune of finding the room equipped with a proper mosquito net, failing which one shared one's bed with insects, including perhaps a large cockroach or two.[4]

This dearth of decent accommodation congenial to the taste of a refined person, along with the slatternly service at such lodges, constituted before 1890 one of the biggest drawbacks to the development of tourism in the colony. What held for Jamaica was just as true in her sister isles. According to John Amphlett, for instance: "I believe that if nice comfortable hotels were supplied and good waiters and servants procured to attend to them, instead of the lazy and independent negroes, the West Indies would be well frequented as a health resort."[5]

The standard at public houses in Jamaica especially, and in the West Indies in general, before the International Exhibition of 1891 left a lot to be desired, or so visitors repeatedly railed.[6] The many taverns in Kingston drew clientele from among persons of moderate means who were not too fastidious about some dirt or a little din. For the more exacting visitor there was another, more expensive type of accommodation—the hall. Located in the lower part of Kingston, these establishments had in the past been erected as private residences by members of the colonial elite.[7] Later, however, whether through debt or movement on the part of their proprietors to cooler and more comfortable districts, they came into the hands of colored entrepreneurs (often women), who converted them into hostels. Despite the higher tariff at the halls, the improvement in the quality of accommodation over the tavern was marginal.

Blundell Hall was perhaps the best hostel in Kingston in 1872 yet, as one guest confided, "if so, the others must be bad." Ducks and poultry kept by the management inhabited a yard in the hotel compound. Carrion crows jostled among the domestic animals in this enclosure, likewise seeking something to devour. The scullery and domestic office, as well as the stables and first floor bedrooms, were arranged along the perimeter of this quadrangle. As for the interior furnishing, the bed on which our informant slept was draped with a tattered mosquito net composed "more of holes than of netting." In consequence,

The Moneague Tavern in 1844. Such taverns provided public accomodation for travelers in inland towns. William Sewell in 1859–60 described the Moneague Tavern as "the best in the island."

Located halfway between Kingston and Spanish Town, the Ferry Inn was a well-known refreshment spot before railways developed and people stopped journeying by coach.
Illustrations courtesy of National Library of Jamaica.

Park Lodge (Kingston).

Date Tree Hall, another old hotel in Kingston (1906).
Illustrations courtesy of National Library of Jamaica.

"in the morning, after my first trial of them, I discovered at least a dozen fat well-fed mosquitoes hanging on inside the curtains, and lazily and contentedly waving their hind legs in the air."[8]

It was such reputed shortcomings in the offerings at most lodgings in Jamaica that Sir John Peter Grant sought to remedy during his tenure as governor. Grant's grand idea was to erect a hotel in Kingston on the model of the best American public houses and to establish a branch of it in the hills organized along the separate cottage plan.[9] In support of his proposal to use public funds for this venture, Sir John argued that it was government's responsibility to take the initiative for constructing the edifice. First, American speculators were not willing to build in Jamaica since they were then receiving a high interest for their money in their own country. Further, his proposal was not without precedent, he contended, for in Nassau (capital of the British colony of the Bahamas) a hotel had been constructed with money from the public purse. Finally, local consensus favored such a hotel as a means of bringing substantial sums of money into the colony, he claimed.

I am convinced that such a Hotel . . . by supplying a want now justly and greatly complained of, would be the certain means of inducing a very large number of persons to come to Jamaica from the United States, and some even from the Dominion of Canada. . . . In every way an influx of strangers in easy circumstances, with the energy and love of progress which the class of visitors that are expected are known to possess, could not but be of infinite benefit to a colony which owes much of its backwardness to a remarkable want of these qualities.[10]

Grant's plan for the construction of the hotel was quite simple. The land for this scheme, he suggested, should be acquired by the government and the building subsequently erected there on an approved plan at public expense. Next, the hotel should be let to a firm or company that was solvent, and the lessee should undertake to operate the hotel at a rent that would provide for the interest on the amount expended, for fire insurance, and for maintenance. Last, the lessee should be entitled to purchase the hotel at any time during the period of the lease. Such an arrangement, he postulated, would be satisfactory to both parties. The government would be assured of the requisite security, and the lessee would have the option to purchase if the business were a success.

Governor Grant's proposal proved stillborn. When he cited the precedent of Nassau to give further weight to his argument, he was evidently unaware that the hotel there had been a financial failure and that, in the words of the colonial office, "very little encouragement can be derived from this precedent." The secretary of state for the colonies was unwilling to sanction a similar undertaking in the case of Jamaica "without much stronger proof than he has yet received that a similar result is not to be apprehended."[11] Following this rejection of Governor Grant's scheme, almost two decades elapsed before the colonial government once more undertook sponsorship of any scheme for the establishment and promotion of modern hotel businesses in the island.

The immediate background to the change in official attitudes was the decision to hold an International Exhibition in 1891. Lodging facilities in Kingston were so limited that "probably one hundred tourists would fill all the recognized hotels in the city," the U.S. consul remarked in February 1890.[12] To prepare for the exhibition, the governor of the island, Sir Henry Blake, enacted legislation that gave a great incentive to domestic hotel development. Under Law 27 of 1890 (the Jamaica Hotels Law), public credit was pledged to the sum of £150 thousand to establish hotels in the island. By its terms, speculators in this enterprise were guaranteed an interest rate of 3 percent per annum on their investment. All the materials needed for the erection and equipment of the buildings were to be allowed duty-free entry into the colony. Critics claimed that the taxpayer would bear any losses under the conditions of the guarantee, whereas the speculators would reap any profits. The terms of the agreement were alleged to be "so temptingly generous as to stir the flame of gambling speculation in the breast of the coolest—most

22222222222222

1111111111111

cold-blooded individual."[13] Great though the expectations were, the government through this largesse was to become saddled with a number of bankrupt businesses in the long run, as their actual performances failed to yield projected results. Under the Jamaica Hotels Law of 1890 the taxpayers were made to contribute generously, and not a few persons were skeptical about the returns that the public at large would receive. Criticism of the Jamaica Hotels Law essentially was based on the contention that land was the foundation of all national wealth. The infant hotel industry, it was protested, had less claim to the grant of government concessions than longer established, land-based enterprises like sugar and coffee.[14] It would have been more advisable for the government to grant concessions to the sugar industry, for example, to stimulate the construction of central factories, than invest in hotels—which are at root "non-productive" or merely "distributive undertakings."[15] If the public money were to be committed, it should as a rule be pledged in that area where it could do the greatest good for the greatest number—agriculture. In the words of one local newspaper:

To suppose that there will always be a sufficient number of strangers in the country to keep the hotels going and even pay the 3 percent that the Government has guaranteed is simply a fallacy. . . . Under any circumstance it is unfortunate, we think, that a country's prosperity should be made dependent upon anything so evanescent and uncertain. National prosperity must come chiefly from the earth. . . . Hotel keeping is but one of the subsidiaries by which the mass of mankind earn their bread, but not in the wildest dream can it be relied on as a source of national prosperity.[16]

Prominent among the objectors was a small number of persons who were distinctly opposed to any course of action that used public funds to benefit private and foreign corporations or to subsidize the comfort and pleasure of itinerants from overseas. If, from an economic standpoint, the Jamaica Hotels Law was at variance with the first principles of politicoeconomic science, from a sociological stance its implied bias was no less reprehensible, in the view of many.[17] As it was, the daily life of the average citizen was spent in an uninspiring cycle of eating, drinking, working, and sleeping. No intellectual diversion of any sort varied the monotony. Should public monies be spent, it was contended, the government, should first administer to the needs of its own population before it catered to the caprices of transients from abroad. As one resident from St. Ann's Parish complained in a letter to the *Jamaica Post:*

There are some few, who, like myself have the opinion firmly rooted in their minds that the necessity for hotels on the large scale now in vogue is purely imaginary, that the country can very well do without visitors of the tourist class, that hotels without external surroundings to make the country a pleasant one to sojourn in are useless and that it is necessary, first to render the country comfortable for our own people. . . . Under present auspices life in this country is not pleasant. . . . we have no theatres, no music halls, no picture galleries, no free libraries; we neglect even to utilize the bountiful gifts of nature by providing large and shady parks in our towns. . . . And yet with immense opportunities and resources whereby to improve in these respects, we thoughtlessly neglect them and squander large sums to raise huge edifices to accommodate strangers.[18]

Following the Jamaica Hotels Law of 1890 a number of hotel companies came into existence, and five modern structures were erected to house visitors to the island.[19] In downtown Kingston two buildings were put up, the Myrtle Bank Hotel and the Queen's Hotel, respectively erected by the Kingston Hotels Company and the Jamaica Hotels Company. In St. Andrew, extra rooms were added to the Constant Spring Hotel, itself built just recently by the American Hotels Company. At Spanish Town, the Hotel Rio Cobre was put up by the St. Catherine Hotels Company. Finally, at Moneague, the Moneague Hotel was erected by the Moneague Hotels Company.

With the exception of the Queen's Hotel, however, these structures all turned out to be money losers, some sooner than later.[20] As early as June 1891, "the Kingston folks" were saying that "hotel ventures are not always a Constant Spring of wealth." Likewise, the directors of the Constant Spring and the Myrtle

(Top) *The old Myrtle Bank Hotel was owned by James Gall, proprietor of Gall's News Letter. It was demolised after being sold in May 1890.*
(Bottom) *The Kingston Hotels Company, which bought the original Myrtle Bank Hotel from James Gall, took advantage of the 1890 Hotels Law to build on the same site this fine structure with seventy-five bedrooms.*
Illustrations courtesy of National Library of Jamaica.

(Top) *The Hotel Rio Cobre, Spanish Town, was built by the St. Catherine Hotels Company under the provisions of the 1890 Hotel Law.*
(Center) *The Moneague Hotel was constructee by the Moneague Hotels Company, also under the terms of the 1890 law.*
(Bottom) *The Constant Spring Hotel was the first building in Jamaica to be lit by electricity. Built in 1888 by the American Hotels Company, it seized upon the Jamaica Hotels Law to erect several small cottages on the hotel's grounds.*
Illustrations courtesy of National Library of Jamaica.

Bank were all chanting this mournful dirge: "Ho-tel me not."[21] Actually, within a mere three months of the close of the exhibition, the Constant Spring Hotel was forced through lack of business to shut its doors for a while.[22] Despite the much-vaunted expertise of American managers, then, neither the Constant Spring nor the Myrtle Bank got off to a successful start. It was almost exclusively upon the "In-Constant" Spring Hotel and the Myrtle Bank Hotel that the brunt of public chagrin was focused. This was because some two-thirds of the £70 thousand that the government had guaranteed on capital invested in the five hotels had been taken by these two buildings.[23] Both establishments were intended to offer the best possible accommodation to visitors in and around the island's capital. However, by mid-1891 it was painfully apparent that "the prospects of the Hotels scheme are not at present particularly bright."

Since a principal purpose of the exhibition had been to propel a takeoff of the tourist industry, what transpired was unquestionably serious enough for W. B. Espeut to raise the matter at the highest levels of government.[24] At a sitting of the legislative council on 22 April 1891, Espeut formally directed the attention of the council to the current state of affairs in the infant hotel business. He had strongly supported the passage of the Jamaica Hotels Law, he said, but if quick action were not taken to erase the unfavorable goings-on in some of the hotels, the guarantee would be endangered and the attempt to provide comfortable accommodation for strangers thwarted.

Of the Rio Cobre Hotel, he claimed, he had heard nothing but praise. He had never visited the Queen's Hotel, but at the Constant Spring complaints of mismanagement were rife. The water in the swimming pool was allowed to remain for two weeks, and it was used by servants as well as visitors. The guests complained of inattention and incivility, and he was told by a person prominent in the shipping business that fewer tourists than expected came to Jamaica because those who had visited the island were so disgusted with the hotel accommodation that they discouraged others from coming. As regards the Myrtle Bank, there were numerous complaints of overcharging and neglect. Indeed, he said, a writer to the London *Globe* of 31 March had been very reproachful in his remarks on both hotels. For these reasons he felt that something should be done speedily to correct this situation.

Espeut's comments in the legislature were revealing. Even though Colonel Ward, another member of the council, charged that Espeut's assertions were designed to damage the hotels, he had to admit that the Myrtle Bank had been mismanaged.[25] Originally it had an American manager and staff, but the manager was in a state of maudlin drunkenness for weeks, and so were some of the staff. They had at last been got rid of and the hotel was, since then, well managed. The acting colonial secretary observed, however, that complaints regarding poor practices at some of the hotels still reached the governor's ear, and the government direcor had been instructed to visit them and stay overnight at times.

If as early as mid-1891 the failure of the hotels scheme seemed imminent, by 1893 it had become a stark reality. From the beginning, neither the Constant Spring nor the Myrtle Bank had been run at a profit. Eventually, in November 1893, the Kingston Hotels Company declared itself unable to keep the Myrtle Bank open any longer, and the government took possession of the building.[26] The legal basis for this action had been stipulated in section 10 of the Jamaica Hotels Law of 1890, which empowered the governor to take possession of a hotel and its equipment upon the failure of the company either to fulfill the terms of the contract or to pay 3 percent interest upon their debentures and certificates for three consecutive years. Owing to this legal provision, the Constant Spring Hotel was taken over by the authorities two years later, and the Moneague and Rio Cobre hotels fell into government hands in 1906.[27]

Of the five hotels set up under the hotels scheme of 1890, only the Queen's Hotel stayed afloat. Unlike the others, which catered to foreigners, the Queen's Hotel had a local clientele of respectable peasant proprietors and country tradesmen who were brought by business to town.[28] By the end of the first phase of the founding of Jamaica's tourism, (that is to say, by 1914), only the Queen's Hotel was still operated by its original company.[29]

By 1893, then, the hotels scheme was on the rocks. The Constant Spring Hotel, which initially had boasted of its cuisine ("the Culinary Department being under the management of a celebrated Parisian Chef, under whom there is a competent staff, consisting of two French cooks and a Viennese baker") had become a white elephant.[30] The Myrtle Bank and the Constant Spring hotels failed ostensibly because of bad management. Their rates had been high, "if not exorbitant." The prices were equal to the highest hotel rates in New York, but the hotels had not offered as luxurious and diversified a menu. Guests had not received good value for their money.[31] Yet, in the opinion of some commentators, failure would still have resulted even if management had been better. The authorities, in their hotels scheme, had unwittingly put the cart before the horse; they had begun at the wrong end.

Given the preoccupation of the authorities with establishing a tourist business, the first thing they should have done, it was suggested, was literally to put their own house in order. The hotels established under the scheme of 1890 were "designed, built and conducted on too large a scale for a small and poor country." Rather than beginning with large, expensive hotels, the government first should have improved the appearance and attractions of the island's capital and established cheaper facilities for getting about the place. These reportedly were among the recurrent complaints of the winter visitors: "Tourists that have been here abhor Kingston; they think it 'a dirty hole' where people are too prompt to take advantage of their ignorance. . . . I have heard many say, do what you will, until you improve your town, give us amusements, and facilities for seeing the Country, you will never induce a large number of Winter Visitors."[32]

A program to remedy these defects, it was contended, would not only have redounded to the benefit of the local people but ought to have constituted "the means first required" to induce visitors to Jamaica. Suitable hotels would subsequently have been erected, simply because it would have then been possible to make money in the hotel business. What was more, people would have been inclined to invest in this sector of the economy without a government guarantee.[33]

If little was offered (whether in the form of attractions in the capital or the quality of service at the hotels) to make Jamaica an attractive environment to the visitor, even less was done in the first place to woo him there. The conspicuous failure of much of the hotels scheme by 1893 was in part owing to the failure to advertise. Following the ambitious effort at organizing the International Exhibition, few measures of any significance were undertaken to call the charms of the island to the notice of the foreign traveling public. In the eyes of many, this neglect was by far the most important failing in the early hotel enterprise, for "advertising is as essential in this respect, as it is to the Manufacturer or Merchant who desires to introduce his class of wares to the buyer."[34] Practical proposals to sell Jamaica were put forward by sundry individuals from time to time, only to fall on deaf ears. One anonymous analyst recommended in 1893, for example:

If we are to expect results, such as we hope for, we must spend a little money; articles on Jamaica must be published not only in New York, but throughout all the Northern States. Advertising of a more direct character must be resorted to; a bureau of information must be established, presided over by one capable of "talking Jamaica," and who would so conduct the office as to render it an attraction for men and ladies to visit, who would seek knowledge respecting this part of the world on which comparatively few know anything.[35]

It was not until the formation of the Jamaica Tourist Association in September 1910 that these measures were actually implemented.[36]

Looking back, perhaps the prime blunder in Blake's administration was the injustice perpetrated against the people of the colony by the passage of the Jamaica Hotels Law of 1890. At a time of recession in the insular economy, the tax burden borne by the struggling people of this poor island was made heavier in order to reduce the risks to expatriate investors in the infant hotel business. Due to this legislation, hundreds of pounds of public money became tied up in hotel failures. Indeed, the colony became bedeviled by what was termed "the hotels loan incubus."[37] What should be done with these "aristocratic alms houses," the Myrtle Bank and the Constant Spring? That question perplexed the members of the legislative council throughout the 1890s. At one time, for example, there was just one lodger at the Constant Spring, and what was more, that prized person was expected to return shortly to the United States. "One lodger," the *Tri-Weekly Budget* declared, "and he is passing out, without an immediate prospect of his place being supplied."[38] On other occasions, occupancy rates were distinctly better. At the height of the tourist season of 1899 there were ten residents at Myrtle Bank and sixteen at the Constant Spring. To serve this number there was a staff of eighty "helps."[39]

Despite all the vaunting of the island's climate and its scenic charm, the early tourist industry in Jamaica exhibited from the start an inferiority complex regarding Jamaicans, their capabilities, and their resources as compared to foreigners. For example, though there had been some element of truth in the charges levied against the public houses of Jamaica prior to the hotels scheme, many of these charges were hyperbolic and mere half-truths. In the words of one tourist guide, the old complaints were in fact "not altogether deserved," for "there have always been a number of well-conducted lodging houses, managed somewhat after the fashion of American boarding houses."[40] Such concerns as the old Myrtle Bank Hotel and the Park Lodge were in themselves "quite worthy of the name of hotel." Creole efficiency in the hotel industry was likewise proven at the Waterloo, at Payne's Hotel in Montego Bay, and at Mrs. Watson's in St. Ann's Bay, notwithstanding the limited resources with which these all operated.[41] But on the assumption of Creole incompetence those hotels set up under the 1890 scheme were placed under U.S. management, even though local capital, private and public, had been sunk into the enterprises.

Under their American managers, these establishments turned out to be fiascos. Regardless of the ascribed expertise of the Americans in hotel management, there was little observable improvement in standards, in efficiency, or in organization—in sum, in the quality of the product offered to the visitor. These mainland managers, some guests complained, would have done better if, instead of chasing after French or Continental cooks, they had acquired a few good Creole cooks and provided good, plain, Creole dishes rather than imitate those of Europe or America and get ridiculed in the process.[42]

At the Constant Spring, in spite of the American management, callers were often compelled to chase from cellar to garret and from office to kitchen to find someone to register them and get them a room. Nobody would be in the vestibule to greet the guest upon arrival. Halls and corridors were dirty; broken bottles lay strewn around the entrance to the billiard room. Even as simple a matter as a boiled egg routinely required three-quarters of an hour to prepare. To crown it all, the servants were insolent and firm in their refusal to know "their place."[43]

Obnoxious as the hotels scheme was to its detractors, nonetheless it had generated some employment for local labor. By 1899, however, even this redeeming quality was in question. As though the structural dependence of Jamaica upon the U.S. vacation market and its functional dependence upon U.S. hotel managers were not enough, the hotel industry deepened the island's subordination by bringing in help from abroad to displace the native staff. In January 1899, cooks, stewards, waiters, clerks, porters, barbers, and others were all imported from the United States to staff the hotels in the colony, irrespective of the depressed state of the local economy.[44] Since it was the public purse that propped up the principal hotels, the plight of the native staff was doubly grievous. As the *Jamaica Post* put it: "the old staff are to tumble out, and kick stones, or else take to the woods and cultivate in order to earn the means to contribute in the shape of taxes to the payment of those brought to take their places."[45] That undoubtedly was the unkindest cut of all.

The burning question in Jamaica as the nineteenth century came to a close was whether the colony was to surrender to U.S. syndicates, retain British dominance, or develop the role of the Creole. As things stood, while the island's economy was under American control, the reins of administration were in the hands of the British, and under Crown government, the Creoles were marginalized in politics. No aspect of the island's economic life was as submissive to U.S. dictation, however, as the trade in bananas, then the chief crop of the colony. From the beginning, the American promoters of the trade were bent on establishing a monopoly so as to be in a position to dictate buying prices to banana growers on the island regardless of the selling price of the fruit abroad. In 1899 this situation had eventually materialized with the formation of the United Fruit Company, a gigantic corporation that dominated the enterprise internationally in production, shipping, and marketing. Submission to U.S. economic hegemonism was the price that Jamaica paid in order to foster economic growth.[46]

It was precisely to counteract this economic dependence of the colony on the United States that the Imperial Direct Line was instituted in 1901 between Jamaica and the United Kingdom.[47] The purpose of this project was to develop a market for the banana trade independent of U.S. monopolists and to promote commerce generally between the colony and its mother country. To this end the British government granted a ten-year subsidy of £20 thousand per annum, and the colonial government did likewise, to establish direct steamer service between the two places. A firm called Elder, Dempster and Company operated this venture, led by Sir Alfred Jones, chief of the corporation, with zeal and optimism.

In 1901, the colony believed that a messiah had come in the person of Sir Alfred Jones to deliver Jamaica from her afflictions. In that year, Elder, Dempster and Company leased from the government the Myrtle Bank and Constant Spring hotels and immediately set about improving, equipping, and advertising them. By September 1902, the company had spent almost £20 thousand to promote its hotel business in the colony.[48] Jones was seen as a savior. He planned not just to establish a new outlet for the Jamaican banana in a market not dominated by the United Fruit Company but also to liberate the colonists from the hotels loan incubus by developing the tourist traffic from England and introducing new and improved managerial skills into running the Myrtle Bank and Constant Spring hotels. The aura of expectancy that enveloped the undertaking was obvious in the address of His Excellency, Governor A. W. L. Hemming, at the beginning of the legislative session for 1902:

During the past year increased attention has been paid to Jamaica in England. For this we are indebted to the Direct Line of Steamers. . . . The Direct Line has demonstrated that fruit can be carried to England, and its promoters have established a paying and most promising market there. . . . The enterprise of Messrs Elder, Dempster and Company has also extended itself to the making known of Jamaica as a pleasure and health resort, and Sir Alfred Jones has leased from the Government the Constant Spring and Myrtle Bank Hotels for the purpose of developing the tourist traffic. The results of this endeavour are already promising, and I believe I shall not meet with a single dissentient voice when I say that this enterprise has the elements of a great future in it.[49]

Elder, Dempster and Company had made a most impressive debut in the Jamaica tourist business. It was reported that the tourist traffic to the colony for the year 1902 showed an unprecedented influx of visitors from the United Kingdom. The newly improved hotel facilities at the Myrtle Bank and the Constant Spring reportedly attracted a large number of Americans.[50] The number of visitors to the island in 1902 was held to be greater than ever before, except for the year of the Jamaica International Exhibition.[51]

So great was the renewed optimism surrounding the hotel business that on 10 May 1904 the government passed a new law, the Jamaica Hotels Law, designed specifically to encourage "the erection and equipment of efficient Hotels in this Island." With the entry of Jones into the Jamaica tourist business, the hotel industry was given a new lease on life. Tremendous developments were anticipated, but for the tourist industry to attain these heights, new and improved accommodation was desirable. Thus, the Hotels Law of 1904 was enacted.

Under the provisions of this law, any person erecting a hotel of forty or more bedrooms could apply to the government for an import license, so that the materials, fixtures, and furniture necessary to construct and equip the building could be brought into the island free of duty. Any such hotel was exempted from paying increased taxation for ten years from the date on which the import license was granted.

Of the five hotels that were erected under the Jamaica Hotels Law of 1890, only the Moneague Hotel was built in the mountains, and the full potential of mountain resorts had remained conspicuously unexploited. In the words of the *Leader,* "we have no large hotels where large hotels ought to be—one for instance in Manchester, one in the Blue Mountains, one in the Santa Cruz Mountains, one in the hills of St. Thomas."[52] The tourist trade of the colony would never become what "it might and could become" unless first-class hotels were set up all over the island. Thanks to the Jamaica Hotels Law of 1904, this could now happen: "if this anticipation is realised, the tourist trade of the colony will be placed on a firmer basis than it has hitherto possessed."[53]

Sir Alfred Jones's entry into the hotel business had once more inflated hopes for the possibilities of the holiday industry. But, contrary to expectations, Jones failed dismally in his attempt to develop the English travel market to alleviate Jamaica's heavy dependence on U.S. visitors. This was blamed on the twin forces of travel-distance and transportation expense. "It has to be remembered," the *Jamaica Guardian* explained, "that Jamaica is too far distant from England ever to become an extremely popular resort for English tourists." Apart from the cost, a fortnight's voyage each way was required for travelers between London and Kingston. It stood to reason that the tourist traffic from England could never be anything but small, the paper concluded. "It is to the winter travellers of the United States and Canada that we must look for the bulk of our trade every season. This island is one of the natural outlets for the residents of these great countries, if only because it can be reached in a few days."[54]

The links that Jones hoped to develop between his passenger service and his hotel business failed to flourish, quite unlike the felicitous experience of his rival, the United Fruit Company. United Fruit always had a full house during the winter months at the company-owned and -operated Titchfield Hotel.[55] One might be tempted to think that Elder, Dempster's lack of success in the hotel business was in part due to the disaster that befell it, as the earthquake that devastated Kingston in 1907 also totally wrecked the Myrtle Bank Hotel. The truth, however, was that the earthquake, regardless of what it had destroyed, had definitely not demolished Jones's faith in the hotel business. Indeed, Sir Alfred remained so committed to this enterprise that he even bought the Constant Spring Hotel from the government the following year.[56] It was not until around 1911 that there was a discernible volte-face in the company's attitude toward hotel keeping. One year later things came to a head with the closure of the Constant Spring due to financial failure.[57]

Whereas the Elder, Dempster hotel business was on the wane by 1911, that of the United Fruit Company continued to thrive. In 1904, the United Fruit Company had taken advantage of the newly enacted hotels law to erect on Titchfield Hill at Port Antonio an elaborate structure with accommodation for some five hundred persons to replace the former edifice that had been gutted by fire. This hotel, the company boasted, was "the finest and most modern hotel in the West Indies."[58] Not only was it patronized by Americans, but it was owned by Americans, run by Americans, and staffed (from chef to waitresses) by Americans—in sum, it was totally symbolic of the new economic imperialism ushered into the Caribbean by Americans.[59] Nor was the

The Myrtle Bank Hotel after the 1907 earthquake. Courtesy of National Library of Jamaica.

Titchfield the only lodge owned by the United Fruit Company in Jamaica; it possessed another at Bowden in the St. Thomas Parish,[60] though information on this is unavailable except for the fact of proprietorship. By 1911, the United Fruit Company was extending its tentacles toward the infant Jamaica hotel industry, while the Elder, Dempster Company, seemed on the verge of expiration. The power of the United Fruit Company extended to the new Myrtle Bank Hotel, rebuilt after the earthquake and reopened in January 1910 in association with the Titchfield Hotel.[61]

In explaining the failure of Alfred Jones's hotel business, consideration must in the end return to the old problem of management. The Elder, Dempster Company's entry into the hotel business had still not stopped the complaints of tourists regarding poor service.[62] The frequency of complaints diminished, but as a visitor's letter to the *Daily Gleaner* put it, "if complaints are no longer heard, it is only because it has long become recognised that it is perfectly futile to make them."[63] Unlike the Titchfield, which from the beginning employed a staff composed almost entirely of Americans, the Elder, Dempster Hotel staff was mainly Jamaican. This itself posed peculiar problems, as the blacks and coloreds in the hotel industry seemed acutely sensitive to racial slurs and infamy. Even to come forward to greet the guest on arrival was frowned upon by the native staff, for "such civility would smack of servility and remind the black or brown person who showed it that his or her colour was once the badge of slavery."[64]

In their face-to-face encounters with visitors from abroad, the hotel staff were the locals most directly exposed to the superciliousness and cultural arrogance of the whites of that time. The hotel industry served to resuscitate the dying master-servant culture of the Great House era in Jamaica. Little wonder, then, that the hotels became an arena of subtle black-white confrontation in which the specter of past struggles came to life in a new guise. For centuries before Emancipation serving as hewers of wood and drawers of water for whites, the blacks on the whole were sensitive about their new status as free men. The subtle struggle for dignity is best illustrated by Trollope in his West Indian travelogue of 1860:[65]

At home, in England, one is apt to think that an extra shilling will go a long way with boots and chambermaid, and produce hotter water, more copious towels, and quicker attendance than is ordinary. But in the West Indies a similar result does not follow in a similar degree. And in the West Indies it is absolutely necessary that these people be treated with dignity. . . .

"Halloo, old fellow! how about that bath?" I said one morning to a lad who had been commissioned to see a bath filled for me. He was cleaning boots at the time, and went on with his employment, sedulously, as though he had not heard a word. But he was over sedulous, and I saw that he heard me.

"I say, how about that bath?" I continued. But he did not move a muscle.

"Put down those boots, sir," I said, going up to him; "and go do as I bid you."

"Who you call fellor? You, speak to a gen'lman gen'lmanly, and den he fill de bath."

"James," said I, "might I trouble you to leave those boots, and see the bath filled for me?" and I bowed to him.

"'Es, sir," he answered, returning my bow; "go at once." And so he did, perfectly satisfied.

Had he imagined, however, that I was quizzing him in all probability he would not have gone at all.

Viewed from a perspective of years later, the ignorance and impudence complained of time and again by guests would seem to have been but manifestations of passive resistance by black hotel staffers. In general, they tended to behave "as if it were gall and wormwood to their haughty souls to have to wait upon the white person." The deportment of these black servants was "in a way unmistakably denoting that they were revenging themselves for the indignity of having to accept such service."[66] It was almost impossible to get prompt service. The hotel guest might ring until he became tired but could never succeed in getting a servant to hear the bell or come. The servant who was asked to do anything invariably concluded that the particular thing was not in his line of duty and most often called upon someone else to do it, and so on.[67]

In Pullen-Burry's opinion, however, much of this was but another index of black inferiority. It was appropriate, she suggested, that the visitor bear in mind that he was in an underdeveloped country, so to speak, and that he therefore should not expect from these colored islanders the quality of hotel and restaurant table service he would get in London or Paris.[68] If, indeed, poor hotel service was "an unavoidable evil not to be cured but endured," did it stem from the natural inferiority Pullen-Burry ascribed, or from the political sociology of the contact situation? "Some of the visitors had rather peculiar experiences. If the negro is abused, or looked disdainfully at as if he belonged to an inferior class, he becomes absolutely useless: he forgets to come back if he is sent away on an errand and becomes ignorant if any information is required. He obviously tries to create as much trouble and annoyance as he possibly can."[69]

At Constant Spring, part of this troublemaking frequently involved standing on one leg and gaping at the guests while they ate or spinning around on it several times while an order was being given.[70] Uppishness, feigned stupidity, clumsiness, and deliberate inefficiency were part of the resistance kit of these early black hotel staffers.[71]

And so the attempt at hotel keeping by the Elder, Dempster Company floundered and failed. But the circumstances of its failure raise some contingent social questions. How representative was the assessed behavior of hotel workers regarding the extent and depth of social sentiment toward the holiday makers? Was the image, then peddled abroad, of Jamaica as a welcoming retreat a mere figment of the imagination of those interested in promoting tourist traffic? Clearly, the first modern hotels in Jamaica were little integrated into the local economy, considering the foreign ownership, foreign management, foreign chefs, foreign waiters and waitresses, foreign foods, foreign furnishings, and so forth. Evidently, too, the private rate of return did not live up to expectation and was generally minimal or even below zero. Yet whatever the verdict on their profit making, according to A. W. Farquharson, the early hotels had been a social boon:

It is hardly necessary for me to state what is a truism, namely that without proper Hotel accommodation a country, however progressive it may be, must remain isolated from the outside world, save to those who are actually driven to visit it by stress of business. The disadvantages which result from such isolation are obvious. . . . a country can in no true sense be in touch with the progress of civilization if communications with it are restricted to the actual necessities of business.[72]

In Farquharson's view, the hotels were crucial to the process of modernization in Jamaica. Still, given that these institutions had been poorly integrated into the local economy, were they any better integrated into the local society? Before the advent of the big hotels in Kingston and in Port Antonio, the retiring hour in Jamaica had been nine o'clock at night. To be out after that time had been hardly respectable unless one was coming from a church soirée, the theater or a private dance.[73] With the arrival of the modern hotels, social recreation was broadened beyond the afternoon teas, small private parties and, for the men, drinking bouts. The hotels brought bright lights, fine orchestras, balls, banquets, billiard contests, and a brand new range of social activities locally.[74] Perhaps, as Farquharson contended, the hotels were essential to keep Jamaica in touch with the rest of the world, but might they also bring new contradictions into the world of Jamaicans? What, for instance, did they bring to the racial situation in the island? And what also did they augur as regards current race relations?

Jamaican tourism was sick from its beginning, and this wining and dining of transient whites simply renewed old social sensibilities. In practice, tourism somewhat rekindled the mores of a bygone period, when sugar was in its golden age and the planter elite was acclaimed for the openness and hospitality with which it received strangers in their land.[75] Such was the sociability and liberality of the West Indian planter class in that era that Bryan Edwards, for instance, asserted one could hardly find a tolerable inn in any of these territories.[76] Similarly, Trollope years later attributed to this much-acknowledged hospitality the lack of hostelries so often noted in the West Indies.[77]

If the Great House spawned the cult of the Jamaican welcome, it also provoked a profound counterculture to it. The ethic in the huts of the dispossessed black toward the white passerby was quite different from what emanated from the manor. Decades after the British slave Emancipation, this difference persisted. As one foreigner fulminated, "the negroes in the English islands are unpleasantly familiar and cheeky . . . and they seldom ask a traveller into their huts. The white residents on the contrary, are hospitality itself."[78]

While the early modern hotels sought to refurbish the traditional welcome and, Midas-like, convert it into cash, they became (much to their bewilderment) veritable frontlines of black resistance. During the ongoing black struggle for racial redemption, complaints that "the black waiters in the hotels are insolent and casual" were still legion well into the twentieth century. This resistance was not confined to the hotels. "Indeed the impudence of all the natives of Jamaica is astonishing to a traveller used to the respect shown to a white man in tropical countries," trippers grouched repeatedly.[79]

In the late nineteenth century, Jamaica emerged as an escape for the weak and weary from the metropoles of Europe and America. These had been told that the colony was not out of the way, just out of this world. All the same, visitors to this island haven more often than not encountered impertinence rather than adulation, derision rather than welcome. That, in the final analysis, was the social end product of a process in which tourism had come to represent a new kind of cash crop—a new sugar.

Chapter 6

The Ratooning of the Plantation

It is beyond doubt that those who live in Jamaica . . . do everything in our power to make the stranger welcome and happy. . . . This old social virtue of ours must never be allowed to deteriorate. . . . it is as much a part of Jamaica as is her soil and climate. And it is as natural and genuine a thing as are her soil and climate.

—*Daily Gleaner*, 3 April 1923

O IDENTIFY fully the sociocultural connotations of the evolving tourist traffic to Jamaica, one must first turn to the past, to a time well before the formal gestation of the holiday industry in the island in 1891. Though the physical climate of Jamaica had customarily been vilified with regard to health matters, its social climate and the generous hospitality of its gentry had won much applause as one of the colony's most pleasing traits. The hospitality of the planter class was proverbial. "Few individuals have resided even a short time in this country, without having experienced the truth of this observation which has been made, or assented to by all writers on the subject," Robert Renny related.[1] Much as hospitality was the Antillean norm in that era, nowhere was it as prevalent as in Jamaica, Bryan Edwards claimed.[2]

In the heyday of sugar should a stranger, without even a letter of introduction, pull up before any of the Great Houses scattered throughout Jamaica, he could expect almost without fail to be treated as an old and esteemed friend of the family and invited to dine and spend the night. Next day he would likely be asked whether he must indeed depart and urged to remain a day or two longer as a houseguest.[3] Accommodation was itself no problem. The typical Great House staff in the second half of the eighteenth century comprised some twenty to forty servants, including seamstresses, storekeepers, footmen, coachmen, and postilions.[4] The warmth of the welcome that the planter class extended to its guests was thoroughgoing and lavish. In the ethos of the times, so ingrained was hospitality that, even in the face of debt, it was still common for many a planter to persist in "the undiminished exercise of their generous hospitality" and regale their guests with all customary magnificence.[5]

Paradoxically, the Jamaican planter was in most cases, like his guest, a mere transient. For most plantocrats, Jamaica was not home but the place where they sojourned during their tropical exile. The planters' ideal was to amass great wealth in these islands and then retire in comfort to their home across the ocean. Few considered the Antilles a fit place to live. As one planter put it, "the climate of our sugar colonies is so inconvenient for an English constitution, that no man will chuse to live there, much

A typical English planter's "great house." Courtesy of National Library of Jamaica.

less will any man chuse to settle there, without the hopes at least
of supporting his family in a more handsome manner, or saving
more money, than he can do by any business he can expect
in England, or in our plantations upon the continent of America."[6] The Caribbean colonies were zones of exploitation, not
settlement.

Life on the plantations was a cheerless cycle of planting, reap-
ing, and replanting—at crop time a planter could be fully occupied from five in the morning till eight at night. His life was
more boring than busy. Nor was the banality of colonial domicile
relieved by the hedonism and materialism of the planter gentry.
Far from it—their intellectual sterility and limited diversions ac-
centuated the boredom:

> As a taste for literature is but little cultivated in this island, so neither do
> any of the polite and elegant amusements of life meet with encourage-
> ment in it. There is neither countenance for the poet, nor employment
> for the painter, the statuary, nor the harmonious son of Apollo. Here is
> no classic ground for the contemplative student to tread on; and as to
> the muses, they are treated as vagrants.[7]

There was little appreciation of aesthetics and little spiritual
edification in the life of the planter class to ease the daily tedium.
Horse racing, gambling, drinking, and parties constituted the
chief forms of recreation.[8] The ladies, in particular, found few
diversions in the colony. Those residing in Kingston had a distinct advantage over their counterparts in the country, as they
could occasionally relieve the monotony by shopping. In general,
however, there was little for planters' wives to do to dissipate their
boredom, except indulge in talebearing and rumormongering.
As a gentleman of long residence in the island remarked, gossip
as a pastime at least had the advantage of enabling these women
to exercise their dormant wit while adding zest to tea.[9]

Although Jamaica is a small island, the geographical distance
between places was in those days greatly magnified by the rugged nature of the terrain and the absence of serviceable roads.
Internal travel was expensive, and during the rainy season many

places lost contact with the outside world for some time. This isolation helped foster a widespread desire for company. The local code of welcome was hence interconnected with both the geography of the island and the difficulties of internal communication.[10] When a planter entertained a guest at his home, it was a big event, for the monotonous rhythm of colonial life was briefly broken. A splendid sideboard loaded with choice wines, a table covered with fine damask, and a dinner of perhaps sixteen or twenty dishes might be produced.[11] Spontaneity and gaiety characterized the entire event. At the end of it all the entertainer, starved as he was for company, probably felt as much obliged as the guest.[12]

This peculiar conjunction of a social code of friendliness and hospitality on the one hand, with the agonizing inhumanity of

A native's wattled hut. Courtesy of National Library of Jamaica.

slavery on the other, demonstrates the harsh extremities in Jamaican planter society. Excess was common among the planter class: excessive eating and drinking, excessive adultery, and to top it off, excessive brutality toward their slaves. That the planters were said to be "hospitable even to excess" was typical.[13] To planter apologists like Edwards or Renny, this prodigality toward strangers was a redeeming quality, whatever the planters' imperfections. To some later historians, however, such beneficence has smacked of not authentic altruism but vulgar ostentation. The spirit of individualism was rampant in that era. "The interests of all were the interests of none." Planter hospitality appears in perspective to have been a semblance of altruism masking the naked fact that the occasion of a visitor constituted a welcome pretext for a parade.[14]

The notion of Jamaica as a welcoming society hence had its genesis in the delight with which the gentry greeted all guests, especially the stranger. Concurrent with this, on the sugar plantations during slavery another conception was nurtured, one based on distinctions of color so deeply implanted in the breasts of white men that it seemed almost natural. According to this notion, black people were a race distinct from and inferior to whites. Providence, this idea ran, had created blacks to be merely hewers of wood and drawers of water for whites. In the prevailing conception of the welcoming society, the black's exclusive role was to serve and that of the white was to enjoy this service.[15] Since the vast majority of Jamaican slaves, however, did not accept these assumptions, conflict was chronic.

In this society whites were by far in the minority, with a ratio of at least ten blacks to one white person in the seventeenth and eighteenth centuries and of more than thirteen to one in the early nineteenth.[16] White ranks were continuously undermined by high levels of absenteeism and the stupendous death rates owing to disease. Thus in slavery days there developed a practice of welcoming white migrants to the colony and encouraging them to settle:

Beggars, those unhappy, and degraded individuals, who swarm in all European cities, are here happily unknown. To a poor man indeed, who in his native land, finds a difficulty in acquiring the necessaries, and little comforts of life, this is the best country in the world. Here, industry not only procures the necessaries, but the conveniences and even the luxuries of life. Turn your attention, then, ye industrious individuals, who are forced to leave your native shores, to this happy island! Here you will find a welcome, a happy and secure asylum.[17]

The gratifying thing about such entrants was that they helped maintain a safe ratio of whites to blacks. Perhaps, as Ragatz noted, these newcomers were often "carpenters" devoid of any working experience with tools, "bricklayers" who scarcely knew the difference between a brick and a stone, and "book-keepers" who were both illiterate and innumerate. In Jamaica, under the prevailing system of stratification they were incorporated into the dominant social group—members of the elite by virtue of skin color, if nothing else.[18] They were heartily welcomed because of the role they played in maintaining the white supremacist system.

The Jamaican traditions of hospitality, up to the time of Emancipation, were the products of the prevailing pattern of racial stratification and displayed an exclusively white bias. The Jamaican welcome, furthermore, had a political function to perform, specifically, to ensure the preservation of that white bias in the social, economic, and political order. Before proceeding, then, to evaluate the characteristics of the welcome and the social responses to it that developed with the birth of tourism, it would be useful to survey the political economy of Jamaica during that interval between the ultimate termination of the slave system in 1838 and the rise of the holiday trade some half a century later.

At Emancipation, Jamaica had a substantial measure of internal self-government, vigorously asserted and jealously protected by the white plantocracy for nearly two centuries. Ultimate control, of course, resided with the British Crown, and all acts of the Jamaican Assembly were sent overseas for final approval. This political constitution was not modified by Emancipation, though the Emancipation Act profoundly altered the physical pigmentation of the polity throughout the West Indian colonies. With Emancipation, the exslave became constitutionally a citizen and eligible as such for both public office and the vote, provided he possessed the respective property and income qualifications required to realize these rights. Of cardinal importance to the advancement of the social and political lot of the freedmen was, therefore, their attainment of economic progress as well.

At the time of the Emancipation, settlement in the Jamaican interior was still sparse. On obtaining their freedom many exslaves eventually withdrew their labor from the plantations and retreated to the highland regions of the interior.[19] There, despite legislation designed to discourage it, they soon succeeded in establishing peasant communities in a bid to secure economic independence from the plantations. As time passed, the black politician also began to surface upon the local scene. This was more than the planter elite could bear. Efforts were made, though in vain, to exclude the black man from the local legislature.[20] The rationale for such recourse was simple. "To suppose that two alien races can compose a political unity is simply ridiculous," one metropolitan critic of the postemancipation constitutional system explained. "One section must govern the other."[21]

Yet the phenomenon of the black politician was not a sudden apparition in the view of the insightful. Not long after blacks in the British West Indies were granted full freedom, Thomas Milner cautioned about the inevitability of black domination in the island:

It cannot but happen that, at a certain period of time, the descendants of the African race must become dominant in the West India colonies. Equal freedom and civil rights, now superadded to preponderance in numbers, must produce this result; and the supremacy heretofore artificially secured to the European colonists will, in the natural course of events, consequent upon the changes in the construction of the social system, pass away.[22]

As whites in the colony ceased to have it their own way, they became less opposed to the abolition of all local legislative powers and the establishment of direct rule from "home." It was not until 1866, though, that constitutional change was effected. Following an uprising among a section of the black population at Morant Bay in 1865, Edward Eyre, governor of the island, astutely seized upon the resulting panic as an excuse to engineer the constitutional change that submitted Jamaica thereafter to direct Crown rule. Although in 1884 a slight modification was made in the system to accommodate a representative element, the establishment of Crown Colony government frustrated further participation of the black Jamaican in the island's government for a considerable time. It was not until 1896 that a full-blooded black man gained one of the unofficial seats for which some allowance was eventually made on the legislative council.[23]

The constitutional change of 1866 is central in accounting for the genesis of the tourist industry in Jamaica. As far as the greater part of the white community was concerned, Crown Colony government, whatever its demerits, liberated the island from the prospects of political pandemonium, social chaos, and total anarchy. In the opinion of many whites, even the warmest proponent of "the man and brother position" would have been hard put to find three or four black men fit to make laws for their own guidance, much less that of others.[24] While in 1860 only seventeen out of the total of forty-seven members in the legislature were black or colored, an assembly 36 percent non-white was still too much.[25] In the island and abroad many whites were of the view so succintly stated later on by one resident: "I am sure that if the black people were the absolute governors of the country, not one white man would remain in the country. It would be impossible; look at Hayti! The blacks are utterly incapable of self-government."[26] According to this vein of thought, white people evidently would not be able to live in Jamaica, much less holiday there, were the blacks ever to become ascendant. Crown Colony government had thus rescued the island from this grave threat.

Judging from the comments of many contemporaries on the Jamaican political scene after 1865, it would appear that the black people in the island were habitually indifferent to political questions in the aftermath of the Morant Bay Rebellion. One journal even claimed that for at least fifty years after that there were no more political questions, only routine administrative issues.[27] Yet, given the prevailing paucity of media for political expression (whether political parties or trade unions), the apparent silence of the masses was no index of their true sentiment. The colonial police certainly did not have any illusions regarding the so-called political disinterestedness of the black masses and were usually as ruthless and repressive in their methods as if the Morant Bay uprising had just occurred.[28]

There was great animosity between the black masses and the colonial police, and at times there were violent clashes between the police and elements of the native population, as in the Montego Bay disturbances (1902) and the Kingston riots (1912).[29] There were, among the masses, many who reacted to this hostility in the political environment by withdrawing from it as much as possible. One reviewer has suggested that, inasmuch as any accommodation to the old order existed, it was due to limits self-imposed by the black masses and intended to reduce friction with the ruling elite.[30]

Jamaica's genesis as a health and holiday spa for the foreigner had been premised in part upon the gestation of what, to many blacks, was but a new form of oppression: Crown Colony government. The early tourist industry itself seemed, from the onset, preoccupied with functions other than merely providing recreational or leisure facilities for visitors from overseas. In the post-Emancipation years, the plantations entered into a prolonged phase of economic decline that reduced the number of whites in the island. This reduction in white numbers was lamented by all who reputedly had the interests of the islanders at heart and who recommended that rebuilding the white community was a vital step for any renewal of colonial, social, and economic development.[31] Tourism was considered a panacea for this problem by a lot of these economic well-wishers, as the numerous handbooks for visitors and prospective settlers attest. The *Colonial Standard and Jamaica Despatch* of 26 March 1895 declared that the function of tourism was basically one of "bringing to our shores large and frequent relays of strangers, who . . . would thus be enabled to form those favourable opinions of its agricultural and other attractions which would not fail in many instances to induce the desire on their part to become permanent residents here."

In the late nineteenth century, *development* as a concept was both racial and climatological. First, it was held that protracted residence in tropical regions tended to sap the energies, morality, and creative ingenuity of white persons. Second, along with the theory that the black man was inherently politically inept was the notion that he lacked the capacity to foster to its fullest potential the physical resources of his economic environment. In view of the decrease in the Caucasian population, it thus seemed rational that the cure for Jamaica's malaise should be the injection of fresh white blood into the prevailing social system, to bolster the perseverance of the remaining whites and to boost their flagging energies. As the *Colonial Standard and Jamaica Despatch* expressed it at the time, "we ask in all seriousness, with the depletion which has for lengthened years been going on from uncontrollable or other causes among our good men and true of days of yore, does not Jamaica sorely stand in need of the infusion in her midst of fresh blood, of men of energy and indomitable perseverance?"[32]

With the hope that the masters of capitalism could be brought into the island via tourism, a climate of welcome awaited foreign capital, thanks to legislative changes that permitted aliens to own local property on terms equal to those enjoyed earlier by British subjects only.[33] This modification of the law facilitated U.S. eco-

nomic overlordship, especially in the banana business. Though
on the surface the growth of tourism and increase in investment
sources diversified the island's economic base, it also widened
Jamaica's vulnerability, deepened its dependence, and lengthened the shadow of the United States over the island.[34]

Presumably it was among the affluent that would-be investors
could be found, and so at the beginning the Jamaica tourist
trade was targeted to this class of persons. The well-to-do, it was
also felt, were usually the trendsetters. Inasmuch as people like
to be fashionable in holiday resorts, it seemed a sound tactic to
concentrate in building the Jamaica tourist industry upon the
rich. Social snobbishness and racial bigotry were two fundamental ingredients of the tourist industry in Jamaica from the start.

One effect of this overall concern to make the local environment attractive to foreigners was the contrasting neglect, on the
whole, of the local black population. While the authorities were
conspicuously occupied with the comfort of itinerant Caucasians, their policy vis-à-vis providing accommodation for the local country people, for example, who traveled to Kingston once
a week or more to market their produce, was callous in the
extreme.[35] Necessity required that peasants put their vegetables
on the Kingston market early in the morning. To get there,
probably half of them had to travel distances of ten to twenty
miles, many carrying heavy head loads all the way. To meet the
requirements of the early morning market and to get some rest
after traveling such long distances, vendors usually came into
Kingston by ten o'clock the night before. These people, the majority of them women and girls, were compelled to find shelter
under appalling conditions. The plight of the country market
people was a blot on the civilization the colonial upper class
pretended to harbor:

No provision whatever is made for the accommodation of so many
hundreds who must spend the night once or twice each week in Kingston. They are left to find whatever shelter they can, chiefly under open
piazzas. . . . Many of them cannot even enjoy the privilege of sleeping
as they have to keep awake all night to guard against thieves. They are

not only exposed to the weather, but they are worried as well. There is no doubt that many of them become ill from this exposure and want of sleep. If they get wet on the way, a thing that happens very often, they have no place in which to change their wet clothes. It seems cruel that they should have no decent shelter within their means.[36]

In the provision of housing, as in the provision of hostelry, the government's neglect was glaring. While the government acted with alacrity to guarantee the construction of elegant lodgings for transient whites, it ignored the housing needs of local blacks. In the capital city, Kingston, it was not uncommon to find at night six or seven people huddled together for shelter in a hut barely big enough for one adult.[37] Overlooking these pressing needs, the government justified its overwhelming concentration on the foreigner's comfort by pointing to the putative benefits tourism development was expected to bring to all Jamaicans. If tourism were properly encouraged, the population would have much to be grateful for, the argument ran. The hotels would all be filled, the livery stables would do a roaring business, vegetable gardeners would have to extend their grounds in response to the increased demand for fresh produce, merchants would find their trade expanding, and so on. In a manner of speaking, the tourist dollar was like manna from heaven: "Every tourist who lands on our shores spends money amongst us; and the money which is thus put in circulation is the most easily acquired money which comes into the island. The raising of our products costs time and energy and labour. The money dropped here by the tourists costs us practically nothing."[38]

For all that, it seemed futile to hope that some of that income that had fallen into the government's coffers might be spent on improving the housing of the blacks. The subject of better housing for the poor was treated by the authorities with "apathetic indifference."[39] While the ruling elite hoped to stimulate contact with external societies through tourism, it did little to reduce the distances between the classes within Jamaican society itself.

Now, according to Melville Herskovits, among the myths about black people in the New World is the belief that they have an adaptable character that can adjust to the most adverse social situations, even to the point of lighthearted acceptance.[40] In contrast to the psyche of the American Indian (who supposedly preferred extinction to enslavement), the black personality is held to have accommodated itself to slavery. Indeed, a portrait of black bondsmen as contented and carefree came into being even in the slavery days, from the pen of apologists who had to support their protestations that the black man was happy with his lot.[41]

The ending of slavery did not entail the destruction of this stereotype. Instead, it was enhanced almost everywhere following the partition of Africa, the development of Jim Crow legislation in the U.S. South, and the global growth of the new imperialism. To justify the subordination of the black man, the thesis was propounded that he possessed the intellect of a child and thus was unfit for freedom. Indeed, this thesis ran, just as it is habitual for children to be cheerful, black people are characteristically happy-go-lucky:

> Quashie's always happy;
> Quashie him don' care;
> Happy when its gloomy;
> Happy when its fair;
>
> Nebber t'ink—what's de use?
> Thinkin' hurt him head;
> If him hab a backache
> Him jus' go to bed.
>
> Quashie's always happy;
> W'y cry 'bout de grave
> When de sun is shinin'
> An de palm trees wave?[42]

That Jamaica (the isle of sunshine) knew no care was corroborated, according to reports, by the smiling faces, joyous laughter, and blithe behavior of the blacks.[43] Happy denizens of an island paradise, the black masses of Jamaica, like the lilies of the field, had neither to toil nor to spin to make a living, since little effort was required to maintain human sustenance in this tropical Garden of Eden. To work like a "nigger" was not to work hard but hardly. Here was a retreat where life was passed in slothful ease and folks were on a perpetual holiday.[44] Even the hovels that were the blacks' homes were presented in fanciful terms. Inasmuch as nature was so bountiful, housing was less necessity than luxury:

Nature in these sunny islands is such an indulgent mother that there is no struggle for existence. . . . In cold climates the negro can, and, as a rule, does work as well as the white man; but he has to do so in order to live. He must have food and clothing, and must live in a house suitable to a cold climate. . . . In his tropic home it is different. The little clothing he requires is worn for decency rather than warmth. . . . an endless supply of ripe fruit that generally grows wild, supplies his simple wants, and like the philosopher that he unconsciously is, he takes life easy—too easy perhaps.[45]

Though, indeed, a number of black men had done well as individuals since Emancipation, freedom had not emancipated the mass of the black population from penury and dependence. In the available documentation on the establishment and growth of the Jamaican tourist industry, one recurring feature was the outstretched palm of indigent blacks soliciting pennies from the foreigner. This request was often preceded by an ingratiating smile and a friendly "Good marning, buckra" or similar salutation. However, the act of begging could at times be pursued with an "amazing" effrontery, impudence, and pertinacity.[46] In a society where the average wage remained a shilling a day in 1914, begging was inevitable. So too were massive emigrations from among the black population to Panama, Cuba, and Costa Rica in the late nineteenth and early twentieth centuries.[47] The concept of Jamaica as a paradise was a fiction, widely and unequivocally rejected by a black population that was constrained to abandon this so-called paradise were they to improve their material lot in life. Jamaica was a fool's paradise, for only a fool could entertain such notions of Jamaicans as carefree and contented.[48]

Had brazen antagonism been the behavioral norm toward the tourists on the part of blacks, that no doubt would have received greater mention by these holidaymakers in their journals. But such irksome conduct as begging aside, few visitors voiced complaints about any unfriendliness from the black masses. Sir Harry Johnston, for example, in *The Negro in the New World*, affirmed that "personally I found . . . all classes and all colours in Jamaica exceptionally civil and obliging to the stranger." This, he asserted, was even more of a surprise because he himself was always prying into backyards, taking photographs of sundry people and objects, and "often in too much of a hurry to request permission or explain the motive." As far as Johnston was convinced, the only exceptions to this deference were the Maroons of northeast Jamaica. These, he complained, were both discourteous and disobliging and "inclined to levy blackmail" on anyone who passed through their villages or sought to photograph them and their surroundings.[49]

While most first-timers to the island were impressed with what in their fancy was the social deference of the local black people, the repeat tripper saw diminishing deference as a societal trend by 1914, when the foundation phase of the industry had come to an end. For Ella Wheeler Wilcox, by her third voyage to the colony much had altered in the attitudes of Jamaican folk toward visitors. On her first trip to the island, she stated, the locals had been remarkably polite, a present of even a halfpenny gave delight, and a copper was fair enough reward for posing before the camera. "Today they demand one or two shillings," she complained, and "where ten gave the pleasant greeting as they passed, one gives it now." To Wilcox, it was clear that more and more islanders were becoming infected by the brusque manners and materialism of the dominant group of visitors, the Americans. "It is a curious fact that wherever American feet make a beaten path," she lamented, "the flowers of economy, politeness and simplicity wither and die."[50]

From as far back, actually, as 1890 the cultural spoor of the American (as businessman rather than tourist) had been manifest, particularly at the North Coast town of Port Antonio. The town was then still in its first flush of contact with American food and figures of speech, but owing to the banana business seemed all set to expand into "a full blown American city with all its virtues and vices."[51] By 1871 Port Antonio had a resident American population of 246, ten years later the U.S. population there was 309, and in 1891, the figure stood at 363—almost all in the banana business.[52] By 1890 the Portland Parish, with Port Antonio as its capital, had also begun to nurture an embryonic tourist industry and to establish for itself an anticipated preeminence as "a very popular resort for winter visitors."

Toward the turn of the century, tourist arrivals in this corner of Jamaica numbered well over one thousand per annum. The table below shows the volume of the tourist trade in Portland Parish from 1901 through 1907.[53]

Year	Number of Tourists
1901–1902	1,201
1902–1903	1,785
1903–1904	1,437
1904–1905	1,673
1905–1906	1,592
1906–1907	607

(Tourism in 1903–1904 was affected by a hurricane, in 1907 by an earthquake. In 1905–1906, only the 1906 season was recorded.)

As a result of this high density of Americans, by 1900 Port Antonio (the first resort town on the island) had begun to exhibit a plethora of social problems that would also torment other parishes as tourism expanded.

Though the larger American presence in Port Antonio generated job opportunities, qualified locals resented the fact that they were offered only inferior positions.[54] At the Titchfield Hotel, for example, with Baker's practice of importing American chefs, waitresses, and so on, only the most menial jobs were left for the local people. Tales of atrocities committed against blacks in the southern United States made many people suspicious of the visitors, and the behavior of these Americans at times resembled the dominance of slave owners.[55] There were, furthermore, isolated physical confrontations, where sailors were attacked for making derogatory remarks about blacks.[56] In sum, notwithstanding that affection for American culture noted by DeLisser,[57] disaffection regarding tourism was rampant. Across the island, black people entertained their own sentiments about the tourist traffic, as recorded in the *Leader* of 5 February 1904:

Tourists! Cou ya Sah! Dem is a confusion set of people. What we want dem for?—An what good dem going to do? All dem idle buckra drive and ride over de mountains in dem buggy and harse wit all dem 'surance, and look down upon we poor naygurs. True, dem say dey brings we money, but when time we eber see it? All de storekeepers dem in Kingston and de big tabern-keeper, dem is de one dat get de money out of dem. . . . An when de tourists come up to de country and see we working in de ground, dem is not goin' to do anything fa we, but take picta and laugh at we. Chu! me bredder, only de buckra dem will profit.

Though still in its infancy in 1914, the tourism industry brought to the black masses in Jamaica the sting of racial prejudice. One Chas Bowlan even had the misfortune of literally feeling its sting on his cheek. The incident occurred when Simeon Grant, a visiting American who had stopped in Jamaica on his way to Colon, somehow got it into his head that Bowlan's laughter, as Grant happened to pass, was directed to him. "You d——d half-starved Jamaica nigger," Grant snarled as he drew his revolver and let fly with his fist.[58] This affair symbolized the tribulations that tourism brought to black Jamaicans. The black community was invited to turn the other cheek and forgive repeatedly the tourists' transgressions against it.

Quantifying the pre–World War I tourist trade in Jamaica is not possible. There appears to be no serial data, for instance, regarding the actual number of visitors to the island. Nor are there statistics on the nationality of these arrivals, their length of stay in the colony, or the occupancy rates at hotels, inns, and so on. While the raw material for a quantitative analysis does not appear to exist, it is still possible to form, from the contemporary commentaries, some crude impressions about the size of the infant enterprise and its secular trends. One of the earliest islandwide statistics is found in a 1906 report by the collector general in which, from a scrutiny of the passenger lists of steamships calling at Jamaica, he estimated the tourist arrival figure for that year at 7,000 (most probably comprising both cruise passengers and long-staying visitors).[59] As for the direct contribution of the travel trade to the economy itself, he reckoned it in the region of £70,000.

Before the September 1910 formation of the first promotional body in the island (the Jamaica Tourist Association), there was little concern for collecting macroeconomic statistics on the holiday business. Thus, only for that period preceding World War I do we have any serial figures regarding Jamaican tourism. The table below lists the tourist arrivals in Jamaica from 1911 through 1914.[60] The figure for 1912–1913 includes cruise ship arrivals.

Year	Number of Tourists
1911–1912	4,023
1912–1913	11,318
1913–1914	3,000

By 1914, there had emerged in the island of Jamaica (and in some other portions of the Caribbean) a new kind of South Atlantic system, with hotel chains and a fresh form of body traffic for profit. If, in the old slavery days, Jamaica had been the most hospitable of the British colonies, with the rise of tourism it soon gained the reputation as the one most prone to exploit the visitor. "For . . . the persons with moderate means who go for a change periodically, Jamaica is too expensive" ran the charge continuously recited by 1911.[61]

The plain truth, T. D. J. Farmer explained, was that "the hotel keeper here has got to look upon the American Tourist as an easy mark."[62] Many Americans reputedly preferred to shun Jamaica and go to Nassau, Bermuda, or Barbados, where prices were said to be much lower.[63] Hence the falloff, recorded in the table above, during the 1913–1914 tourist season. Lewis Clemens, secretary of the Canadian Travel Club and representative of the Jamaica Tourist Association in Canada, claimed, "I do not think that the average hotel rates in Jamaica are complained of, but the large hotel rates are certainly driving the people on to Barbados, who would rather pay the difference in ocean fare and spend a longer time on shore where the rates are not so steep. I think about 25 per cent of the people I have sent on to Jamaica this winter have gone on to Barbados."[64] In its greed, Jamaica, it seemed, was apt to kill the goose that laid the golden egg.

Perhaps the tourists were the economic victims of the early trade, but the black masses were, unmistakably, its social casualties. The color question had always hung over Jamaica, but with the growth of tourism it festered further, for the industry revitalized distinctions of color that had faded with the widespread planter destitution since Emancipation. Sired within the structures of plantation society, tourism in Jamaica bore from its inception all the socioeconomic features of its geniture and in essence soon became a new kind of sugar. As things stood "only de buckra dem" profited.[65] It is a sad irony that tourism spread unsavory external influences all over this Caribbean island, 145 miles long and, in the language of the tourist brochures, a smile wide.

Chapter 7

Paradise on the
Auction Block

A tourist resort, which does not advertise its attractions
intelligently and persistently, is like a horse that winks in the
dark—the horse itself knows that it is winking, but no other
living creature in the world does.
    —Anonymous, in the *Jamaica Guardian*, 16 January 1909

NOTWITHSTANDING the expectation that the Jamaica International Exhibition of 1891 would propel the takeoff of tourism in the island, one of the biggest obstacles to growth in the number of vacationers to Jamaica was still, at the turn of the twentieth century, the dearth of information abroad concerning the colony. Once the exhibition had come and gone, the ad hoc committee formed to promote Jamaica overseas disbanded, and no organization was left to sustain the publicity it had generated or to extract the maximum advantages from the tourism possibilities it had opened up.[1] There was no specific organization to maintain Jamaica before the gaze of the globe-trotter. Nine years after the exhibition, at the end of the nineteenth century, the island still lacked both a tourism policy and a tourism agency.

If, in the nature of modern tourism, advertising a place is critical in stimulating a demand for it, this is even more important when the resort in question is a new one, as was Jamaica when the twentieth century began. In typical laissez-faire fashion, the colonial government insisted that the business of selling the island to overseas travelers was "one best left to private enterprise."[2] But Jamaican private enterprise, in classic colonial style, lacked the wherewithal and the cooperation to achieve such an end, however desirable they considered it.

Some of the media, like the *Jamaica Daily Telegraph and Anglo-American Herald,* even felt that there was no need for an organized tourist bureau in a colony the size of the island.[3] In the paper's contention, were such a body established it would achieve little that could not be accomplished anyway by simply publishing pamphlets or leaflets. Jamaica's supreme need in tourism, it continued, was not an information office but improved facilities for guests—good boardinghouses and sanatoria, more modern hotels, cheaper and better domestic transport, et cetera. Until the accommodation and conveyance questions were settled satisfactorily, a tourist bureau would be of little or no use to either the colony or its visitors, the paper postulated. In the words of another tabloid, the *Leader,* "What is more ridiculous than inviting people to come to dinner and setting before them a dish of herbs?" Kingston, for instance, did not even have a theater or much else to entertain visitors. Jamaica, the paper argued, should first get its own house in order before inviting guests.[4]

With this lack of enthusiasm for a tourist bureau articulated by major opinion makers, it is not surprising that the gestation of such a body was slow. It was not until almost two decades after the 1891 exhibition, in fact, that any organization came into being. In the interim, in spite of the basic tourist potential of its natural assets, Jamaica lingered in the minds of several persons abroad as simply "a place or kind of machine into which you empty planters and niggers at one end, and draw out rum, sugar, and molasses at the other."[5] The Caribbean islands attracted international attention only when there was some catastrophe, like the 1902 eruptions of Mount Pelee in Martinique and of the Souffriere in St. Vincent or the 1907 earthquake that demolished Kingston. "Poverty stricken islands, barren of riches, planted somewhere in some tropical sea. . . . That," one Englishman affirmed, "is all that is generally known of the great islands of the Caribbean Sea."[6]

This information vacuum on Jamaica was filled, if at all, through the proliferation in print of travel anecdotes recounting the island's delights as a winter resort for northerners and perhaps serving to woo a few would-be travelers to the colony.[7] Of course any prospective visitor first had to shed the preconception that the island was swarming with dangerous reptiles and wild animals. These travelogues assured the timorous that Jamaica was a land free from poisonous snakes, the mongoose allegedly having devoured all of them. Nor should trippers fear fever, as that had now become an anachronism, considering the discoveries regarding the etiology of the disease. Finally, the local black people gave no cause for disquiet. Jamaica, it was held, was a fecund island where anything once planted in the ground grew in the most prolific manner. Thus the sting of hunger had no place in the character of domestic class relations on the island.

If food, clothing, and shelter were assuredly satisfied in this most genial setting, so too was personal safety.[8] The white woman visitor had no need to fear the possibility of rape. To begin with, the Jamaican police and law courts were held to be effective as deterrents. It was claimed, moreover, that the island's blacks had internalized an "almost divine affection" for the white woman because during the reign of a woman they became freedmen.[9] Above all, Jamaicans were quite different from their black brethren in the United States, where life was unsafe and lynch law was "a necessary evil." In Jamaica, in contrast, the social situation was acclaimed as the polar opposite of that in Mississippi: "Rape does not occur in Jamaica because there are many black women with whom the bruitish negro can have companionship. It is a hilly country where every Jack can have his Jill, and where many neglect to go to a clergyman or a magistrate before living together."[10] Given this supposed ease in satisfying sexual appetites, Jamaica's "best crop," so the travel-

ogues claimed, was the production of "piccaninnies." So benign
was nature that it did not visit the islanders with epidemics severe enough or earthquakes calamitous enough to carry off the
"superfluous nigger babies."[11] With such guaranteed benevolence of nature and the ostensible friendliness of the people,
Jamaica was touted as the ideal vacationland.

Apart from the stereotyped docility of the people, their manners, superstitions, idiosyncracies, and modes of thought were
invaluable to instituting and developing tourism. One of the
most entertaining recreations in Jamaica, was observing the
"bruitish" blacks in their habitat.[12] A trip to Jamaica was like a
visit to a huge zoo to watch herds of black-skinned bipeds. The
black Jamaicans were observed as primitives.

A memorable spectacle for the sightseer was to observe the
Jamaican black at "feeding time." "There is a great licking of
lips, rolling of eyes and heavy munching by strong jaws."[13]
When he had succeeded in gorging himself, the negro's grace
was then said: "thank you, me fadder, fe all me na swallow.
Hope we may lib, fe nyam smo' (to eat some more) tomorrow."[14]
Equally worth the while of the nature-loving white tourist was to
view the mating habits of the blacks. The scenes of such intimate
encounters were framed in tropical moonlight, waving palm
trees, and flashing fireflies. On Forrest's and Henderson's recommendation, the voyager to Jamaica could become a voyeur as
he pursued the anthropological delights of the island in their
most delicate detail: "For an accurate picture of the love scenes
you must visit the island of rivers and take your place in one of
those quiet corners of the banana field and wait for George and
Jemima, or James and Mrs. Agostiss R—I cannot describe the
scene. Go to Jamaica and see it for yourself."[15]

The black people of Jamaica were depicted in these accounts
as curios, like the objects they made to sell to the tourists.
Though the sociology of the black inhabitants was described ad
nauseam by itinerant scribes with a professed concern for promoting tourism, it was their sociability that was the real promotional key. This is well illustrated by the controversy that arose

over the film that the British and Colonial Kinematograph Company attempted to shoot in the island in 1913. The story broke when, in mid-January, a representative of one of the local tabloids visited the site of the company's operations. The reporter saw some scenes acted with such realism that he began to wonder what effect the picture would have on the people overseas who saw it.[16]

Since New Year's Day the Kinematograph Company had been shooting local scenes for the film, which featured an uprising in which black rebels decide to besiege and burn the home of a white missionary. The company director recruited a group of laborers from a nearby plantation and instructed them to bring along their cutlasses and forks. The fictive uprising was portrayed as taking place on a day when "Lieutenant Daring," an officer on one of His Majesty's frigates, happened to be at the house paying court to the missionary's daughter. Though Daring, the hero of the story, time and again warded off fierce attacks by the insurgents, the whites were rescued only after the brave girl managed to escape on horseback and return to the house with help.

So great was the outcry from some sections of the public when the company's doings were printed in the newspaper in question that the project apparently had to be discontinued. Reverend Ernest Price, principal of Calabar College, felt that when the publics of England and America saw the film they would believe that the black people of Jamaica were bloodthirsty and that white islanders lived in dread of their lives, finding relief only by the fortuitous presence of any passing man-of-war.[17] The film would be most injurious to the infant tourist industry; it was not the type of advertising that Jamaica needed. Another irate Jamaican made the point with more force:

I know of some countries where such a libel on their inhabitants would never be allowed to leave their shores. If it is a criminal offense for a man to publish pictures defamatory of another, ought it not to be so for a Company which libels a whole island? We know of the ignorance and the gullibility of the average foreigner as regards things West Indian. I hope the Government of Jamaica will exercise a rapid censorship on this and similar attempts to belittle the people of this island, and will order the destruction of the series of pictures to which attention has been directed.[18]

Even the least insinuation that the people were discontented or that the tourist could suffer some insecurity of life or limb was incompatible with the goal of making Jamaica a winter spa for white folk from Europe and North America. The vaunted image of the contented Jamaican masses was, however, undermined by the frequency of begging. This was particularly true in the urban areas, where begging posed a persistent source of vexation to the visitors.[19] By 1913, begging abounded almost everywhere on the island. At Castleton Gardens, for example, even little children could be found standing by the gates and pestering the tourists, as they entered or exited, for a threepence or a shilling.[20]

Bad as mendicancy was for Jamaica's image, the behavior of curio sellers was no better. By the end of the first decade of the twentieth century, the city of Kingston was overstocked with these peddlers. While one could not complain about the desire of these vendors to turn an honest penny, their zeal in pursuing a living was so excessive that the public felt something had to be done to regulate their activities. They swarmed everywhere, "dogging the steps of the harassed visitor,"[21] insisting that their victims buy Job's tears, liquorice seeds, lace bark, puffs, and postcards. They were said to become abusive when their wares were rejected.

The streets teemed with another set of activists—those youths who foisted themselves as guides upon touring parties from cruise ships that stopped at Kingston for a few hours. It was astounding the ludicrous things these self-imposed conductors imparted to the visitor as "reliable information." To the *Daily Gleaner* it seemed absolutely necessary that a system of licensing be instituted, so that the business of showing visitors around could be limited to competent and professional guides.[22] Such a system, the paper claimed, would not only prevent visitors from being pounced upon by idlers eager to earn easy money but would ensure that the tourists received information that was at least fairly accurate. When they departed it would be with a somewhat more favorable impression of Jamaica and its populace.

All told, the masses must be stopped from such unsavory practices as begging and harassing the tourists, and this S. C. Burke, the supernumerary magistrate of Kingston, solemnly resolved upon. One Monday morning in February 1912, for example, "a section of the ignoble army of vagrants, popularly known as beggars," was arraigned before Burke. Among those arrested was an old woman named Rose Ann Walters, who might have been sent to jail like her fellow "craftsmen," if not for her impassioned appeal. The constable who arrested her claimed that she attacked the tourists:

"People going from Jamaica will probably be thinking that it is a land of beggars," the Magistrate rejoined.

"Do, massa, do, gie me a chance," the old woman pleaded, while tears rolled down her cheeks.

"No, no," the Magistrate retorted. "The first thing you people teach your children is to say, 'beg you a quattie, massa.' All these things must be stopped."

"Do, massa, have mercy on the poor old woman," was the persistent supplication. "Do, bucky massa."

"Well, you are an old woman," the Magistrate concluded, "and I will give you a chance, but the next time you will go straight down to the Penitentiary."

"I am going to start locking up everybody else" was the proclamation as the old woman left the dock.[23]

So intolerable did the situation become by 1913 that the authorities launched a crusade against curio vendors, "street arabs," and others who pestered the tourists. The police put on special duty a few constables in plainclothes to keep a close watch for such proceedings, and Burke fined, or more readily confined, any adult brought before him for that offense. Juveniles convicted on such a charge had an option of six strokes with the tamarind rod.[24]

In the advancement of Jamaica as a holiday resort the colonial administration played an influential role. The entry of visitors into a territory, their safety, the import of goods, and questions pertaining to investment by foreigners all, of course, fall within the normal function of government. It was felt that the government ought to encourage the infant tourist trade by reducing the import duties on a long list of items used by hoteliers as well as householders. Critics of Jamaican hotels insisted that their charges were too high, and this was said to be having a considerable adverse effect upon the tourist industry.[25] But how could hotel charges be low when the import duties on foodstuffs, wines, spirits, and other consumer goods were "extraordinarily high"? The corrective seemed obvious enough: "Jamaica will never become a popular winter resort for northern travellers until the cost of living is reduced. . . . When our tariff is as low as that of Bermuda, the Bahamas, Barbados and other islands, and our hotel charges are correspondingly reduced, then—but not till then—will Jamaica be visited every winter by crowds of health and pleasure seekers."[26]

Yet the government was reluctant to do more for the infant enterprise than pass incentive legislation for building and equipping hotels on the island. This had been first done in 1890 as part of the preparations for the Jamaica International Exhibition held the following year. In April 1904, the government once again enacted legislation to foster hotel development in the island. Through Law 15 of that year, persons erecting a hotel of more than forty bedrooms were allowed an import license that permitted materials for establishing and equipping the edifice to be brought into the colony free of duty. Such persons were also exempted for ten years from increased taxation of hotel buildings. Though this law lapsed on 30 June 1907, it was revived in 1910 and again in 1914 so that some of its provisions might be extended to three hotels then under construction.[27]

Such support for the erection of hotels was far from enough to absolve the authorities of the blame that they were idle and unenergetic in promoting Jamaica as a holiday resort. On this subject the *Jamaica Guardian,* for example, was explicit: "What has our Government done to popularise Jamaica as a winter resort among Americans and Canadians, or even to let them know that there is such a resort so close to their doors? It has done nothing—absolutely nothing."[28]

Local dissatisfaction with the quality of government support for the infant tourist industry was of some years standing. There was repeated animadversion, for example, at Governor Blake's refusal to grant an annual subsidy to Colonel Headley Plant to promote tourist traffic to the island.[29] During the 1890s, when Cuba was caught up in the renewed nationalist struggle against Spanish rule, martial law had prevailed for some time in Havana. Colonel Plant, who had been instrumental in pioneering the tourist industry in Florida, had also been in business taking American tourists to Cuba.[30] With the growing turmoil there, however, Plant was forced to find an alternative island resort and chose Jamaica. Around 1894 he approached the colonial legislature with a business proposition, whereby in return for an annual subsidy of £2,000 for five years—all of which would be spent in advertising the attractions of Jamaica in the United States—he would commit himself to running a regular service of luxury steamers between Key West and Kingston. In addition, he would endeavor to build up a big tourist trade for the island.

In Jamaica, many influential people considered this a splendid offer, particularly when it seemed that the colonel was also interested in entering into the hotel enterprise there. It was anticipated that after five years or so of advertising by Colonel Plant the tourist traffic would be on such firm footing that the annual subsidy would no longer be necessary. But Governor Blake apparently felt that, with Cuba closed to him, Plant would bring his tourists to Jamaica whether he got a subsidy or not. In defiance of advice to the contrary, the governor turned down Plant's proposal. The colonel's boats did come to Jamaica, but only for a brief while, since Nassau was soon "discovered." When Sir Henry Blake realized that Jamaica was not indispensable in the winter travel business it was already too late.[31]

Given the government's laissez-faire stance, it was left to private individuals who desired to advance the colony as a resort to band themselves into an organization, which might itself act to promote the island and might also pressure the authorities to do the same. The first tentative moves to form such a body date from around mid-1903, when a public meeting was held in the rooms of the Merchants' Exchange to devise practical methods for regulating and protecting the tourist traffic. At this gathering the participants unanimously agreed that this business was "one of the greatest importance to the material welfare of the Island" and that a tourist board should be established with a paid executive as director.[32] This meeting even included a discussion about the means to raise the finances necessary for funding the projected office. It wound up with a resolution that the chairman appoint a fifteen-man committee (with power to add to their number) to continue the work begun in drafting a plan for a tourist association.

In February 1904 the Merchants' Exchange convened an even grander meeting in Kingston, impelled by a deepening sense of urgency regarding the advancement of tourist traffic.[33] A disastrous hurricane in 1903 had gravely affected the banana and tourist trades of the colony, laying bare the frailty of the economic order in Jamaica. "Tourists can only come here," the tabloids pointed out, "if there are the steamships to bring them; and the hurricane has had the effect of putting the overwhelming majority of the fruit steamers out of service." Under the pressure of economic dislocation, however, and spurred by the suffering engendered by the temporary rupture of external communications, the value of tourism had become "thoroughly appreciated."[34]

Early in February 1904, the mass meeting of gentlemen interested in developing the tourist traffic convened under the auspices of the Merchants' Exchange. At this gathering a consensus plan for founding a tourist bureau crystallized.[35] The proposed bureau would register hotels and lodging houses throughout the island and keep a record of all livery stable keepers. It would consider measures to foster hotel construction and perhaps intercede with government in that respect. Both the central government and the parochial boards were to be induced to take an interest in the tourist traffic. The value of lighting the streets in several towns should be urged upon both of these authorities, and something had to be done to improve the water supply, so that when visitors to the country wanted a bath they would not be impeded because the water was locked off.

It was recommended that the proposed bureau should be put under the management of an intelligent man with good address and that he should be well paid.[36] The parties at the bureau should be thoroughly disinterested and unbiased in favor of any hotels. The bureau would also use the services of a few ladies, who could offer suggestions periodically to hotel managers, lodging house keepers, and others as regards entertaining guests with as much as possible of the produce and products of the country. Finally, regarding the question of funding, all at the meeting realized that they could not rely entirely upon the public purse to make this proposal a success.

By February 1904, therefore, the tourist industry in Jamaica was poised to embark on a new phase in its growth, one of sustained promotion via an association of interest groups. This association was an index of the new prestige of the holiday business. Even the colonial government felt enough persuaded of its significance to bestir itself in the circumstances and pass the Hotels Law in April 1904.

Despite the solemn speeches about the value of the industry, however, the merchants made no perceptible moves to implement the proposals that had germinated in the February 1904 convention. "This is Jamaica all over," one paper declared. "A big outcry—great bustle and excitement—marvellous and impracticable projects—and then silence as unbroken as that of the grave."[37] Nor did the drought of tourists in the aftermath of the

1907 earthquake alter this state of things. The infant tourist industry continued to suffer from promotional apathy until, at last, in September 1910 the Jamaica Tourist Association became a reality. Reporting on the incarnation of this body the tabloids prophesied: "We shall not be surprised if, in future years, the 15th September, 1910, will be looked upon as the beginning of a new era in the history of the tourist trade of the colony."[38]

The primary purpose of the Jamaica Tourist Association was to enhance the claims of the colony as a health and pleasure resort at home and abroad and to give "reliable" information to both prospective visitors and those already holidaying in the island. Membership in the organization was open to all persons interested in developing the tourist traffic of the colony; and because the active cooperation of as many people as possible was desirable, membership was in the names of individuals, not firms.[39] There was no entrance fee, but all members were required to pay an annual subscription of twelve shillings to aid in the work of the association.[40] Every year a general meeting was held at which the members elected a committee to take care of business for the new year, including a president, treasurer, and secretary. The secretary was responsible for managing affairs at the association's headquarters and may have received a stipend, and the other offices were honorary.

The headquarters of the Jamaica Tourist Association was in downtown Kingston and was well equipped with reference books on Jamaica and the entire West Indian archipelago. Picture postcards, pamphlets, folders, steamship information, and other bits of information were displayed at the office. The ordinary routine at headquarters entailed answering all enquiries personally or by mail, which kept the secretary and his assistant busy. Information given by the association was free of charge. It is proof of the growing outreach of the association that, by April 1913, it established branch information offices at Port Antonio, Montego Bay, and Mandeville. By 1914, the association had even acquired representation in Canada and the United Kingdom.[41]

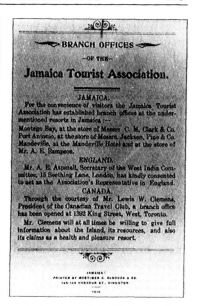

Founded in 1910, the Jamaica Tourist Association not only had branch offices in Montego Bay and Mandeville but abroad, in England and Canada, by 1914.
Illustrations courtesy of National Library of Jamaica.

One of the first acts of the Jamaica Tourist Association was to make its existence and functions known to the visitor. Framed placards were hung in the different railway stations, in stores, and in other public places inviting visitors to make use of the association's office for information about the island. A large number of printed postcards were sent abroad to the different steamship offices and tourist agencies, with a request that when intending visitors wrote for information about Jamaica, the agency would, along with its literature, send a card inviting the recipient to write for data to the association's office in Jamaica.[42] Thanks to this mode of advertising, it was subsequently claimed that the association was in receipt of enquiries from prospective visitors and settlers from all parts of the world and on all subjects.[43]

To finance its work the Jamaica Tourist Association depended

heavily upon the subscriptions of its members, but the size of its
membership and the readiness with which members paid the
subscription were far from satisfactory. Five months after the
inception of the association, membership stood at 100;[44] six
months later it was merely 120. With an annual subscription of 12
shillings per person, this meant a mere £72 to carry on the work
of the association, assuming that all the members had paid up.
This was not the response anticipated by the president of the
association, because in his view there ought to have been at least
400 on the rolls by then.[45] Instead of improving, it appears that,
over time, the financial position of the association may have
grown worse. In 1914, for example, although 73 new members
joined the association and paid the required subscription, this
brought to 76 the total number of members in good financial
standing.[46] Clearly, such paucity of funds retarded the work of
the association.

Fortunately, ever since the association's inception the government usually reserved for it a provision of around £300 on the
annual estimates. This amount was considered by the association
to be "totally inadequate" for the effective advertising of the
island. In 1911, the second year of its operation, the body asked
that £2,000 be placed on the estimates for promotional work,[47]
but this request was rejected by the government. With such
constraints of finance there were severe limitations upon what the
association could do.

Nonetheless, the organization showed itself most active and
alert to every chance to expose Jamaica overseas as a haven for
vacationers. At the end of its first year of operation, the tourist
association issued an illustrated guide book on Jamaica containing data on places likely to be visited by sightseers, tidbits on the
island's history, and information on its folklore. Five thousand
copies of this guide book were published and distributed, free of
cost, to visitors and to people abroad. In the subsequent edition
for the 1912–1913 tourist season, 7,500 copies were published;
for the 1914 and 1915 seasons the figure mounted to 10,000.[48]

Beside its annual guide book, a number of other publications were issued by the Jamaica Tourist Association. For the 1913–1914 tourist season, for example, ten thousand illustrated leaflets entitled *Come to Jamaica* were printed by the association and distributed overseas. An equally large number of leaflets was also printed for distribution among visitors on incoming steamers at Port Royal. Entitled *Welcome to Jamaica,* these offered helpful information on such subjects as customs procedure, porterage, and the rates of buses and taxicabs, and listed hotels and boarding houses. According to the president of the association, this leaflet was much appreciated by visitors.[49]

In the pursuit of its objectives the Jamaica Tourist Association brought its attention to bear upon such diverse questions as the licensing of motorcars plying for hire, the provision of signposts along the country roads, and the preservation of the island's natural beauty spots.[50] Beginning in 1913, the association even instituted a daily weather report service between Jamaica and North America, which proved "distinctly successful" in impressing the tourist with the contrast in weather conditions. The Special Weather Report Service operated from January to March and was arranged with the Direct West India Cable Company, Limited. Cables giving the temperature and weather conditions in New York, Montreal, and Halifax were sent daily to Jamaica and published in the local press. The weather conditions in Jamaica were cabled each day to New York and published in the *New York Herald* and the *New York Sun.* The cost of this service in 1914 was £20. Of this amount, £18.6.6 was subscribed by the merchants and others in Kingston and £1.13.6 was paid out of the funds of the association.[51]

The association was not intent on selling Jamaica only as a winter resort. On the contrary, opportunities for developing summer traffic were readily seized, and even academic institutions abroad were tapped as a potential source of visitors. Literature was circulated among students and teachers recommending Jamaica as a place to pass their vacation.[52] When in August 1914 a party of English schoolteachers visited the island, "the best efforts" of the organization were invoked so that their stay in the colony might be "as instructive and enjoyable as possible."[53] The idea was to iron out the fluctuations in the infant industry, since from the very start seasonality had been a problem.

Overseas there were opportunities to advertise the island via various exhibitions and these the association pounced upon. In 1912, for example, the association sent two exhibits at large.[54] One went to the Travel and Vacation Exhibition in New York, and the other was displayed at the Toronto Exhibition. The exhibits included large framed photographs of some of the island's beauty spots and an album containing pictures of the principal hotels and boardinghouses in Jamaica. There was also a large map depicting the motor roads in the island and places of interest seen en route, the latter represented by inset views. Participation in expositions drew attention to the island and advanced its claims for international recognition as the ideal vacationland.

The courage of the Jamaica Tourist Association in attempting so much with so little at its disposal was much to the credit of E. Astley Smith, a Kingston merchant-proprietor who specialized in the sale of sports equipment and was the association's first president. Smith believed in Jamaica's potential as a tropical island resort so much that, almost a decade before the foundation of the Jamaica Tourist Association, he set up his own private agency catering to the interests of overseas visitors.[55] Smith's Tourist Information Bureau was a room set aside in his store with picture postcards, guides, curios, and other items on sale. There he gave information to the visitors free of charge, and organized excursions and tours for small parties wishing to visit various parts of the country. Smith, on his own initiative, kept a list of hotels and lodging houses in and around Kingston, noted complaints made against establishments, and informed those inns with discredits against their names.[56] As the tourist association's president (and subsequently its secretary), Smith tried to move the mountains in the path of the island's realization of its potential.

In selling Jamaica as a tropical winter resort, numerous steamship companies also played a significant part. After 1901, the Im-

E. Astley Smith ran the Tourists' Information Bureau from his store in Kingston. Courtesy of National Library of Jamaica.

perial Direct Line, for example, assumed management of two of
the principal hotels in the colony and did its utmost to encourage
passenger traffic from England to the island. Actually, with such
zeal did the company exert its efforts to this end that the *Jamaica
Guardian,* though taking cognizance of Sir Alfred Jones's gross
failures in the banana business, acknowledged in a 1909 issue the
deep interest that he had displayed vis-à-vis the colony's tourist
trade:

> whatever criticisms may be passed on the manner in which Sir Alfred
> Jones has fulfilled his commercial obligations to the colony, he has done
> infinitely more than the contract calls for in the matter of advertising
> Jamaica as a winter resort, and encouraging English tourists to come
> here. Sir Alfred may not have proved the benefactor to our fruit trade
> that he was expected to do; but he has spent money lavishly in bringing
> the scenic and climatic attractions of this Island to the notice of his fellow-
> countrymen. . . . It is only fair to state that in this respect he has far ex-
> ceeded his duty; and due credit should be given to him for it.[57]

Notwithstanding Sir Alfred's efforts, his company's attempts to
develop a large English clientele for the Jamaica tourist trade
were unsuccessful. It was upon North America that Jamaica relied for its tourism, and it was mainly North American travel
agents and shipping companies that were prominent in advertising the island overseas.

On different occasions between 1910 and 1914, varying sums
of money were granted to internation travel and shipping companies to advertise the island abroad. At the time the Jamaica
Tourist Association was established, the sum of £300, for example, was granted to the firm of Thomas Cook and Son to
popularize the island as a resort.[58] Of this sum, £200 was subscribed by the merchants of Kingston and £100 by the government. Seven months later, in April 1911, another foreign firm
received funds to publicize Jamaica, when the government,
urged on by the tourist association, granted £150 to W. G. Foster,
a key figure in the tourist trades of Florida and Cuba.[59] The
strategic intent behind these tactics was to secure the patronage
of highly skilled advertisers with an already established network

of travel bureaus throughout the North Atlantic. What Cook and Sons had long been in Europe, Foster was to travelers on the American continent—their guide and adviser.[60] Gaining the good offices of Cook and Foster seemed likely to prove "of much more service to this colony than the spending of a similar sum on Jamaican exhibits at some obscure exhibition, where the name 'Jamaica' is forgotten within a week of its closing."[61]

Even without a subsidy, some of the steamship lines that did business with Jamaica advertised the island on their own account. The United Fruit Company, for example, periodically issued a pamphlet entitled *Jamaica: The Summer Land,* which brought to the attention of the traveling American public the varied attractions of the island. This company was one of the first interested in developing a summer tourist traffic to the colony. Because the summer temperature of Jamaica is much cooler and more exhilarating than in many parts of the United States, the idea was postulated to induce American schoolteachers and pleasure seekers to spend their summer holidays on this island. In 1912, the United Fruit Company arranged for an excursion service between New York and Jamaica during the months of June to September "at special reasonable rates."[62] That effort to initiate a summer traffic was the last act in the drama of the evolving tourist business of Jamaica before the outbreak of the First World War.

By 1914, then, Jamaica had buried its past ignominy as a godforsaken tropical island spurned by the wise traveler. Instead, with its promotional paraphernalia in gear, the colony sought to consolidate its image as the new Riviera just when completion of the Panama Canal promised a future with much more in store for the travel trade. Concomitant with the economic evolution of the colony was the gestation of a veritable tourism psychosis, which held it libelous—almost treasonous—to revile the climate of the island, physical or social, so engrossed had the community become with the accumulation of tourist dollars.[63]

By 1914, this preoccupation had permeated all social strata to the extent that, in Kingston for example, during the tourist season it was "altogether impossible" for black or colored Jamai-

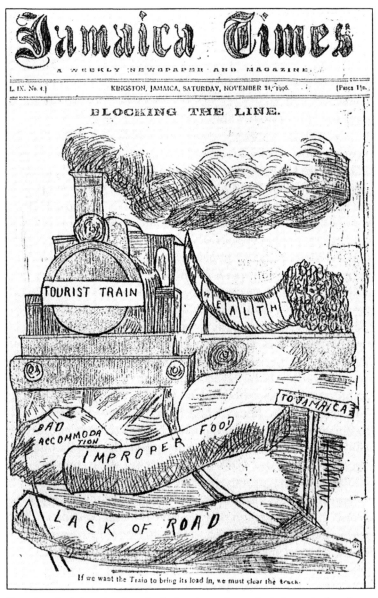

Drawing depicting the obstacles facing the early tourist industry in Jamaica.
Courtesy of National Library of Jamaica.

cans to get a hackney carriage driver to pick them up, so rapt were these city Jehus with pursuing the tourist dollar.[64] Some half a century earlier, Sewell, describing the economic behavior of people in the capital toward strangers, noted that "the Kingstonians remind me much of the Bahama wreckers. Having little or nothing themselves, they look upon a steamer-load of California passengers, cast away in their harbour for a night or a day, as very Egyptians, whom it is not only their privilege but their duty to despoil."[65] By 1914, this observation held true for the entire island.

Part Two

THE AFTERMATH

Chapter 8

Resurrection
and Revival

I F T H E generation before World War I saw the Jamaican tourist industry in its infancy, that after 1919 watched it attain its adolescence. But in the beginning, after peace came in 1919, visitor arrivals were well below the numbers of the prewar period.[1] In a sense this reduction in tourist traffic was only a reflection of the radical rupture in the island's communication links during the war. Up to 1914, there had been two steamship companies transporting English trippers to and from the island in well-equipped steamers. By 1919, however, steamers from the Royal Mail Steam Packet Company were no longer crossing these waters with passengers from England, that being left to the firm of Elders and Fyffes (a subsidiary of the United Fruit Company).[2] As for the North American trade, there had been at least three passenger outfits connecting Jamaica before 1914. Five years later, apart from the White Star Line and the Canadian Pacific Railway, whose cruise ships came this way, regular weekly communications were the virtual monopoly of the United Fruit Company. Jamaica was under the stranglehold of two firms—the UFC and its subsidiary, Elders and Fyffes. Since freighters from both had been requisitioned during the Great War and some had been lost to enemy action, tonnage to Jamaica was naturally smaller after 1919 than it had been earlier.

Were the Jamaica holiday trade to assume anything like its prewar level, it was felt that the colony should, in the circumstances, subsidize other companies to increase steamship facilities.[3] Beyond that, a great publicity campaign was imperative to bring Jamaica once more to the attention of the holidaymaker.[4] With its limited resources, though, the Jamaica Tourist Association was underequipped to manage that big push in advertising. Since the eruption of the war the association had faced official indifference and neglect. At one time the government had voted the sum of £250 per year for the work of the association. During the war, that had sunk to £50, then to £10, and finally to nothing.[5] Now that hostilities were over, the association itself needed a subsidy if there was to be a resurrection of the tourist trade to the colony.

While the Jamaica tourist trade languished in the doldrums immediately after the First World War, elsewhere holiday travel was noticeably on the increase with the beginning of peace. The Canadians, for example, by 1920 were spending an estimated $20 million each winter at vacation resorts in the United States, in places like California and Florida. This $20 million, it was felt, could well be diverted into the coffers of Britain's West Indian colonies if communications with Canadian ports were developed with a view to making the islands "the winter playground for Canadians."[6] Possibly no other country in the world generated as large a proportion of tourists per capita as did Canada, the *Canada-West India Magazine* claimed, basing the explanation for this upon, first, the general prosperity of the people and, second, the climate.[7] Canadians in the postwar era were, more and more, taking their holidays in the winter. Their employment was often seasonal (like growing grain, for example), occupying them in the summer and leaving them free for the winter. Thousands of Canadians had begun taking winter vacations in the warmer climates to the south (in Florida, California, etc.), unaware of what the West Indies had to offer.

If the Canadians were spending millions, the Americans for their part were spending billions on holiday travel at home and abroad in the early postwar years.[8] In Florida, for example, by 1926 the seasonal influx of winter visitors from inside and outside the United States numbered, as a norm, well in excess of the state's resident population. These visitors annually spent a sum of money ranging from $600 million to $1 billion. Similarly, California by 1928 could consider its golden sunshine to be worth more in currency than its oil or, for that matter, the gold that had lured so many in a previous era. Overseas, this holiday mania was reflected in a surge in foreign spending by American trippers, from an estimated $175 million in 1909–1910 to around $770 million by 1927. In France alone, for example, there were 220 thousand American tourists by 1925, with a total expenditure reckoned in the region of $226,160,000.[9] Such was the outlay in Europe by U.S. holidaymakers that President Hoover declared in 1928 that their overseas expenditure was enough to cover "the entire amount" of that continent's annual debt payments to the United States.[10]

Were Jamaica to cash in on this travel bonanza, it had to get its house in order—that is, develop such natural assets as the mineral baths, improve the general condition of Kingston, the gateway of the island, expand the accommodations in the colony, provide funds for overseas publicity, and, interest more shipping companies in putting Jamaica on their itinerary.[11] To advance all this, there was appointed by law on 10 July 1922 a body known as the Tourist Trade Development Board. Much as a precedent existed in the Jamaica Tourist Association, this new body was a novel departure in that it was the first promotional team constituted by government fiat. Since the tourist association itself had been lobbying for some time for such a body, from the outset there was close collaboration between both entities. While two members of the Tourist Trade Development Board sat upon the committee of the Jamaica Tourist Association, the board enjoyed on its seven-member executive board the services of the honorary secretary of the association.[12] Initially, according to Law 15 of 1922, under which it had been established, the Tourist Trade Development Board was to remain in force for just three years. Legislation was enacted in 1925, however, to provide for the development board's continued functioning, and in 1926 the Jamaica Tourist Association was amalgamated with it.[13] In fact, the development board was not abolished until 1955, when the Jamaica Tourist Board was set up in its stead.

Now, although after 1914 the Jamaica tourist industry tetered on the brink of "an almost complete cessation," by 1923 the tide had turned and visitors were again calling at the colony.[14] Whatever the vicissitudes of the holiday traffic since the Jamaica International Exhibition of 1891, it had still been a vehicle for bringing into the island, over the years to 1925, a sum that one guesstimate totaled at £3,500,000.[15] There were also instances where individuals came to the colony at first as visitors and later acquired "a permanent interest" in it through investment and settlement.[16] Because of the postwar increases in health and pleasure travel on the part of North Atlantic nations, the Jamaica tourist industry was felt to be far more capable of contributing to domestic economic growth than it had in the past. In 1924, the tourist trade was positioned in fourth place among the island's industries. Contemporary projections, however, postulated that the trade could readily be expanded to assume first or second place as a source of income to the island, provided that the infrastructure of amenities were developed and adequate publicity measures were procured. The table below lists the chief trades in Jamaica in 1924.[17]

Fruit	£2,131,555
Sugar	911,812
Coffee	203,882
Tourist trade	158,540
Coconuts	139,851
Cocoa	138,315
Dyewoods	117,711
Rum	80,903

In contrast to before 1914, when Jamaica's mountain air figured at the top of her appeal to tourists, in the interwar years it was sea- and sunbathing that surged ahead as her prime allure. Throughout the North Atlantic by the early 1920s, the virtues of

the sun were sung by growing numbers of physicians and sur-
geons convinced that heliotherapy would prove to be "one of the
greatest therapeutic agents of the future."[18] At sanatoria in
parts of Europe and even in England extraordinary cures were
effected by sun treatment, and indeed, the famous English osteo-
pathologist, Herbert Barker himself, found that several weeks of
sunbathing in the Caribbean "has left me in a state of wonderful
health, strength and rejuvenation." One British tycoon wanted to
see facilities established in Jamaica for people to take "altogether
sun-baths" (i.e., nude sun baths) and announced his own willing-
ness to invest in the holiday business with an outlay for a giant
hotel complex to be erected at Montego Bay.[19] In an era that had
begun to glorify the suntan, there was unbridled optimism that
Jamaica could benefit from tourism even to the tune of £1 million
per year, comprised as follows:[20]

1,000 Visitors staying 4-6 months, (average 5 months) at, say, £40 per month	£200,000
2,000 Visitors for periods of from 1 to 3 months (average 6 weeks), at £15 per week	£180,000
4,000 Visitors, 1 to 4 weeks (average 2 weeks), at £20 per week	£160,000
5,000 Cruise Tourists, about 2 days, (some accommodated on board whilst in Port), at say £7 per head	£ 35,000
5,000 Summer Visitors of 5 days to 4 weeks—average of about £25 per head	£125,000
17,000	£700,000
1,000 Permanent Residents at an average of £300 per annum	£300,000
	£1,000,000

The Jamaican tourist trade never attained such dimensions
during the pre-World War II period. While most government
officials were not unenthusiastic about tourist trade development, there were still some (such as the governor, Sir Henry
Stubbs, and Sir Arthur Jelf, his colonial secretary) who seemed
peeved at the prospect that the colony might be transformed

into "a nation of hotel-keepers."[21] Whether or not the governor approved of tourism, the question of its development was neglected. For the most part the funds allotted to the Tourist Trade Development Board by the governors were far too little for it to carry out its work.[22] The explanation for this lay not so much in the prejudices of individual governors toward tourist trade development as in the question of who should finance it— private entrepreneurs or the government.

Some circles felt that provisions to advertise Jamaica should be made primarily by private enterprisers rather than by the government, as it was the former, particularly the hoteliers and the gasoline and automobile dealers, who received the lion's share of the benefits from the existing trade. Since these organizers found tourism so desirable, it was in their interests to take the initiative and advertise the island themselves, the argument went.[23] The private entrepreneurs, for their part, felt that the greater the business done between themselves and the visitors, the greater was the sum of money that accrued to the government. They claimed that the whole island benefited, as it turned out to be chiefly a matter of the cash first passing through their hands (the so-called multiplier process). From their viewpoint, the responsibility of advertising the island, therefore, lay with the government and not its corporate subjects.

The issue was eventually settled by a decision to make the tourists themselves finance the promotion of tourism in the island. According to Law 16 of 1935, "a Law to impose a duty on passengers transported to Jamaica by ship or aircraft," a tax of ten shillings was imposed on those visitors who remained in the island beyond three days, and one of four shillings was imposed upon those whose stay was shorter. The object of the tax was to obtain funds specifically for advertising the island abroad and for otherwise promoting the tourist traffic. By the end of the tourist season of 1939, a mere four years after the introduction of this tax, £43,041 altogether had been collected from it.[24] Tourist trade development in the island was given a tremendous boost by the substantial increases in funding accruing to the Tourist Trade Development Board after 1936, as the following table shows. It lists government grants to the Tourist Trade Development Board from 1923 through 1938.[25]

1923	£2,630
1924–1926	1,000, each year
1926–1929	1,250, each year
1929–1931	1,500, each year
1931–1936	1,000, each year
1936–1937	7,000
1937–1938	10,459

(Funds for 1936 through 1938 were granted from passenger duty collections.)

Although Jamaica was not deluged by tourists to the point where its traffic was worth £1 million per year, tourism nevertheless grew steadily during the interwar period. By the end of this period, tourism occupied third place in export value, after bananas and sugar, and was "conservatively estimated" to earn for Jamaica half a million pounds each year.[26] As indicated in Table 1, between 1922 and 1937, there was an unbroken progression in the numbers of visitors to the island. Of the 65,269 visitors in 1937, 66 percent came from the United States, 25 percent from Great Britain, and about 9 percent from Canada and the rest of the world.[27]

Considering the widespread economic depression during the 1930s, this steady growth in the number of visitors to Jamaica was remarkable. In the opinion of the secretary of the Tourist Trade Development Board, the explanation for it lay largely in the successful publicity overseas promoted by the board itself as well as by some of the steamship companies and travel agencies.[28] The departure of England from the gold standard was also significant, as it offered the opportunity to advertise the island in "certain other countries" to the greatest good.[29] Finally, the increases in tourist arrivals were to some extent a

TABLE 1. TOURIST TRADE IN JAMAICA,
1922–1940

Year	Stopover Visitors	Cruise Tourists	Total
1922	1,872	—	—
1923	2,734	—	—
1924	3,114	—	—
1925	3,378	—	—
1926	3,668	7,951	11,619
1927	4,016	8,208	12,224
1928	3,906	10,550	14,456
1929	4,850	13,763	18,613
1930	4,461	21,726	26,187
1931	4,079	22,474	26,553
1932	5,062	27,669	32,731
1933	6,360	26,994	33,354
1934	5,149	34,113	39,262
1935	6,192	43,608	49,800
1936	6,886	49,007	55,893
1937	10,432	54,837	65,269
1938	9,908	52,782	62,690
1939	7,493	42,413	49,906
1940	4,319	10,828	15,147

SOURCES: Tourist Trade Development Board, *Report for the period from 1st January, 1936, to 31st March, 1937;* Ministry of Trade and Industry, Ministry Paper 4 (April 1954), app. 9.

N. B. *Stopover visitors* applied to tourists remaining over three days in the island. *Cruise tourists* included all visitors remaining three days and under. (A record of cruise tourists was not kept until 1926.)

happy reflection of a growing intra-empire sentiment and travel, as Britishers were evidently becoming alive to the idea of "seeing the Empire first."[30]

No less consequential were the effects of international politics in explaining the continued growth of the Jamaican tourist traffic despite the economic turbulence of the 1930s. For instance, with the grave unrest in Cuba that accompanied the overthrow of Machado in 1933, a great part of the tourist traffic to Havana was temporarily deflected to its neighbor, Jamaica.[31] In another example, the leisured classes of Europe and America had for many years passed the winter in Italy. With its Mediterranean climate and magnificent art treasures and historical monuments, Italy had long been one of the principal tourist centers on the Continent. But following the development of Italian fascism and the growth of the conflict with Ethiopia, this portion of the Mediterranean became uncomfortable for tourist travel. No doubt it was possible that Jamaica gained part of the trade that Italy lost.[32] Whatever the reason, one out of every four visitors to the island in 1937 came from England.

With the steady growth of the tourist traffic to Jamaica in the interwar years came a steady development of the facilities available to visitors. Actual figures on the growth of hotel accommodation are hard to come by, but Gisela Eisner states that between 1910 and 1930 the number of hotels and boardinghouses in Jamaica increased by over 100 percent from 54 to 114.[33] This reflected a deepening interest by the local private sector in the hotel business. Many of the structures established for tourists were Jamaican Great Houses transformed into hostels by adding new rooms and installing more up-to-date appliances.[34] With the golden age of sugar in the distant past, a number of the ancient landed families saw a new era of profit making looming on the horizon, thanks to tourism. In view of the growing profitability of the holiday industry since 1923, local capital resolved not just to increase the extent of its involvement in the enterprise but, if possible, to develop it for their exclusive benefit.

Before 1914, a considerable amount of the capital invested in the hotel industry had been acquired from sources overseas. The belief at the time had been that tourism in the island could be developed only by providing large, elaborate hotels for the visitors. In the postwar years, however, this began to change. In Montego Bay, for instance, then emerging as a resort, the general feeling was that small hotels of, say, ten to twenty rooms would better serve the needs of the growing tourist traffic than some gigantic building erected by a large company.[35] Small hotels would be homelike and more in keeping with the local surroundings, and there was no reason in the world why they could not be as comfortable and as efficiently run as a large establishment. Besides, their overhead expenses should be considerably less, and they were likely to be more viable, when business slackened in summer, than a large enterprise. Finally, if need be, some small hotels could even close during the off season without doing any damage to the tourist trade.[36] As one gentleman asserted, "We want no Titchfield or Myrtle Bank here [in Montego Bay] but small hotels that will pay their way and keep open all the year round."[37] Many popular resorts had started in a modest fashion and then grown to fame and opulence, and Montego Bay could do likewise.

For many years, local entrepreneurs had solicited government support with a view to increasing hotel accommodation but had met with little success. At Montego Bay, for instance, there were only three popular hotels in 1925 to take care of the tourist traffic, and these had a total of only about seventy-six rooms.[38] Some years earlier there had been only one or two lodging houses of the old Jamaica type. For many years after the war, government had procrastinated on the question of hotel accommodation, but it eventually responded with the passage of the Jamaica Hotels Aid Law, Law 10 of 1936—itself an amended version of the Jamaica Hotels Law of 1904. Under the terms of this new enactment, hotel proprietors were permitted to import, free of duty, building materials, furniture, and equipment for any new hotels or for the reconstruction or enlargement of existing plants, provided that the building contained not less than ten bedrooms when completed.

The government also initiated a scheme whereby any hotel proprietor who wanted to enlarge his plant, or alternatively, to build a new one, might apply for a free grant not exceeding 1.5 percent per year for seven years on the capital outlay. Expenditure under this head was provided out of passenger duty collections and was limited to a total of £1,500 per year for seven years.[39] What this really represented was a free grant to hotel proprietors of 1.5 percent per year on sums up to £100 thou-

sand. At last, it seemed, government had begun to give the tourist industry something of the "New Deal" that the Tourist Trade
Development Board had long been urging. That, however, fore-
boded a continuation of the old deal for black Jamaicans. Given
its accompanying discriminations of race and class, in the contemporary assessment of one columnist, "this tourist trade boom
is the greatest encouragement for the development of an inferiority complex that the island has ever suffered."[40]

In the years before World War I it had not been too difficult for
dark-skinned Jamaicans traveling between New York and the
colony to obtain accommodation on a ship or to secure decent
treatment while on board. At the time, active competition existed
between the Royal Mail Line, Hamburg American Line, United
Fruit Company, and the many small steamship outfits plying that
route. In the post-World War I years, however, the situation had
changed dramatically, in that the United Fruit Company came to
exercise a virtual monopoly over the passenger service between
the city of New York and Jamaican ports. With the growth in
popularity of the Caribbean cruise trip among Americans, it
became exceedingly difficult for black Jamaicans to secure rea-
sonably humane treatment on ships belonging to the company.
Though most persons kept silent about it,[41] this racism was visible
to all who traveled on the company's steamers, so blatantly was it
carried out. The following is a concise account of the situation
that had developed in the postwar period:

Whenever a coloured passenger applies at the office of the United Fruit
Company for a berth he or she is told that all the cabins are gone except
those located in the stern of the boat where the vibration of the pro-
peller makes it a none too comfortable voyage. Besides, the cabins are
smaller and less comfortable.

Should the intended passenger be a bit suspicious and step outside
and use the telephone to inquire about booking, the same clerk, now
unable to see the colour of the questioner, will tell him that cabins are
available in the very sections which he had just been told were already
booked up. It is rumoured that a similar condition prevails in Kingston.

If he returns and protests he meets with adamant resistance. . . . On the ship itself the coloured passengers are often asked to eat and leave the dining saloon BEFORE the rest of the passengers and have to hurry through their meals within a specified time. If they refuse to co-operate in their own humiliation they will find that they are segregated at the tables and put by themselves in some out of the way corner. On the ship itself some of the crew treat the coloured passengers with disdainful discourtesy.[42]

It should be noted, nevertheless, that the United Fruit Company was not exceptional in this respect. If it was the biggest offender, that was because it controlled the bulk of the passenger service between the United States and Jamaica. In some respects the United Fruit Company might even have seemed more "generous" in its policy toward black people than the Standard Fruit Company. The latter, it appears, absolutely refused to accept colored passengers on their boats.[43]

The colored person was unwelcome in the hotels as well as on the boats.[44] Nor was the position any better when the proprietor or manager himself happened to be colored. In general no noise was made publicly about color discrimination in the hotels or in the wider Jamaican society,[45] but the color complex was there all the same. For instance, prior to the emergence and development of Montego Bay as a tourist resort, it had been the age-long right of the people to bathe at the beautiful White Sands Beach, the pride of the township. Apart from the scenic beauty of Montego Bay, its greatest attraction as far as visitors were concerned was that incomparable stretch of white sand bordering the famous Doctor's Cave. This beach was the general property of the public and therefore under the control of the municipal authorities, the parochial board of St. James. The Doctor's Cave itself was the property of an exclusive bathing club that bore the same name. For years the Doctor's Cave Bathing Club had been trying to get exclusive rights to the White Sands, but it was not until the mid-twenties or thereabouts that this attempt really blossomed.[46]

First came a notice from a commissioned land surveyor claiming ownership of the White Sands Beach in the name of the

Montego Bay (1924).

Doctor's Cave, Montego Bay (1924).
Illustrations courtesy of National Library of Jamaica.

bathing club. The club had no evidence to support this contention. Indeed, they had no idea where the land they actually
possessed began or ended, as no diagram accompanied the title
that they produced.[47] It might generously be assumed that they
made a "mistake" in claiming parochial property as their own.

Having failed in this respect, the bathing club next sought
to gain control of the beach by leasing it from the parochial
board.[48] The White Sands, they claimed, was one of the most
valuable assets of Montego Bay from the tourist point of view.
Unfortunately the place was not always all that could be desired,
as order and decency were at times absent, due to the lack of
effective control of the beach. If this absence of regulation continued, they argued, tourists would not be likely to frequent the
place, and thus the entire tourist trade of the town would be
endangered. In fact, what many members of the club feared,
though they did not publicly say so, was that the visitors would
be driven away if the place were left open to all and sundry.[49]
Their ostensible public-spiritedness in seeking the protection
and development of the economic interests of the community as
a whole was a fig leaf behind which they sought to cover their
naked desire for control of the White Sands Beach to satisfy
their own prejudices.

Naturally the public was not prepared to relinquish its rights
without a struggle, and the attempt of the Doctor's Cave Bathing
Club to encroach upon the privileges of the people caused quite
a stir. It seemed to some that the matter revolved around issues
no higher than those of color and class. According to the *Northern News,* for example, the rights of the general public were
neither for rent nor for sale; more, the board had no moral
authority to lease the public rights to any select group of people.
"The beach is public property and not for any exclusive section
of the community. The beach is also not belonging to any
Church to be disposed of at will. Let all these facts be distinctly
understood at once," the paper cautioned from the outbreak of
the question.[50]

The beach was a material asset to the town and ought to be

well managed. While in a technical sense the bathing club committee was better qualified to do that than the parochial board, it was unacceptable on purely social criteria. A compromise was reached wherein the White Sands Beach was to be managed by a joint committee consisting of three members of the parochial board and a like number from the Doctor's Cave Bathing Club Committee.[51] Such a body, it was felt, could best provide for the improved administration of the place and at the same time protect public rights and privileges. But what occurred in actual practice was rather different.

It had, for example, been the habit for people from humble walks of life to shelter among the trees and there divest themselves of their clothing before going on to the beach for a bath. To discourage such persons from using the beach any further, the bathing club committee had all the trees on the site cut down without even consulting the parochial board.[52] Furthermore, a bathhouse that had stood on the beach and that could have been used as a screen was moved to a position where it could not serve the same purpose. Under the umbrella of the joint committee, the bathing club thus set about to run the place exclusively to its own taste. This behavior was, of course, condemned at a subsequent meeting of the parochial board, but despite such indications of the trend within the bathing club committee, a proposal to lease the premises to it came up again in the parochial board.[53]

In a meeting of the board at the beginning of May 1927, the chairman suggested that the board should rent the place to the bathing club, as it was a great asset to the town and ought to be well cared for. Again the proposition was turned down. However, it was clear that, despite the existence of the joint committee, the matter of the management and control of the White Sands Beach was far from settled. With tourism, the White Sands Beach had become of inestimable commercial value, whereas the rights of the people were clearly (in some circles) a trivial question of sentimental value.[54] The grand finale of the whole affair eventually came when, in April 1929, regardless of public feeling on the issue, the parochial board resolved to lease the White Sands Beach.[55] This lease to the Doctor's Cave Bathing Club Committee was to run for twenty-one years, and the rental was set at £25 per annum, payable half yearly. The covenant of the lease stipulated that the public had the right to use the sands for promenading and the water for bathing, provided that persons so doing were decently dressed, decently behaved, and paid whatever fee was charged by the bathing club for the privilege of using the property. Furthermore, no discrimination was to be made among the various users of the beach.[56] In view of the reputation that the club had acquired, public misgivings that these conditions might not be respected were not without foundation. As it stood, the lease in effect legitimized discrimination on the basis of class while rejecting its application on the grounds of color.

The tourist trade was not only dehumanizing, it was demoralizing, it seems. It brought to the island the "standardised fripperies of Palm Beach" along with the canned entertainment of Hollywood—its values and vulgarity. Critics vigorously contended that tourism cheapened the morals of Jamaican youth, who mimicked the observed behavior of the American tourists with drinking, smoking, and public "necking."[57] Prostitution too had mushroomed throughout the chief ports of the island, compliments of the holiday business. Reports had it that Montego Bay was besieged by "an epidemic of homosexuality" by 1940.[58]

Little as the local population benefited from the morality of the tourists, it had even less to gain from them as models of manners and courtesy. The bulk of Americans who visited the island were arrogant, ostentatious, and coarse, and many Jamaicans themselves assumed such traits.[59] "The more energy is devoted in Jamaica to making the Island 'attractive' to tourists in the methods that are commonly understood to be inviting to them (night clubs, 'Lidos', etc.), the less attractive does the Blessed Island become," one former governor confessed.[60] Confronted by the foreign exchange preoccupations that had engendered this seeming tradeoff between popular dignity and the tourist dollar, critics of public policy were left with little recourse other than the passive resistance of satire and caricature:

> Montego Bay . . . is one gigantic farce. But Jamaicans believe there is something in it all. In Kingston they congregate in horrible little night-clubs a beetle would be too fastidious to frequent. They assume the bovine loud aggressiveness of the tourist manner. They mortgage their properties to buy expensive cars. They give themselves grave-yard faces by dancing all night or slim to resemble their celluloid film-heroines. . . .
>
> Jamaicans have a genuine and glorious sense of humour when they are not over-awed. When will they use it? When will they take off the blinkers of a self-assumed inferiority and, looking at these preposterous car-loads of commercial rats on the spree, of melodramatic baby-faces and fleshy lobsters—when will they look and lift up their voices in one magnificent roar of mirth?[61]

The social reality of what tourism brought, of course, was far from a laughing matter. All over the island it elicited an out-break of touting, begging, and multifarious forms of parasitism. Even children hardly able to walk hurled abusive epithets at visitors when their demands were not met.[62] Proof of the degree of the problem is evidenced from the court records of Kingston. Between December 1936 and September 1937, 630 persons were apprehended and prosecuted in petty sessions for selling on the streets. In each case the charge was the result of visitors being pestered in downtown Kingston. Altogether, 504 convictions were recorded, and total fines amounted to £98.5.6—that is, four shillings per person convicted.[63] As for begging from cruise passengers, fifty-two arrests were made in the capital city during 1937, and of these, forty defendants were convicted and fined a total of £9.12.6. Tourism created an interaction between the overwealthy of the earth and its wretched, and with it there sprang to life sundry odious and degrading behavioral patterns among the Jamaican masses. The pearl of the Antilles was, in the language of one local publication, "a perverted hell."[64]

Advocates of tourist trade development had always claimed that the industry would win enormous profits. But for whom?

And at what price? Looking back, in the opinion of some observers the trade was of benefit primarily to a few hotel keepers, but these were not wont to invest their profits within the colony,[65] nor were they famous for paying high wages to their staff. The opposite pertained, where "in Jamaica, we pay our own people, the labourers, less than anywhere else in the world, and charge the visitors more!"[66] The colonial government did receive a fair amount of income each year from the tourist tax, but this money was spent primarily on projects advertising the island abroad or on schemes for improving facilities for visitors. Almost none of these receipts, it seemed, was spent on relieving conditions among the masses of the people and thereby making their lives in the colony less uncomfortable.[67]

A little seasonal employment had been derived from the development of the tourist trade, but persons who earned money just during the tourist season could only be adversely affected by the other months of idleness. To crown it all, it was suspected that businessmen had a tendency to mark up the prices of their goods during the tourist season, in which case the native himself was also a victim of this particular kind of opportunism fueled by tourism.[68] The colony at large, it was claimed, was being exploited for the sake of certain vested interest groups, local and foreign—the hoteliers, the merchants, the car rental and transportation agencies, and so on. To the bulk of the population the value of the tourist trade was practically nothing, many a critic contended.

At the close of the interwar period the Jamaican tourist industry had developed neither social legitimacy nor, among large segments of the population, even economic credibility. Yet Jamaica had already begun to anticipate the eventual coming of a new era, when people would be able to travel from New York to Kingston and vice versa by air. The arrival in the island of the *American Clipper* during November 1931, with Charles Lindbergh and its designer, Igor Sikorsky, on board, was an event of great significance for Jamaica.[69] Given its trade dependency, the welfare of Jamaica's citizens had always been closely connected with the quality of the transportation facilities at its service. From the standpoint of tourism, the most important feature of the visit of the *American Clipper* was its demonstration of the speed with which the island could be reached, bringing the colony closer to the homes of holidaymakers. "One often hears business people say that they do not want to be far away from home. This has been the drawback with Jamaica in the past," Philip Olley, secretary of the Tourist Trade Development Board, protested.[70] Without question it would take a few years before air routes to the island were built up and Jamaica could receive an augmented tourist traffic via this medium. "But," Olley exulted, "the point is that we know now that it is possible and only a matter of time."

Just as the pre–World War I years in Jamaica concluded on a note of optimism that the opening of the Panama Canal would be a great boost to the colony's tourism, the pre–World War II era closed with an analogous sentiment. Thanks again to its geographical position, the feeling was that this time around Jamaica would boom through the development of aviation. When he landed in the island in 1931, Lindbergh had pointed out that, in terms of any putative air routes between North and South America, the fastest of these would necessarily pass through Jamaica. The colony lay in the way, as it were, and was therefore expected to become a critical connecting point between both continents.[71] In any case, with its location just a few hours by air from the shores of the United States, the population of which luxuriated in the highest income per capita on this planet, it seemed indeed Jamaica's manifest destiny to become "God's paradise for tourists." In 1928 a total of 14,456 persons visited the island; but a mere ten years later, on the eve of the Second World War, the number of visitors stood at 62,690—an increase of 430 percent (see table 1). The advent of the airplane patently promised more. First, however, the colony needed to get its house in order, as it turned its gaze skyward in anticipation of this second coming by tourists that aviation portended.

Chapter 9

The Second Coming

BEFORE the outbreak of the Second World War, insofar as Jamaica had been a favorite holiday retreat for westerners, it had been so for the wealthy almost exclusively. It was not until December 1930, when Pan American World Airways first linked Jamaica with the outside world via its Clipper service, that Jamaica began to emerge as a leading destination for the average middle-income vacationer. According to the *Daily Gleaner*, mass tourism in the island commenced with the appearance of Pan Am.[1] The airline did not just invest in the creation of links between the island and the mainland, but through its advertising campaigns in newspapers, magazines, posters, film travelogues, et cetera, actively promoted Jamaica as a tourist mecca. The story goes that the airline company was only three years old when on 2 December 1930 it inaugurated service through Kingston on its Miami-Panama route. With its original four-engine Commodore flying boats or seaplanes, Pan Am carried twenty passengers per trip from Kingston to Miami in about six hours.[2] A quarter of a century later, however, Pan Am's Clippers were carrying two or three times as many people twice as speedily to the island.

When the company began operating in Jamaica at the end of 1930 it had four employees, but by 1955 its personnel at the Kingston office numbered sixty-two, and at Montego Bay the staff amounted to a dozen.[3] By 1955, Kingston was only three hours distant from Miami by daily round-trip Clipper flights. Jamaica was on two main Clipper routes—one between Miami and Puerto Rico and the other between Miami, Colombia, Venezuela, and Trinidad and Tobago. Indicative of Pan Am's interest in the promotion of Jamaica was the fact that the island was featured among twelve countries on the pages of its 1955 calender, which was distributed all over the world. Proof too of Pan Am's desire to bring mass tourism to Jamaica was its willing participation in 1950 in initiating the first "Know Jamaica" tour—a scheme that brought over one thousand travel agents and travel editors on familiarization visits between 1951 and 1953.[4] Finally, there was PAA's practice of "installment travel" (10 percent down, up to twenty months to pay)—an initiative that by 1954 had made Jamaica accessible to many who would otherwise have lacked the financial means to visit the colony.[5]

Before 1940 there was no landing field in Jamaica, and so when Pan Am began its operations in 1930 the company used Sikorsky Clippers and continued that practice throughout its first business decade on the island. In the heat of World War II, in 1940, the military authorities in Jamaica started the construction of an adequate airport on the Palisadoes Peninsula south of Kingston harbor. Following the completion of this field, it became technically feasible for other aviation companies to open links with the island, and among the first to do so was the Royal Dutch Airlines (KLM).[6] Using diplomatic channels, a request for a permit was made and received, thus permitting KLM on 19 August 1941 to land its first airplane on the island.

On that first flight KLM carried among its passengers the personnel managers of all the oil companies engaged in refining in Curaçao. The idea was for them to see for themselves the many attractions offered by Jamaica: good hotels, beautiful scenery, and cool mountain air—things not found in Curaçao, and especially appreciated by the Dutchmen there since they could not repatriate to wartorn Europe for their holidays. Subsequent to this maiden flight, so many employees and their families from the Dutch oil companies flocked to Jamaica via KLM to spend their vacations that the airline, in October 1941, increased the number of its weekly flights between Curaçao and Kingston from one to two.[7]

Besides PAA and KLM, the British Overseas Airways Corporation (BOAC) also played an active role in the postwar promotion of Jamaica's beaches and other resort charms. In May 1952, BOAC's stratocruiser brought to Jamaica on a six-hour, nonstop flight from New York about sixty of the leading travel agents and hotel personalities in the United States.[8] The intent of this initiative was to promote the island's summer tourist traffic, which in the years after World War II had begun to assume a significance that it had not before possessed. In 1948, for example, 42 percent of the tourist traffic occurred in the months of May through September, as compared with only 23 percent in 1938. In 1951, the proportion of business represented by the summer trade stood in the region of 39 percent of the overall traffic.[9] It was BOAC's hope that, by bringing a select who's who of the big names in travel and showing them the island's equable summer climate, it could contribute to the generation of a year-round tourist trade. Though there was no higher motive than the expansion of business for its carriers, BOAC's salience in seeking to enlarge the summer market was not without substantial macroeconomic merit. As one observer remarked at the time, "the importance of the summer trade cannot be exaggerated . . . taking into account the spread of employment in the industry and the all-the-year-round tourist spending which circulates throughout the whole economy."[10]

While prior to the Second World War visitors to Jamaica had arrived almost exclusively by sea, in the years after the war it was by air that most tourists came. By the mid-1950s the island was serviced by eight international airlines—PAA, KLM, Trans Canada Airlines, Delta, Avianca, Avensa, BOAC, and British West Indian Airways (BWIA). So brisk was the volume of business conducted by these airlines that between 1954 and 1957 all saw fit to increase their regular schedules to Jamaica.[11] With this rise of air transport in the postbellum years came a dramatic shift in the centers of Jamaican tourism. Port Antonio, the island's leading banana port, had once been its leading tourist resort. After 1945, however, Port Antonio sank into the background as a travel destination because it lacked an airfield and was, considering its mountainous environs, unable to build one. Montego Bay rose into preeminence, thanks in part to the airstrip laid out there during World War II. That the air rather than the sea had become the mode of travel in the Jamaican tourist industry by 1950 is revealed by the following travel statistics, which list Jamaica tourist arrivals from 1951 to 1960, by mode of travel.[12]

Year	Air	Sea
1951	78%	22%
1952	81	19
1953	78	22
1954	67	33
1955	71	29
1956	73	27
1957	71	29
1958	72	28
1959	72	28
1960	69	31

In the postwar years the Jamaican tourist industry grew by such leaps and bounds that by 1951 it had already become second only to sugar in economic significance to the islanders.[13] In 1949 its reported value was £2.7 million; in 1950, £3.2 million; in 1951, £4 million; by 1957 it was worth almost £10 million and still rising in value (see table 2). On the eve of international conflict, in 1938, the annual number of visitors to the island stood at 62,690. Barely six years, in 1951, after the cessation of hostilities, it had risen by about 50 percent to 93,626. Despite fleeting reversals in 1954 and 1957, by 1960 the yearly arrivals figure was some 240 percent of that of 1951, such was the momentum of tourism development in the postbellum period (see table 2). If, in international perspective, the 1950s, and 1960s were a veritable golden age of a global tourism boom,[14] in that gilded era Jamaica's North Coast was literally its gold coast, pulsating with tourism development. Among the British West Indian islands, Jamaica was the acclaimed leader in establishing mass tourism. Since it lay on the doorstep of the United States, it came considerably faster to the fore as a pleasure destination for mass recre-

TABLE 2. JAMAICA TOURIST ARRIVALS AND
ESTIMATED EXPENDITURE, 1945–1960

Year	Long Stay (more than 3 days)	Short Stay (3 days and less)	Total	Percentage Distribution		Estimated Tourist Expenditure
				Long Stay	Short Stay	
1945	3,625	30,745	34,370	12	88	—
1946	6,461	34,145	40,606	19	81	—
1947	10,653	42,817	53,470	25	75	—
1948	12,860	48,971	61,831	21	79	—
1949	13,720	54,908	68,628	20	80	—
1950	17,983	56,909	74,892	24	76	£3,266,540
1951	24,799	68,827	93,626	26	74	£4,022,476
1952	24,532	80,254	104,786	23	77	£4,249,172
1953	28,100	93,632	121,732	23	77	£4,860,135
1954	36,377	76,431	112,808	32	68	£5,196,805
1955	45,318	76,831	122,149	37	63	£6,718,190
1956	50,960	110,426	161,386	31	69	£8,876,230
1957	58,480	102,195	160,675	36	64	£9,837,125
1958	65,689	103,756	169,447	39	61	£10,166,820
1959	72,326	118,977	191,303	38	62	£11,478,180
1960	80,420	146,525	226,945	35	65	£13,616,700

SOURCES: *Annual Report of the Jamaica Tourist Board, Year Ended 31st March, 1960* (Kingston, 1960), pp. 6–7; *Annual Report of the Jamaica Tourist Board, Year Ended 31st March, 1961* (Kingston, 1962), pp. 6–7; John Jones, "Tourism as a Tool for Economic Development with Specific Reference to the Countries of Jamaica, Trinidad and Guyana," Ph. D. diss., University of Florida, 1970, p. 220.

ationers than Trinidad or Barbados.[15] Also, being larger than the others, it had more miles of beaches available for building its burgeoning hotel industry upon. By 1960, Jamaica had passed the quarter-million mark for annual tourist arrivals, and as table 2 details above, their expenditure was a record high of over £13,600,000.

Perhaps the most striking characteristic of these statistics is not the growth in the annual totals of Jamaica's tourist arrivals but the changing composition of the island's long-stay and short-stay visitors. Between 1950 and 1960, for instance, long-stay visits grew by nearly 447 percent, from 17,983 to 80,420. In these same years the short-stay category experienced a much smaller

increase of 257 percent, from 56,909 to 146,525 (see table 2).
Though the long-stay visitors category was evidently the faster
growing segment of the Jamaica tourist trade, it continued to
constitute the smaller proportion of the total visitor traffic until
1965. In this year, for the first time ever, long-stay visitors came
to comprise the bulk of arrivals, accounting for 59 percent of the
total (see table 3). This development heralded the coming to full
maturity of the Jamaica tourist industry, since it is the long-stay
as compared to the short-stay vacationer who establishes the
basis for viability in the holiday business. As though to mark that
"coming of age," as tourist trade officials termed it,[16] 1965 was
also the year in which tourism surpassed the declining sugar
industry as a foreign exchange earner in the economy.[17]

Allied to the postwar surges in the numbers of Jamaican tourist arrivals was the mushrooming of the island's tourism plant
and infrastructure. So ebullient was the growth in capacity in the
hotel industry that it outpaced the annual rate of growth in
visitor arrivals between 1955 and 1962, for example.[18] In 1950
Jamaica had 1,040 hotel rooms, or a total bed occupancy of
1,680.[19] By 1962, however, the island possessed 74 hotels, 46
guest houses, and 106 resort cottages that together represented

TABLE 3. JAMAICA VISITOR ARRIVALS AND
TOURISM FINANCE, 1959–1968

Year	Long Stay 3 nights and more)	Short Stay (less than 3 nights)	Total	Estimated Tourist Expenditure, in U.S. $1,000	Tourist Board Budget, in U.S. $1,000
1959	72,326	118,977	191,303	28,000	840
1960	80,420	146,525	226,945	40,320	980
1961	76,000	148,492	224,492	40,880	980
1962	78,468	128,352	206,838	36,668	1,126
1963	80,939	121,390	202,329	37,800	1,462
1964	97,230	134,960	232,190	43,680	1,733
1965	175,769	124,489	300,258	64,960	2,338
1966	212,673	132,615	345,288	78,400	2,870
1967	219,547	113,291	332,838	79,800	3,157
1968	239,961	156,386	396,347	87,800	3,264

SOURCE: *Jamaica Tourist Board Annual Report 1968/69.*

a tourist capacity of about 7,000 beds and a gross investment of some £20 million. Between 1945 and 1962, the number of hotels in the island increased twofold. Before the war, in the North Coast town of Ocho Rios, for example, where there had been but one notable hotel, in the late 1940s a brand new holiday resort suddenly emerged with the building there of a nucleus of hotels and beach cottages.[20] Almost everywhere miscellaneous services materialized in response to the bustling numbers of tourist arrivals. Free port shops proliferated, as did nightclubs, sports facilities, car-rental agencies, and so on. It is also noteworthy that, by 1960, tourism had ceased to be the one-season affair it had been before the war and became a year-round commerce.

In contrast to the past, when Jamaica's tourist clientele came from the moneyed classes, the advent of air transport opened up Jamaica to mass travel, making it imperative that the island adjust its marketing appeal to a wider range of vacationers, a lot of whom were budget conscious. To accommodate this shift from class to mass, a formula was adopted in the early 1960s that reorganized the industry on a twelve-month basis with two distinct economic time spans: the winter and the summer seasons.[21] Winter season ran from 16 December to 15 April and targeted the rich, who are financially capable of holidaying at this time of year. The summer season followed immediately after and catered to middle-income holidaymakers lured to Jamaica by the drastic reductions in hotel rates, sometimes as much as 40 percent, that took place during the period from 16 April to mid-December of each year. Whereas the major prewar hotels operated for about twenty weeks a year, by 1950 the operating period had extended to thirty weeks, and by 1954 it was even longer—some forty weeks per year. By Jamaica's independence in 1962 the hotels no longer closed their doors at all.[22]

Crucial as private sector decision making was in fueling the process of Jamaica's postwar tourism development, the contribution of government should not be underestimated. One factor that had certainly helped to energize Jamaica's postwar expan-

sion had been the Hotels Aid Law of 1944.[23] Passed to replace
the earlier laws that expired in 1943, the new legislation gave
numerous financial concessions for the construction of resort
hotels. Among these were the waiving of customs duties on im-
ports of building materials and various items of hotel equipment
(including furniture, linen, silverware, kitchen utensils, etc).
Hotel proprietors were also permitted, for income tax purposes,
to set off against revenue from their hostelries one-fifth of the
capital expenditure upon the operation "in each of five years of
an eight year period."[24] At the time of independence in 1962,
this law (periodically extended) was still in force, having to its
credit attracted into the building of the island's tourism plant
substantial American, Canadian, and British capital, along with
local investment.

It was to the Hotels Aid Law of 1944 that Jack Pringle, president of the Montego Bay Hotel Association, attributed the
breakneck speed with which this North Coast town developed in
the postwar era. For 1958 alone, he credited the Hotels Aid Law
of 1944 with securing the capital expenditure of well over £2
million on hotel construction.[25] Pringle quantified tourism
growth, thanks to the Hotels Aid Law of 1944, in this section of
the island between 1946 and 1956 in terms of the statistics
shown in table 4.

Another significant measure taken by the government to enhance tourism development was the setting up of a more sophis-
ticated organization to attend to the industry's needs and
promote Jamaica overseas. Since 1922, the promotion of Jamaican tourism had been in the hands of the Tourist Trade Development Board, a body with limited membership appointed by
the island's governor. The board had been financed partly by
passenger duties and partly by annual government grants.
Though the resources of the board had been increasing, they
were still inadequate to meet the potential of the postwar era,
wherein rising incomes and cheaper air fares meant that more
and more people were finding it possible to come to Jamaica. By
1952, the Tourist Trade Development Board had lost much of

TABLE 4. TOURISM STATISTICS IN MONTEGO BAY,
1946 and 1956

	1946	*1956*	*Percentage Increase, 1946–1956*
Accommodations in hotels (rooms available)	229	1,350	489.5
Weekly salaries paid to workers (excluding managerial and executive staff salaries)	£216	£5,870	2,617.5
Annual water rates paid to parish council	£211	£8,318	3,842.0
Other annual taxes paid to parish council	£1,158	£26,290	21,702.5
Workers employed (excluding managerial, executive, and entertainment staff)	c. 200	1,587	693.5

SOURCE: *Daily Gleaner,* 4 March 1959.

its original dynamism. "At present most of the people actively engaged in the industry regard the board as ineffective and they accordingly take little interest in its activity," a mission of the International Bank for Reconstruction and Development reported in September of that year. "Only a board directly representative of the industry can be expected to promote tourism with maximum vigor and effectiveness," it added, urging that the development board be reconstituted.[26] This recommendation was implemented when, by Law 61 of 1954, authorization was granted for the creation of the Jamaica Tourist Board.

A notable feature of the new board was its representation. Membership was offered to most of the private interest groups involved in tourism—hoteliers, shipping and airline representatives, ground transportation and travel agents, and the like. Government too had a voice, as it had the privilege of appointing nominees to represent the state sector. The new body operated under the auspices of the Ministry of Trade and Industry and was supported by annual grants from the government treasury. In addition to a generous subvention each year, the tourist board was given special borrowing powers. Such dispensations enabled it to maintain its head office in Kingston, augment full-time staff, and open sales offices in New York, Miami, Chicago, and London.[27] With these resources it immediately launched a blitz campaign of advertising and promotion to stimulate travel to the island. In fact, in April 1955, when the tourist board was inaugurated, the target it instantly set for itself was to double the island's tourist business within five years.[28] In terms of both tourist arrivals and visitor expenditure, that goal was achieved by 1960, as table 2, above, reveals.

If Jamaica's new board of tourism planners intended to explore fresh promotional methods, it decidedly did so in its subscription (however hesitant) to a regional, rather than a purely insular, approach to tourism development. The possibilities of tourist travel within the Caribbean Basin as a whole had been perceived by many at least since the turn of the twentieth century, but it was not until 1945 that a regional approach to tourism development was accepted or appreciated. Near the end of World War II, the Anglo-American Caribbean Commission (subsequently called the Caribbean Commission) undertook a survey to assess the potential value of the West Indian islands as vacation resorts and reported its findings in a 1945 publication entitled *Caribbean Tourist Trade—A Regional Approach*.[29] Tourism in the islands of the Caribbean Basin had grown from 45 thousand visitors in 1919 to a high of 204 thousand in 1937. Apart from lapses in 1922–1923 and 1932–1935 (years of globally depressed economic conditions), the interwar period had witnessed a sustained growth in Caribbean tourist arrivals.[30]

It was to accelerate this trend that the Caribbean Tourist Association (CTA) was founded, funded by subscriptions from those member countries that incorporated it within a year or two of the 1945 study. The Caribbean Tourist Association comprised the British, French, and Dutch territories in the West Indies, as well as the island nations of Cuba, Haiti, and the Dominican Republic. In addition to research, the association conducted publicity programs for the entire archipelago, thus complementing the microlevel efforts of each territorial tourist board. Initially, Jamaica held only observer status at the annual meetings of the CTA, but in 1958 it decided to become an affiliate member. As explained by a spokesman of the Jamaica Tourist Board at the time, the reason for joining the CTA was that "this organization is a very useful and valuable one, and with the present state of Caribbean development and unification, Jamaica should not be the only West Indian territory outside the ranks of the completely regional body."[31] Notwithstanding such verbiage, Jamaica's decision to become a member of the CTA was not motivated by some newly felt regionalism in the outlook of the Jamaican powers that be. Rather, the stimulus seems to have been the expressed desire of many vacationers to partake in island hopping, and that required some measure of regional cooperation, were Jamaica to maximize its gains from this segment of the travel market.

It was not horizontal but vertical integration that came to characterize Caribbean tourism in the years after 1958. Placed in a global perspective, such an outcome is not surprising. Throughout the world, tourism continued to advance during the decade after 1958, and 1967 was designated by the General Assembly of the United Nations as International Tourism Year. Tourism accounted for a turnover of $14.1 billion in 1968 and emerged thenceforward as the world's foremost trade item, its market value greater than oil, steel, copper, or any other commodity.[32] The evolution of jet travel spurred this progression of tourism, along with the rise in the discretionary incomes of North Americans and Europeans and the introduction of charter flights and package tours by airlines and travel agencies. Given the multiple elements that a visitor plant entails and the potential for earning huge incomes, international tourism thus became a major magnet for transnational investment all over the planet.[33] Hand in hand with this came increasing concentration of ownership.

A case in point concerns the U.S. airlines. In 1966, after having invested millions of dollars in jumbo jets, U.S. airline companies began to tighten their grip on the tourist market, buying up hotel chains and building travel accommodations for their clientele. The precedent for this had been set in the immediate postwar era when, in 1945, the president of PAA, Juan Terry Trippe, established the Intercontinental Hotel Corporation to build hotels along Pan Am's routes.[34] A quarter of a century later, that was the standard practice of firms in the airline business. For example, Trans World Airlines (TWA) in 1968 purchased the Hilton International hotel chain; United Airlines in 1970 bought the world's largest hotel syndicate, Western International; and American Airlines and Eastern Airlines owned and operated hotels in various countries by the early seventies.[35] In the Caribbean, the presence of these and other transnational conglomerates was manifest in the string of Hiltons, Holiday Inns, Intercontinental Hotels, Sheratons, and so on across the region. Undoubtedly tourism did bring an increase in the gross national product. Yet was Jamaica the nation that enjoyed this ostensible increase in the GNP?[36]

Inasmuch as Jamaica is endowed by nature with a superb climate, spectacular scenery, and gorgeous sand beaches, it was in the opinion of many the obligation of the government to do all in its power to enhance the cash value of the island as a playground for tourists. In 1959–1960, the government had granted to the Jamaica Tourist Board as its annual subvention the sum of U.S. $840 thousand to carry on its operations, the minister of trade and industry having repeatedly expressed himself as being "more than satisfied with the work of the Tourist Board."[37] But after the great leap forward in the fifties and the record high number of visitor arrivals in 1960, holiday traffic suddenly fell by almost 11 percent between 1960 and 1963 (see table 3). To reverse this decline, the Jamaica Tourist Board was streamlined by the designation, in 1963, of a full-time director of tourism, a veritable industry czar, since the person so appointed also assumed the post of president of the Jamaica Tourist Board. Besides this, the government allocated an even bigger amount of funds for the board to carry out its functions. When in 1964–1965 the trade bounced back, the government's annual spending on the tourist board was as much as U.S. $1,733,200— more than twice the outlay in 1959–1960.

Since the numbers of long-stay visitors had, by 1965, come to surpass that of the short stays in Jamaica, and since the tourist trade in the main showed a profit margin superior to that of any other government investment, the tourist board could by then feel assured that the vitality of the industry was more secure than ever before. Following an estimated visitor expenditure in 1964 of U.S. $43,680,000 (see table 3), the board could with confidence announce that for every dollar it was disbursing the tourists for their part were spending $25. Further, it could boast that the amount earned by tourism for Jamaica in 1964–1965 was, all in all, the equivalent of over 75 percent of the island's balance of trade deficit.[38] When, in the four-year period between 1964 and 1968, Jamaica's visitor arrivals figure expanded almost twofold and estimated tourist expenditure more than doubled, the tourist board was delirous with self-adulation, as table 3 suggests.

Another indication of the maturation of the tourist industry by the mid-1960s was the sudden proliferation of sundry organizations representing the various sectors of tourism. Since its genesis in the late nineteenth century, the intrinsic condition of the Jamaican tourist industry had been disorganization, except for the successive bodies formed to market the holiday product. In 1961, however, the hotel operators formed the Jamaica Hotel and Tourist Association (JHTA) to tackle the common problems of hotels and to represent the interests of hoteliers to the tourist board and to the Jamaican government.[39] The JHTA had an elected council and a permanent staff overseen by a general manager. Villa and apartment owners also set up a special interest organization, the Jamaica Association of Villas and Apartments (JAVA). Formed in 1967, JAVA acted as a clearinghouse for the rental of privately owned villas and apartments.[40] Other special interest groups created were the Jamaica Association of Travel and Tour Agents (JATTA), the U-Drive Operators Association, an In-Bond Merchants Association, miscellaneous taxi operators' associations, and so on.[41] Whatever differences existed within and between these organizations, a united front usually surfaced in the face of any challenges to the tourist economy's total image, so substantial were the investments jeopardized. From the viewpoint of such vested interests it was, if not sheer seditiousness, most unpatriotic to criticize the holiday business in any fundamental way.[42]

Its seeming monetary successes notwithstanding, Jamaicans from all walks of life continued, well beyond the island's independence, to harbor a substantial ambivalence toward tourism, some seeing it as, at best, a necessary evil and some not even seeing it as necessary. Many Jamaicans persisted in regarding tourism as a new form of imperialism. The director of tourism admitted in a 1966 interview that "the biggest problem that we are facing isn't 'selling' Jamaica to the tourist, but 'selling' tourists to the Jamaicans."[43] So worrisome was the extent of unfriendliness, disagreeableness, and downright aggressiveness stalking the streets of Jamaica that in November 1969 the minister of trade and industry appointed a Montego Bay Liaison Committee to investigate the hostility in the island's main tourist city. While Montego Bay could claim the dubious distinction of being the first to form a committee to inquire into the inhospitality of its residents, Kingstonians for their part were said to have been so unamiable for so long that "anything short of mass psychological brainwashing would be a waste of time."[44] Among the causes of this lack of rapport between the locals and the tourists was the feeling that festered among the former of somehow being excluded by the holiday business. "It is as if one part of Jamaica were reserved for Jamaicans, and the other part for tourists, and both are separated by a forbidding and confusing screen," the *Daily Gleaner* editorialized.[45]

However great the financial benefits brought by the travel trade, many in the island still felt as if their birthright was being bartered for a mess of pottage. That was certainly the sentiment regarding the fate of the island's best beaches. As explained by one commentator, under British law private landownership of beaches is demarcated by the normal high tide watermark; below that lies the public domain.[46] While in England this ensured a sizable public preserve because the tide in some places goes in and out for nearly a mile, in the Caribbean (where there is little tide) it had different ramifications. Colonial Jamaica had been subject to English law, and many beaches had become private property.

Before the increasing tourist traffic had placed a premium on the beaches, few proprietors had bothered to enforce their property rights by shutting out casual bathers and fishermen; but not so after 1945. With the postwar tourist explosion, several of the good beaches were converted into private enclosures by hotels and clubs, provoking much public resentment. It is perhaps noteworthy that, in 1955, the same year in which the reconstructed tourist board began its operations, the government set up a Beach Control Authority. Though the function of this body was to grant licenses for the use of the foreshore and to secure the interests of "John Public" in some measure,[47] it was of little avail in stemming the exclusion of the ordinary folk from some of the best beaches.

As late as 1971 that situation was not rectified, in spite of the tourist board's claims that the prerogatives of the people were not up for sale. On the contrary, a mounting crisis was exposed by one observer in a 1971 analysis of public estrangement from the holiday business.

Where is the Jamaican holiday-maker in all this? Fifteen years ago if you were black you were nervous about going to one of our big hotels because you weren't sure of your reception. At the rate things are going, the ordinary Jamaican cannot take his family for a holiday to any of our developed resort areas. He can't afford it. If he doesn't want hotel accommodation but just a safe swim on a good beach, he finds that large chunks of the island's beaches are closed to him.

Here and there on the North Coast one sees signs put up by the Beach Control Authority saying "Reserved as a Public Bathing Beach." Usually they are not the best kind of beach available in the area.

I believe that fundamentally it is wrong to have our beaches locked away by private interests and guarded against Jamaicans by armed guards. Jamaica is a small country—our shore line is not unlimited. The day could come when the ordinary Jamaican doesn't know what a good beach looks like![48]

Throughout the years there had been many voices criticizing the hell-bent quest for the tourist dollar and exposing the hidden social menaces it entailed. For instance, in April 1959 the lord bishop of Jamaica cautioned that the tourist industry should be changed by the island rather than the island changed by the tourist industry.[49] This caveat had been ignored. As more and more men with capital saw a gold mine in tourism, it seemed incontestable that the interests of the people would be given short shrift. Still, on at least one subject—casino gambling— Jamaica was not bowled over by those who were, in this case literally, wheeling and dealing. Even the 1959 loss of Havana as the gambling capital for tourists in the Caribbean did not entice Jamaica into catering for this market. A firm line was drawn against these dens of iniquity by church, state, and community organizations in the island. "Once you've got gamblers you've got gangsters—and that's that," the director of tourism vouched.[50]

A most disturbing feature that accompanied mass tourism around the Caribbean Basin was its solicitation of a wide range of undesirable fringe businesses like gambling, drug trafficking, prostitution, and the like. Jamaicans had actively resisted casino gambling, but the authorities were a dismal failure as far as halting the spread of other social menaces like prostitution and narcotics dealing. As jet travel brought hordes of tourists to Jamaica, both pimp and peddler found a bigger market wherein to ply their professions. The state of affairs rapidly degenerated until, in the early seventies, the visitor could hardly walk through the streets of Jamaica at any time without being pestered by either the prostitute or the pusher. The classic attitude among the Jamaican multitudes was to view the teeming numbers of tourists as idle whites who were "over-rich, over-sexed, and over here."[51] Critics of tourism and all it entailed thus denounced it as a "prostitute's trade," nicknamed it "whorism," and decried it as sheer "trafficking in human flesh."[52]

The gigolo psyche was not the monopoly of scufflers and loudmouths but manifested itself even at the highest levels of the society through what seemed to be coded messages in advertising Jamaica's tourist product. For instance, when in 1968 Jamaica inaugurated a national carrier to cash in on the profits to be made in taking visitors to and from the island, it gave the airline the somewhat suggestive sobriquet, the *Love Bird*. These *Love Birds* brought throngs of northerners to what a 1968 Jamaica Tourist Board advertisement portrayed as literally a fantasy island, where visitors could rent whatever the heart desired—a villa, a maid, a cook, a nanny, a gardener—whatever. This isle of romance was alleged to be under a covenant of innocence, at least environmentally. "In a world of bad air, poisoned water and litter, there are still a few virginal places," the Jamaica Tourist Board solicited trippers in a 1971 advertisement. "Enjoy Quickly!"[53]

Thus, thousands of tourists pounced gleefully upon this exotic island to enjoy the vaunted gratifications that, it was claimed, its virginal je ne sais quoi provided. Success was measured in heads counted on arrival at Jamaican ports, and by that measure the tourist industry had done marvelously. Once upon a time the atmosphere in Jamaica had been almost that of a South Sea island asleep in the sun, but by the dawn of the independence era in 1962 the genie of modernization was manifest everywhere, released by the arrival of mass tourism.[54]

The big hotel owners, travel agencies, and others profited from tourism. Its benefits were also alleged to trickle down to the so-called village boys—"the barefoot boys from country villages in Jamaica who today are respected, well paid, well-shod members of the industry, in the hotel service and the entertainment trade."[55] Thanks to tourism, one writer maintained in a 1955 article, these village folk were able to "learn sanitation" and expand their social expectations. Proof of the said change in vistas was their reluctance in the North Coast areas to work for

Jamaica's rent-a-villas come with rent-a-cooks, rent-a-maids, rent-a-nannies, rent-a-gardeners, and even rent-a-cars.

You can rent a lovely life in Jamaica by the week.

It starts with a country house or beach cottage or hilltop hideaway that comes equipped with gentle people named Ivy or Maud or Malcolm who will cook, tend, mend, diaper, and launder for you.

Who will "Mister Peter, please" you all day long, pamper you with homemade coconut pie, admire you when you look "soft" (handsome), giggle at your jokes and weep when you leave.

A kind of Nannyhood for Grownups, actually.

They'll spoil you.

But you'll also spoil yourself.

For more about renting the Life You wish You Led, see your local travel agent or Jamaica Tourist Board in New York, Miami, San Francisco, Los Angeles, Chicago, Toronto or Montreal.

This is an abbreviated version of an original Jamaica Tourist Board advertisement

Advertisement by the Jamaica Tourist Board (1968). Courtesy of National Library of Jamaica.

the old pittance as pimento pickers or to serve the Jamaican elite as houseboys and maids when they could earn higher wages at hotels. "Jamaicans, who ten years ago [at the end of World War II], had nothing to look forward to save years of poverty in isolated mountain villages, are now becoming self-respecting earners in an expanding business, tourism."[56]

Yet in many quarters doubts lingered as to whether the cash windfall wrought by tourism might not result in the ensnarement of the people within some new species of thralldom. In the slavery era, the peaceful folk who later formed the mountain villages had been legally bought and sold as chattel. But judging from the Jamaica Tourist Board promotions in the late sixties, for example, one discernible index of progress was that, in modern times, working hands could be procured for service through rental rather than purchase. According to the rhetoric of the tourist board, from these mountain hamlets came scores of Jamaica's hotel workers—"gentle people named Ivy or Maud or Malcolm who will cook, tend, mend, diaper, and launder for you. . . . admire you when you look 'soft' (handsome), giggle at your jokes, and weep when you leave."

This portrait of the "village boys" as happy hewers of wood and drawers of water for whites was a virtual recreation of the Quashie image by Jamaica's tourism gurus to complement the paradisal landscape that they marketed. Taking a cue from tourist board propaganda, in April 1971 one local agency advertised that it could furnish these "gentle people" for long-term labor leases and invited visitors to select from among its stocks whomever they might wish to procure for toil back home: "ATTENTION! ATTENTION! VISITORS: American and Canadian tourists and other visitors and business people to the island, visit McCartney Legal Services Bureau, 14 Retirement Road, Cross Roads, Kingston 5, and select any category of domestic and other farm workers you are interested in to work with you in your homeland. Phone 69835."[57]

No part of Jamaica exhibited the manifold problems inherent in postwar tourism development as much as did Montego Bay, the holiday capital of the island. Nicknamed by the locals "the little Republic" because it was so saturated with U.S. citizens, Montego Bay was more like a little Miami than a part of Jamaican territory. Though Jamaica may have been a British colony until 1962, in many of its shops prices were quoted not in pound sterling but in U.S. dollars, and often change was returned in U.S. currency as well.[58] To many locals that quote-the-dollar technique in hotels, restaurants, and stores appeared as another way of saying, *if you are not spending dollars, you are not welcome*— thereby excluding a category of Jamaicans.[59]

It was the local person who felt like an alien rather than the holidaymaker from abroad, for blacks were not welcome in the principal establishments of Montego Bay and its environs. "I found a bit of this coolness," one author wrote of a November 1955 incident, "when I walked into a big hotel for tea later in the afternoon. There were very few guests but I was made to wait an unnecessarily long time. And the price of my pot of tea made me wonder whether I was paying a 'colour tax' as well."[60] When it came to service in a restaurant, for example, persons of color— particularly Jamaicans—experienced the greatest difficulty in catching the waiter's eye. That apparently was not because persons of color were less generous as tippers. "As to service that one Jamaican might perform for another Jamaican," the island's first director of tourism offered in explanation back in 1966, "I think this is the attitude: Why should I, since I am on the bottom, turn myself into a step on the ladder of this other Jamaican who is progressing?"[61]

Given the country's past, it was unlikely that the postwar tourist industry in Jamaica would create any but the peculiar ambience it in fact did, neoplantation enterprise that it intrinsically was. As more and more whites swooped down upon this supposedly idyllic spot for a holiday in the sun, diverse problems surfaced throughout the island. It was not holidaymakers alone who descended upon Montego Bay and the other resort centers; hard on their heels came the big developers and the land speculators. Crusaders for the tourism enterprise had contended that its natural assets were inexhaustible, unlike bauxite, for example. Yet they were decidedly not inalienable. With colossal caravansaries springing up to accommodate the rising numbers of tourists, and with the superrich beginning to purchase winter residences in Montego Bay, land prices shot way up in an orgy of speculation. In the end, with the vast territorial transfers and the denationalization that occurred through land sales, Montegonians, for example, were left with little more than an intense feeling of claustrophobia and a sense of being less and less the masters of their own land.

The member of Parliament for the Montego Bay area, in an address to the House of Representatives of Jamaica, gave voice to such sentiments in his constituency when he warned of the grave situation created by the tourist industry:

The foreign interests have come down like Philistines in Montego Bay and they have bought hundreds and thousands of acres of land. The town is circumscribed and surrounded, and in a little while there will be no room for the middle class people and people in the low income bracket. It is a situation that Government needs to examine. It is a serious situation. Between Montego Bay and Falmouth most of the lands are bought up by foreign interests and in a little while when we are arriving from Montego Bay to Kingston, we will be passing through foreign land."[62]

And so, in its desire to win popular endorsement and support, the Jamaican tourist industry found itself faced with as much of a dilemma in the second half of the twentieth century as it had at its beginning in the late nineteenth. The government sought to do everything in its power to bring to all Jamaicans an awareness of the benefits of tourism, and in 1970 teaching tourism to schoolchildren as part of the social studies curriculum was explored as one possible way to gain social approval for the industry.[63] To the government, the tourist industry was the frontline of Jamaica—the place where the outside world and the visitor got their first and often most lasting impression of the island. Since the hotels were the main places where Jamaica's guests were accommodated, part of the struggle for the social legitimacy of tourism entailed winning the hearts and souls of the workers in the industry.

The opening of the Jamaican Hotel School in Kingston in 1969 was considered "a major achievement," as it was expected to improve not only the proficiency of workers in the hotel industry but their morale as well. In order to establish the school, the government leased the premises of the Hotel Casa Monte, invested a large sum of money in modifying it, and built classrooms and dormitories on the compound.[64] It then turned the facility over to the tourist board to operate. In the classrooms students were exposed to theory and in the hotel to practical training. By November 1973, the school had produced some six hundred graduates for the hotel and catering industry. These had been required to pass the external examinations prepared by the American Hotel and Motel Association.[65]

As the authorities saw it, Jamaicans had to become tourist minded.[66] The Jamaica Tourist Board agreed and in January 1969 launched its Meet the People program. Copied from a project started in Denmark after World World II, under this scheme any visitor who desired to meet Jamaicans had merely to contact the Meet the People desk at the tourist board office. There, the names of Jamaicans interested in making the acquaintance of foreigners were kept on file, thus enabling visitors to be matched with local individuals who had similar (for example, professional and recreational) interests.[67] Through such contacts it was hoped that some of the tensions that plagued the relations between foreigners and locals would be eased. That was also the logic of the various Tourism Matters to You campaigns:

> Who benefits from Tourism?
> You. Me. Everyone. . . .
> The more tourists we have,
> the more money Jamaica earns.
> And the more we have for all. . . .
> By being here they are helping us
> to build our country.[68]

Despite all that had transpired in tourism development since World War II, it was still a question in some quarters whether tourism was "helping to build" Jamaica's economy, much less its society. The government was convinced that tourism was to the national credit, and so the authorities busied themselves with such legislation as the Hotel Incentives Act of 1968, expanding the realm of incentives and granting generous tax holidays to excite even greater construction fervor in the hotel sector. In consequence, between 1969 and 1973 room capacity doubled, and villas and apartments expanded the range of accommodation available.[69] In January 1970, the government made entry stipulations for visitors to Jamaica so low that it boasted of having perhaps the most liberal entry requirements on the planet.[70] That, for its part, enabled the industry to pass the half-million visitor mark by 1973.[71] However liberal Jamaican entry laws did become, the structure of the Jamaican economy also ensured the most liberal outflow of whatever monies tourism brought into the island.[72]

Jamaican tourism, in the final analysis, reflected a colossal contradiction. On the one hand, postwar tourism development was meant to relieve the problems of Jamaica's colonial past. On the other, tourism reinforced many essential features of that original condition and entrapped the island in the clasp of neocolonialism.

Chapter 10

Conclusion

BETTER Must Come. It's Time For a Change. With such slogans as these the People's National Party (PNP) of Michael Manley won the February 1972 national elections in Jamaica by a landslide. Given tourism's past, it is remarkable that the development plans of the Manley regime envisioned this change for the better as comprising not less but more tourism. With the gravity of the island's balance of payments predicament, and with its acutely high level of unemployment, the Manley government felt that it had little real economic option other than to accept tourism and to urge that the nation as a whole acknowledge its intrinsic economic value.[1]

While change away from the tourist industry was not envisaged, the regime was committed to changing numerous unsalutary features within it, thereby activating tourism's fullest potential as a developmental engine. After the PNP had held power for just under half a year, P. J. Patterson, the minister of trade and tourism, was constrained to warn the Jamaican populace in August 1972 that the holiday business was on the verge of crisis.[2] "I AM WELL AWARE THAT it has become fashionable in certain circles to dismiss the tourist industry and to spend all the time in condemning its social effects," the minister said. "I prefer to take the positive view that these are problems we can control, particularly once we take the decision—as I now take— to put the industry in our own hands—to manage it as we see fit to determine its shape and direction."[3] He unveiled a package of measures aimed, first, at delivering the tourist trade from its immediate difficulties and, second, at laying down a new blueprint for tourism development in the island.

179

For some time, actually, the idea of a new tourism had been gestating in the Manley administration, but prior to the minister's announcement on the subject in August 1972, the public at large seems to have had little inkling of any intended change of approach. To start with, the new tourism called for a fundamental change in the historic social tenor of the Jamaican industry. In the past, the local folk had been shut out of the tourist hotels and beaches. In this climate of exclusion there had naturally been little fondness for tourism among the ordinary people. Indeed, maintaining the industry in an atmosphere of isolation from the masses of the population had built up a store of resentment against it, and this was one of the key factors that brought tourism, by 1972, to what the minister termed "a point of collapse." A new tourism could only be constructed, it would seem, in a social context where the Jamaican people were given a new deal.

As the minister visualized it, there were at least three cardinal principles to be observed, if tourism was to become all that it could be. First, "We must be careful to distinguish service from servility. They are not to be confused." Second, "We must not in our advertising demean the status of our people or compromise their dignity as human beings." Third, "the only sort of tourism we will have is one devoid of all forms of racial discrimination or social snobbery."[4] In light of these guidelines, the Manley regime sought to develop domestic tourism, for example—something that had been negligible prior to this initiative. The object here was to remove some of the barriers that had long existed between the tourists and the Jamaican public, thus allowing for a greater interchange between both groups. It was in this regard that the Jamaica Hotel and Tourist Association, as well as the Jamaica Tourist Board, began negotiating with hotels, villa owners, and operators of visitor attractions to obtain special rates for locals desiring to spend their vacations on the island.[5] In addition, the tourist board entered into discussions with the Jamaica Civil Service and with business groups to give local vacations as production incentives and rewards to their staff.

Finally, in keeping with the concept of a new tourism, the government expressed an intent to create a number of amenities in the country, especially in the resort areas, that would be open to enjoyment by all. Though parks and other recreational facilities were to be provided primarily for Jamaicans, the idea was to make these so attractive that they would appeal to visitors as well and become meeting points where both locals and visitors could socialize.[6] Social exchange, as the regime saw it, was as important as foreign exchange.

That the government was indeed committed to creating a new tourism was made clear when, on 3 December 1975, the minister presented before the House of Representatives a forty-three-page charter for the future development of tourist traffic in Jamaica. Entitled "Growth Through Integration," the document left no doubt that the government's goal was to integrate the tourist trade into the fabric of the Jamaican society and economy.[7] Integration meant broadening the racial base of Jamaica's holiday clientele by capturing a big slice of the African-American travel market. It also meant harmonizing tourism with the local culture; hoteliers were urged to hire Jamaican musicians and cultural performers, for example, instead of importing foreign entertainment at great expense. Likewise, hoteliers were urged to stop decorating their rooms with prints of paintings from Europe or other countries and to display instead the work of Jamaican artists.[8]

Clearly the public also needed to enjoy some tangible material benefit, if successful integration of the tourist traffic were to be effected. To ensure this, small businessmen and craftsmen, for instance, were to be brought more into the mainstream of tourism through the establishment of more craft markets, craft stalls, and craft production centers in the principal tourist areas.[9] Greater participation of local people in the enterprise as small entrepreneurs and not just as workers was one of the primary goals of the new tourism.

Attainment of the growth element in the slogan "Growth Through Integration" meant supplying vacationers with a much improved tourism product. A more efficient service was imperative at the hotels. From the start, the minister proclaimed it his intention to appoint a Man of Standards—that is, a hotel inspector whose job it would be to assess the quality of the accommodation and service available at the various hotels. Where hotels consistently failed to meet required standards of service, the minister vowed to revoke their operator licenses.[10] Beyond that, ensuring product excellence meant augmented training, staff seminars, and the like for hotel personnel. Finally, if the tourism product had deteriorated, it was in part owing to the mounting misdeeds against visitors when they ventured outside the hotel environs. Hand in hand with the effort to create a new tourism, therefore, went an intensified campaign to weed out crime and persuade the nation that the tourist industry was essential to its survival.[11]

Whereas the 1950s and 1960s had been a golden age of tourism, the 1970s were an age of gall and wormwood. Though the Manley regime had set tourism the herculean task of earning more and more foreign exchange, between 1974 and 1977 it earned less and less. In U.S. dollar terms, Jamaican tourist trade earnings in 1974 were $132.9 million; in 1975, $128.5 million; in 1976, $105.8 million; and in 1977, $72 million.[12] In visitor arrival statistics, stopovers declined by almost 40 percent between 1974 and 1977; meanwhile, the figures for cruise passenger arrivals between 1975 and 1977 dropped by almost 20 percent (see table 5 below). It is indicative of how calamitous the decline of the tourist industry was during the Manley period that, at the end of his administration's tenure in office in 1980, the number of stopovers was, on the whole, lower than it had been at the start in 1972.

Miscellaneous internal and external factors help to explain the spectacular slippage that tourism suffered during the 1970s. Already, even before the PNP's accession to power in 1972, the writing was on the wall for the profitability of the hotel industry. In consequence of the building orgy that occurred in the later part of the sixties, tourist accommodation found itself growing at a faster rate than visitor volume. For example, between 1969 and 1972 stopover visitors had increased by 47.3 percent, but during that same period, room capacity had grown by over 60 percent.[13] This, together with the fact that the average length of stay of visitors to Jamaica had declined by 7 percent, precipitated a fall in the room occupancy percentage, from 62.1 percent in 1969 to 48.9 percent in 1972.[14] In fact, even though Jamaica had welcomed growing numbers of tourists annually, in 1971, after six years of continuous decline in room occupancy percentage, the president of the Jamaica Hotel and Tourist Association warned of possible bankruptcies among many of the nation's hotels should the current trend remain unchecked.[15] It needed only the energy crisis that erupted in late 1973 to push the Jamaica hotel industry over the edge.

Throughout the world, the onset of the energy crisis after the 1973 Arab-Israeli war dealt the travel trade a grievous blow, as airfares were pushed up owing to the steep increase in oil prices. Accompanying the rising energy costs was an inflationary spiral everywhere, including inside the United States and Canada, which together accounted for 87 percent of Jamaica's tourist market in 1972.[16] With stagflation haunting the First World countries, these societies became cautious about spending money on such leisure activities as travel overseas. What is more, the United States and Canada, while they form the source of Jamaica's largest visitor market, are also among its strongest rivals in the field of international tourism. One reason why Jamaica's tourism languished in the midseventies was precisely the heavy spending within the United States on its See America First program, as a means of keeping the travel dollar at home.[17] Many U.S. citizens were unwilling to venture abroad at a time when there were myriad attractions connected with the bicentennial celebrations of U.S. independence to keep them in the country. Canada was also spending copiously on its own tourist industry in the early seventies, and Montreal was the locus of the 1976 Olympic Games.

Jamaica felt the effects of all this in the precipitous drop its stopover tourism suffered from 1975 to 1977 and again in 1980 (four of the eight years that Manley was in power). Much as the shortcomings of its tourism infrastructure contributed to this (through unreasonable prices, lousy service, crime, political violence, et cetera), by far the most salient reason for the travails of Jamaica's tourism under Michael Manley was the country's foreign policy. In the era of the cold war, the diplomacy of nonalignment and relations with Cuba that Manley opted for was hardly compatible with the strategy of tourism development that his regime supported. As one critic expressed it:

EVERY GOVERNMENT has a sovereign right to decide what its foreign policy will be. . . . As is its right, this Government opted for a shift in the very cordial relations which traditionally existed between the United States and Jamaica, towards an alliance with Cuba. . . . COMES the inevitable payoff—as naturally as night follows day. American investments for Jamaica dry up; the American press burn us at the stake; our tourist industry, which is almost totally sustained by the American market, begins to die on its feet, and we find that the world has suddenly become a much more difficult place to make our way in.[18]

Yet if Manley's new tourism did not succeed in catapulting the industry to the heights hoped for, it did change the image of the enterprise, at least for a while. "We set out to break the old elitist pattern in which tourist hotels were like enclaves, shut away from the local population by psychology as much as by price," Manley later boasted, claiming success in this endeavor.[19] The emergence of a substantial domestic market for holiday facilities was a highlight of the Manley era (1972–1980). This development was encouraged by his government's Domestic Holiday Program, its tight foreign exchange restrictions on travel abroad by Jamaicans, and the Discover Jamaica promotional campaign by the tourist board to entice locals to spend their vacations in the island. Actually, some 131,089 Jamaicans stayed in the island's hotels in 1977, for example—a figure equal to 49.5 percent of the total foreign stopover arrivals for that year.[20]

Jamaica may have faltered in the international travel market, but it made notable strides in domestic tourism during the second half of the 1970s. The local vacationer may have proved to be the vital difference between a profit and a loss position for many hotels. The irony, however, is that these two sides of the tourist business appear perhaps to contradict more than they complement each other. If, on the one hand, the domestic holiday market flourished while the external demand for Jamaica's tourist facilities floundered during the 1970s, on the other hand, when international demand recovered in the 1980s, domestic tourism literally went to the wall. The outcomes of the repeated currency devaluations that Jamaica suffered during the 1980s were quite dissimilar regarding the domestic and international demand for the island's hotels. Thus, whereas devaluation lowered the actual costs of food and drink for foreign guests at the hotels, it caused prices for these items to soar more and more beyond the pockets of local clientele, shutting many out again.[21] As it was in the beginning, so in the end; for the multitude of Jamaicans, there remained no room in the inn.

Since 1981, the external demand for Jamaica's tourism has grown rapidly, and for some years now the industry has surpassed bauxite as the prime earner of foreign exchange for the country. In 1987, total visitor arrivals exceeded the one million mark for the first time (see table 5). In that year gross visitor expenditure was estimated at U.S. $595 million, whereas in 1980 it had stood at U.S. $241.7 million.[22] Considering the havoc wrought by Hurricane Gilbert in September of the following year, not many individuals thought it likely that Jamaica would soon host another million-plus visitors, yet it did so in 1988, and the upward spiral of numbers continued into 1989 and 1990. By 1990, gross visitor expenditure was estimated at U.S. $740 million, or nearly 25 percent more than the 1987 figure, and total arrivals were almost 20 percent higher than in 1987. Within a generation, between 1970 and 1990, Jamaica's tourism had grown by some 300 percent, as table 5 shows.

In retrospect, Jamaica's tourism had come a long way since 1950. Yet large as these figures were in 1990, they were still not

To Hell with Paradise

TABLE 5. VISITOR ARRIVALS TO JAMICA,
1970–1990

Year	Stopover Visitors	Cruise Tourists	Armed Forces	Total
1970	309,122	86,247	19,351	414,720
1971	359,323	66,366	22,875	448,564
1972	407,806	71,450	14,232	493,488
1973	418,257	91,450	7,703	517,410
1974	432,987	92,675	5,064	530,726
1975	395,809	150,433	7,016	553,258
1976	327,706	141,494	1,514	470,714
1977	264,921	120,982	611	386,514
1978	381,818	148,644	2,402	532,864
1979	426,540	159,577	7,454	593,571
1980	395,340	133,423	14,325	543,088
1981	406,355	139,672	5,851	551,878
1982	467,763	194,430	8,009	670,202
1983	566,151	210,153	6,639	782,943
1984	603,436	231,039	9,299	843,774
1985	571,713	261,508	13,495	846,716
1986	663,593	278,507	12,521	954,621
1987	738,827	292,156	6,651	1,037,634
1988	648,873	367,732	3,688	1,020,293
1989	714,771	444,054	4,411	1,163,236
1990	840,777	385,205	10,093	1,236,075

SOURCES: Ministry of Mining, Energy and Tourism, *Annual Travel Statistics 1987*, p. 8; Ministry of Tourism, *Annual Travel Statistics 1990*, p. 9.

enough for some Jamaicans. In comparison, the Virgin Islands had fewer than 50,000 visitors a year during the early 1950s but by 1988 their tourism had expanded to over 2 million cruise-ship travelers and long-stay visitors.[23] Considering its proximity to the international tourist markets, Jamaica was sitting on a veritable gold mine and should therefore have been doing better, former president of the Jamaica Hotel and Tourist Association, Gordon 'Butch' Stewart, felt. Hawaii, with a population of 1 million persons, was by the late 1980s attracting more than 6 million tourists per annum, while Jamaica with its population of 2.5 million attracted only 1 million. Provided common sense reigns, the possibilities facing Jamaican tourism were innumerable, Stewart opined.[24]

One hundred years after tourism made its official debut at the Jamaica International Exhibition in 1891, the industry has evolved to a point where, with the collapse first of agriculture, and then of bauxite, it finds itself the lifeblood of the Jamaican economic system. While in economic terms the tourist trade has reached new heights, so have its accompanying social problems. For example, in 1987 a small beachfront hotel on Jamaica's southern coast circulated an advertisement that invited visitors to partake of its nudist facilities and discover "the uninhibited, the unspoiled and uncovered beauty of Jamaica" in a discreet setting free from "gawking."[25] According to the twelve-page, foldout color brochure published by the hotel, its facilities included a freshwater pool with an adjacent bar and dining area "for your full measure of sun, sea, sand, libation and food." The ad was withdrawn after several persons in the tourist trade in that area expressed shock and disgust at the publication.[26] Still, the policy of nudism, per se, was not withdrawn by the hotel's administration, because naturism or nudism is big business in the world of modern tourism. It is nothing new in Negril, for example, where (with absolution from a financially strapped government) bathing in the buff is sanctioned on some stretches of public beach.

To lure more tourist dollars into their coffers, not only did a few Jamaican hotels commence catering to naturists or nudists, but some hotels solicited business from the many high rollers who play games of chance. "We're doing something fabulous to do the country proud," was how tourism specialists summed up their November 1989 plan to introduce gambling into Jamaica's tourism product.[27] According to their proposal, chambers equipped with slot machines were to be set aside as so-called games rooms within as many hotels as desired them. For several years previously, slot machines had been outlawed because of the government's qualms about the impact of gambling on the morals of the public. Still, by a ministerial order of 17 November 1989, permission was given to hoteliers to operate these devices on their premises for the entertainment of their guests. To those who feared that this order might open the door to casino gambling in Jamaica, it was no retreat from the stand of earlier governments on that subject. Compared to a games room with its array of slot machines, a casino by definition was a more complex undertaking, characterized by a variety of table games like blackjack, Nevada craps, poker, and roulette.

In the 1990s, tourism may have acquired a new status as the backbone of the Jamaican economy, but a host of old problems continue to haunt the industry at almost every turn. For instance, among the grassroots people in Jamaica the feeling persists that the average man is excluded from a fair share of the financial benefits derived from the tourist business.[28] Citizens in the resort areas see the enterprise as imposing manifold social costs upon the residents of these localities. As listed by one Jamaican analyst, the social downside to tourism includes drug trafficking, prostitution, pimping and hustling, high prices, acute housing shortages, overcrowded streets, police harassment of vendors and small traders, water and pollution problems, and environmental sewage.[29] Whereas visitors may speak rapturously about Jamaica as a holiday paradise, the locals still look askance at the tourist industry and all its works. Moreover, many of the employees in the hotel trade still complain of feeling exploited and underpaid.[30]

In all, the primacy that sugar once held in the Jamaican economic system has long been handed over to tourism. It is ironic, then, that "just as the soils of many formerly fertile areas of the world have become exhausted or totally removed by exploitation without thought to the future, so are many tourist areas being ruined by thoughtless exploitation."[31] This caveat, issued some years ago by one student of Jamaican tourism, pertains with even more poignancy to this island nation in the 1990s.

APPENDIXES
NOTES
BIBLIOGRAPHY
INDEX

Appendix 1

WELCOME TO THE TOURISTS

Here's a welcome to the tourists
On this fair West Indian Isle,
May you find the skies above you
Just one bright eternal smile;
May the mountains and the valleys,
And the climate, and the sea,
Prove as full of balm and beauty
As you fancied they would be.

But remember in your seeking
After pleasure, this one thing:
You will find no more contentment
Anywhere than what you bring.
If you take your pack of troubles
Always with you while you roam,
You might better save your money,
And your time, and stay at home.

So just drop it in the ocean
As you sight this summer port,
And come smiling into harbor
With a heart for any sport.
Just forget the snows and blizzards,
And the worries left behind,
Meet the Eden of Jamaica,
With an Eden of the mind.

SOURCE: Ella Wheeler Wilcox, quoted in *Sailing Sunny Seas*. Chicago: W. B. Conkey, 1909, p. 54.

AN ARGUMENTUM BOASTANDUM

MYRTLE BANK LOQUITUR

If Constant Spring were Myrtle Bank,
It might aspire to highest rank,
But Myrtle Bank o'er Constant Spring,
Reigns all supreme as Hotel King!

For Myrtle Bank is on the sea,
Enjoying breezes cool and free,
While Constant Spring is miles away
And no sea breezes o'er it play!

And Myrtle Bank is close to town,
Near Rail, near Bank, Cars up and down,
Buses each moment—nothing wanting
To make its standing all-enchanting!

And once a week the Kingston Band,
Plays sweetest strains within its stand,
While menus of the daintiest food
Supply its guests with all that's good!

In short, it stands that Myrtle Bank
With Tourists holds the highest rank,
And Constant Spring—good of its kind,
Must be content to stand behind.

• • •

CONSTANT SPRING ANSWERETH

Must I indeed? I don't admit
That all your brag my merits fit,
For though your sea breeze may be rare
'Tis nothing like my mountain air!

And Myrtle Bank, when breeze is high,
Has dust that blinds all passers-by,
While Constant Spring is ever green,
For dust ne'er lies on verdure green!

And Constant Spring tho' far from town,
Has Cars that run oft up and down,

But once located there each guest
Forgets the town and stays to rest!

And if there be no Kingston band
To play upon its sea side strand,
Sweet Mountain birds the whole night long,
Warble their notes in native song!

In short bold Constant Spring declares
That it stands Primus inter pares
Its cuisine's FRENCH, and Myrtle Bank
Must only claim a LYNCH law rank.

SOURCE: "Your Neighbour," quoted *Colonial Standard and Jamaica Despatch*, 6 June 1892.

• • •

DE TOURIST

Deys a pile a' millionaire!
Massy bra, dem nuf dis 'ear.
Ebery one bring motor car
Fe dribe when dem want go far.
You tink tourist no hab money?
Top me massa, you too funny.

Ebery one you see come out
Nebber lef' New York wid out
Couple tousan' poun' a' cash—
Gole an' silva jus as trash.
Ef you want see somet'ng bra,
Go hotel an' see, me bredda.

Billiard ball 'pon table roll;
Man dah tek dem hat ketch gole;
Dolla bill dah tun napkin;
Gole an' silva mek hat pin;
Di'mon 'pon dem finger res,'
'Pon dem shut-front numberless.

Walking stick mek out a' gole,
Dem eat out a' silva bole;
Nuttin but champagne dem drink;
Lard, me bredda, wha' you tink?

Wan Jew man ben tell me say
"Some get tousan' poun' a day."

When dem tired fe stan yah
Dem go back dah 'Merica,
From deh back to Englan' Town;
All de whole wull dem go roun.'
Dem don' hab no time fe wuk
Yet you see dem nebba bruk.

A which-part dem get dem money
Only Gawd can tell—no' me.
When dem pass we in de day
Brukkin stone along de way
Some a' dem tek photograph
Den dem look 'pon so laugh.

Listen wha' I gwine go tell:—
"Is we pitcher dem dah sell
When dem go dah furrin lan'
Show dem how black nayga stan'
Don't you see dem all hab tac'
Why dem come yah in a flack."

We can't betta, bra, we cuss,
Jus' as well we bear de wuss.
All we hab fe do yerri
Is fe lib till we bury
Den we all meet ober dere
Where divishan is quite fair.

Source: Norman Palmer, Toll Gate,
quoted in *Jamaica Times*, 2 March 1912.

Appendix 2

The following is from *Public Opinion*, 29 January 1938.

PUBLIC OPINIONS
OBTAINED BY THE ENQUIRING REPORTER

Question
What do you think of the tourist trade in connection with Jamaica?

Replies

Mr. T. A. Aikman—Journalist, Kingston. 'It can be of great benefit to Jamaica economically. A lot of persons are against it, but I feel that a lot more should be done to foster it, and not only by Government, but all interested in the progress of the country.'

Dr. R. S. Hall—Physician, Orange St., Kingston. 'I don't think there is much in it. All the noise of the council re Holiday Tourists, and where were they? These Americans getting $10 to $25 per week can barely afford to make the trip, and when they do come, they neither spend much nor stay any time, and I am sure that won't do us much, if any, good.'

Mr. L. A. Thoywell-Henry—Merchant, 107 Water Lane, Kingston. 'I think it a very good thing for Jamaica, if the comforts of the citizens and the finances of the country are not sacrificed to make it a success.'

Mr. Rupert Meikle—Accountant, Port Maria. 'The Tourist Trade is de-Jamaicanizing the Jamaicans. By this I mean they (the Government) are endeavouring to subordinate things of more vital interest to the Island community for the seeming benefits of this Tourist Trade, and in the last analysis, how many people in Jamaica are benefited from this Tourist business?'

Mrs. Morris Knibb—Teacher, Woodford Park, Kingston. 'I do not think it has been very profitable to this Island. Discrimination has been already evident, and the greatest good is not being done for the greatest number, and the improvement of our masses should be a first thought of the Government, and not the tourist in the question of expenses.'

Rev. E. McLaughlin—Councillor, St. Andrew. 'From a matter of publicity the Tourist Trade, if properly handled, is good so that people will come and see what we are; but in an undeveloped country such as we are, the Tourist Trade simply benefits a small section of the community, that is, the parties with whom the tourists do immediate trade. If the Government of the country is tourist-minded and will use the Tourist Trade for the development of the country's resources, then it will bring distributed good to the population. It is, however, distressing to know that even where government support is given, neither native foods nor native labour is being utilised, except in very menial positions. This cannot be of use to us.'

Mr. Victor Bailey—Teacher, Gayle. 'In my opinion the Island is being exploited in order to benefit certain sections of the Island's business groups. The intelligent observer of the trend of present day tourists' activities can come to no other conclusion than that special arrangements have been made by Government to cater to merchants and transportation agencies; hence the circulation of money expended by tourists is confined to a very small section of the taxpayers and this money seems to go out of the island for dry goods and gasoline. The Island's public questions are ignored during the tourist season by the daily press in order to give useless and ill-considered interviews from people whose opinions matter very little and affect the Island less. The only kind of tourist who is of any intrinisic value to this country is the one who stays for a season, and he refuses to be called a tourist.'

Mr. K. G. Hill—Journalist, Kingston. 'A menace to the country. How can you expect us to develop into a nation if all our interests are to be subjected, as they are, to the interests of foreigners who don't care a damn about us except to use us to fill their recollections of the natives of some undeveloped Island which they have visited for sheer sport and pleasure? Develop the tourist trade and perhaps you may have a 'nation' of waiters. We will become more servile and be further away from self-government. I am glad to observe a substantial decrease in the revenue yielded by the passenger tax.'

Mr. A. R. Hart—Articled Clerk, Kingston. 'I think that the pecuniary advantages to the few hotel keepers and taxi drivers hardly outweigh the advent in Montego Bay of the barren sport of homosexuality and the sharpening of colour prejudice.'

Mr. O. A. Isaac-Henry—Ex-Teacher. 'I think it's a damn good thing, only I am not so sure that the resultant benefits are as widely diffused as they might be.'

Mr. R. W. Thompson—Journalist, Kingston. 'I think it's very useful, and as one of our best minor industries, should be given every encouragement.'

Miss E. C. Collymore—Stenographer, Kingston. 'I think it's good and in no way detrimental to the country.'

Mr. Percy J. St. A. Reid—Secretary, Jamaica Contract and Carriage Association, Kingston. 'The Tourist Trade is in a bad state of affairs owing to the lack on the part of Government in seeking advice from the right parties who are directly connected with the transportation of tourists on their arrival in the island. For that reason the Association is formed to bring forcibly to Government the horrible state of affairs now existing generally in connection with the Tourist Trade; and they desire to submit a definite means whereby the drivers could exist by way of a standard scale of charges, as also proper and adequate parking places, and to assist the police in keeping proper regulations among the drivers so as not to slur the good name of the Island.'

Mr. H. S. Burns—Restaurateur, Octavian Coffee House, 86 Slipe Road, Cross Roads. 'The Tourist Trade could be of incalculable benefit to the island provided that we do not sacrifice the liberty of our people and their national spirit to foreign influence.'

Notes

Chapter 1. Introduction

1. Robert Hill, *Cuba and Porto Rico, with the Other Islands of the West Indies* (New York, 1898), p. 186.

2. Rupert Boyce, *Health Progress and Administration in the West Indies* (London: John Murray, 1910); Richard Dunn, *Sugar and Slaves: The Rise of the Planter Class in the English West Indies, 1624–1713* (New York: Norton, 1972), chap. 9.

3. Quoted in Otis Starkey, *The Economic Geography of Barbados: A Study of the Relationships between Environmental Variations and Economic Development* (Westport: Negro Universities Press, 1971), p. 132. On the beginnings of this, see G. J. Sutton Moxley, *An Account of a West Indian Sanitarium and a Guide to Barbados* (London, 1886).

4. Starkey, *Economic Geography of Barbados*, pp. 131–32.

5. Paul Albury, *The Story of the Bahamas* (London: Macmillan Education Limited, 1975), p. 223.

6. Ibid.

7. *Jamaica Post,* 21 March 1898.

8. See chapter 2.

9. A. Burkart and S. Medlik, *Tourism: Past, Present and Future* (London: Heinemann, 1974), p. 5 ff.; George Young, *Tourism: Blessing or Blight?* (Middlesex: Penguin, 1973), pp. 18–19.

10. Burkart and Medlik, *Tourism,* pp. 14–16.

11. Peter Murphy, *Tourism: A Community Approach* (New York: Methuen, 1985), p. 19. On Cook's exploits, see Edward Swinglehurst, *The Romantic Journey: The Story of Thomas Cook and Victorian Travel* (London: Pica Editions, 1974); also see Louis Turner and John Ash, *The Golden Hordes: International Tourism and the Pleasure Periphery* (New York: St. Martin's, 1976), chap. 3.

12. See chapter 2.

13. Burkart and Medlik, *Tourism,* p. 3.

14. Albury, *Story of the Bahamas,* p. 219.

15. Murphy, *Tourism: A Community Approach,* p. 18.

16. J. G. Bridges, "A Short History of Tourism," in *International Travel and Tourism: Readings Book,* Examination, part 4 (Washington: Institute of Certified Travel Agents, 1967), p. 4.

17. Richard Pares, *Yankees and Creoles: The Trade between North America and the West Indies before the American Revolution* (Hamden, Conn.: Archon, 1968).

18. R. W. Beachey, *The British West Indies Sugar Industry in the Late 19th Century* (Oxford: Blackwell, 1957), p. 128. As for Jamaica, some 83 percent of its sugar was sold in the United States in 1890. Gisela Eisner, *Jamaica 1830–1930: A Study in Economic Growth* (London: Manchester University Press, 1961), p. 273.

19. Lord [Sydney] Olivier, *Jamaica, the Blessed Island* (London: Faber and Faber, 1936), pp. 248–49.

20. Eisner, *Jamaica 1830–1930*, p. 268 ff.

21. Louis Meikle, *Confederation of the British West Indies versus Annexation to the United States of America: A Political Discourse on the West Indies* (London: Sampson Low, Marston, 1912), chap. 12.

22. C. Vann Woodward, *The Strange Career of Jim Crow* (New York: Oxford University Press, 1955); Gunnar Myrdal, *An American Dilemma: The Negro Problem and Modern Democracy* (New York: Harper, 1944), p. 449.

23. Sterling Stuckey, *Slave Culture, Nationalist Theory and the Foundations of Black America* (New York: Oxford University Press, 1987), p. 249; James Olson, *The Ethnic Dimension in American History*, vol. 2 (New York: St. Martin's, 1979), p. 301; C. A. Wilson, *Men with Backbone, and Other Pleas for Progress* (Jamaica: Educational Supply, 1913), p. 80.

24. Woodward, *Strange Career*, pp. 54–56; Thomas Gossett, *Race: The History of An Idea in America* (New York: Schocken, 1965), chap. 13.

25. Meikle, *Confederation Versus Annexation*, chap. 9.

26. William Sewell, *The Ordeal of Free Labor in the British West Indies*, 2nd ed., 1862 (London: Frank Cass, 1968), p. 207.

27. N. B. Dennys, *An Account of the Cruise of the St. George on the North American and West Indian Station, during the Years 1861–62* (London: 1862), p. 92.

28. For this, consult issues of the black nationalist Jamaican newspaper, *Jamaica Advocate*, January 1900–December 1905.

29. Herbert L. Hiller, "Tourism: Development or Dependence," in *The Restless Caribbean: Changing Patterns of International Relations*, edited by Richard Millett and W. Marvin Will (New York: Praeger, 1979), p. 54.

30. Tom Barry, Beth Wood, and Deb Preusch, *The Other Side of Paradise: Foreign Control in the Caribbean* (New York: Grove, 1984).

Chapter 2. The Deliverance from Hellshire

1. For instance, see map of the island of Jamaica dated 1894 in Frank Cundall, ed., *Jamaica in 1895: A Handbook of Information for Intending Settlers and Others* (Kingston: Institute of Jamaica, 1895). In the course of the twentieth century one may note a reversion to the use of the old name "Hellshire." This reversion is a telling affirmation of the strength of confidence that the island has come to enjoy internationally as a tourist resort, and thus it needs no longer rebut, through its nomenclature, obsolete notions about its climate.

2. Jas [James] Johnston, *Jamaica, the New Riviera: A Pictorial Description of the Island and Its Attractions* (London: Cassel, 1903).

3. Edward Bancroft, *A Sequel to An Essay on the Yellow Fever: Documents that the Fever Called Bulam, or Pestilential, Has No Existence as a Distinct or Contagious Disease* (London 1817), p. 248. On the region's health history, see Boyce, *Health Progress*.

4. *Gall's News Letter*, 4 February 1896.

5. Quoted in Frank Pitman, *The Development of the British West Indies 1700–1763* (Hamden, Conn.: Archon, 1967), p. 389.

6. Dunn, *Sugar and Slaves*, p. 334.

7. Ibid.

8. Boyce, *Health Progress*, pass.

9. William Lempriere, *Practical Observations on the Diseases of the Army in Jamaica as They Occurred between the Years 1792 and 1797*, vol. 1 (London, 1799), pp. 91–93.

10. H. Harold Scott, *A History of Tropical Medicine*, vol. 1 (London: Edward Arnold, 1939), p. 85.

11. Olivier, *Jamaica*, p. 53.

12. On the health history of the army, see S. E. Maunsell, *Contribution to the Medico-Military History of Jamaica: A "Retrospect"* (Kingston, 1891).

13. George Frederick Bone, *Inaugural Dissertation on Yellow Fever and on the Treatment of That Disease by Saline Medicines*, with an Appendix by Hugh Bone (Edinburgh, 1846), p. 21. Also see Boyce, *Health Progress*, pp. 17–18.

14. Eisner, *Jamaica, 1830–1930*, p. 128.

15. John Hunter, *Observations on the Diseases of the Army in Jamaica; and on the Best Means of Preserving the Health of Europeans in That Climate* (London, 1788), p. 23. Izett Anderson, *Yellow Fever in the West Indies* (London, 1898), pp. 1–3. Of 19,676 men sent to the British West Indies in 1796, no less than 17,173 (i.e., 87 percent) died within five years, according to Lowell Ragatz, *The Fall of the Planter Class in the British Caribbean, 1763–1833* (New York: Octagon, 1977), p. 32.

16. Hunter, *Observations*, p. 23.

17. Ibid.

18. Ibid.

19. Olivier, *Jamaica*, p. 53. Also see Anderson, *Yellow Fever in the West Indies*, p. 5. For comparative data on tropical fever within a wider sphere, see Philip D. Curtin, "Epidemiology and the Slave Trade," *Political Science Quarterly* 83 (1968): 201 ff. Also see K. G. Davies, "The Living and the Dead: White Mortality in West Africa, 1684–1732," in *Race and Slavery in the Western Hemisphere: Quantitative Studies*, edited by Stanley L. Engerman and Eugene D. Genovese (Princeton: Princeton University Press, 1975), pp. 85–89.

20. Boyce, *Health Progress*, p. 6.

21. Hunter, *Observations*, p. 58.

22. James Lind, M.D., *An Essay on Diseases Incidental to Europeans in Hot Climates. With the Method of Preventing Their Fatal Consequences. To Which Is Added, an Appendix Concerning Intermittent Fevers and a Simple and Easy Way to Render Sea Water Fresh, and to Prevent a Scarcity of Provisions in Long Voyages at Sea*, 5th ed. (London, 1792), pp. 130–31. This letter, dated 24 October 1762, was written to Dr. Lind.

23. Rupert Boyce, *Mosquito or Man? The Conquest of the Tropical World* (London: John Murray, 1910), p. 18.

24. Bone, *Inaugural Dissertation on Yellow Fever*, p. 18.

25. Lempriere, *Practical Observations*, pp. 6–9, 58. Also see Hunter, *Observations*, pp. 31, 33.

26. Edward Long, *The History of Jamaica. Or General Survey of the Ancient and Modern State of That Island: With Reflections on its Situation, Settlement, Inhabitants, Climate, Products, Commerce, Laws, and Government*, 3 vols. (London, 1774), vol. 2, p. 514.

27. Boyce, *Health Progress*, pp. 7, 23.

28. Roger Buckley, *Slaves in Red Coats: The British West India Regiments, 1795–1815* (New Haven, Yale University Press, 1979), p. 4.

29. Long, *History of Jamaica*, vol. 2, pp. 505–506.

30. Bone, *Inaugural Dissertation on Yellow Fever*, p. 19.

31. Ibid.

32. Boyce, *Health Progress*, p. 23.

33. For a word of caution as to this figure, see Douglas Hall, *Free Jamaica 1838–1865: An Economic History* (New Haven: Yale University Press, 1959), pp. 102–103.

34. Robert Baird, *Impressions and Experiences of the West Indies and North America in 1849*, vol. 1 (London, 1850), p. 157.

35. Charles Plummer, *A Concise Catechism of the Geography, History, Soil, Climate etc., etc., of the Island of Jamaica and Its Dependencies* (Kingston, 1862), lesson 11.

36. James Scott (Commissioner of Health), *Papers Relating to the Present Sanitary State of Kingston* (Kingston, 1874).

37. Ibid.

38. On the Public Medical Service, see A. C. Sinclair and Lawrence R. Fyfe, comp., *The Handbook of Jamaica for 1887–88. Comprising Historical, Statistical and General Information Concerning the Island* (Kingston, 1887), pp. 157–59.

39. Scott, *Papers*.

40. Eisner, *Jamaica 1830–1930*, pp. 341–42. On the earlier situation as regards quarantine, see Mary Elizabeth Thomas, "Quarantine in Old Jamaica," *Caribbean Studies* 4, no. 4, (January 1965): 77–92.

41. Ibid.

42. Eisner, *Jamaica 1830–1930*, p. 340.

43. Maunsell, *Contribution*, pass.

44. C. J. Bartlett, "A New Balance of Power: The 19th Century," in *Chapters in Caribbean History 2* edited by Douglas Hall, Elsa Goveia, and Roy Augier (Kingston: Caribbean Universities Press, 1970), p. 68. For the earlier period, see Richard Pares, *War and Trade in the West Indies, 1739–1763* (London: Frank Cass, 1963).

45. Maunsell, *Contribution*, p. 34.

46. This is a system under which excreta is mixed with dry earth or ashes. "Where there is no general system of water-carriage sewage, an earth closet will in careful hands give perfect satisfaction," *Encyclopedia Britannica*, 13th ed., vol. 23, p. 737.

47. Anderson, *Yellow Fever*, p. 3.

48. Charles Singer and E. Ashworth Underwood, *A Short History of Medicine* (Oxford: Clarendon, 1962).

49. Scott, *History of Tropical Medicine*, vol. 1, p. 356. Also see Boyce, *Mosquito or Man?* p. 27.

50. W. T. Prout, "Malaria," in *Annals of Tropical Medicine and Parasitology*, edited by Ronald Ross, series T. M., vol. 3, no. 4 (17 November 1909), pp. 478–81.

51. Ibid., p. 476 ff.

52. "Far from being hotbeds of pestilence and disease, we found Colon and Panama most enjoyable Cities. . . . the States have purified the Augean stables, and life on the Canal Zone now proceeds smoothly and safely. The American portion of Panama, with its Hotel Tivoli, is fast becoming a favourite halting-

place for tourists." R. M. Overend and Walker Overend, *Wintering for Invalids in the West Indies* (London: Spottiswoode, 1910), p. 60.

53. Reprinted in the *Daily Telegraph and Jamaica Guardian*, 2 February 1912.

54. C. Ernest Fayle, *A Short History of the World's Shipping Industry* (London: Allen and Unwin, 1933), chap. 9.

55. Boyce, *Mosquito or Man?* p. 120.

56. Singer and Underwood, *Short History*, p. 188.

57. Boyce, *Health Progress*, p. 80.

58. James Phillippo, *The Climate of Jamaica* (London, 1876), p. 5.

59. David King, *The State and Prospects of Jamaica: With Appended Remarks on Its Advantages for the Cure of Pulmonary Diseases, and Suggestions to Invalids and Others Going to That Colony* (London, 1850). Also see William Wemyss Anderson, *Jamaica and the Americans* (New York, 1851).

60. Anon., *A Winter in the West Indies and Florida: Containing General Observations upon Modes of Travelling, Manners and Customs, Climates and Productions, with a Particular Description of St. Croix, Trinidad de Cuba, Havana, Key West, and St. Augustine as Places of Resort for Northern Invalids* (New York, 1839), p. 173.

61. Anderson, *Jamaica and the Americans*, p. 6.

62. King, *State and Prospects of Jamaica*, p. 225. In this context consider, for example, the *Prospectus* of the Jamaica Mutual Life Assurance Society (1844). Generally an amount was charged in excess of the premium in England. The amount in excess was determined by the length of residence within the tropics, those who had resided for over five years paying a smaller amount. An extra premium also had to be paid if a sea voyage were undertaken. This was to cover the additional risk, and the money had to be paid before the risk was incurred. See *Prospectus of the Jamaica Mutual Life Assurance Society, with the Rules and Regulations to be Observed by Parties Desiring to Assure, and the Table of Premiums Adopted by the Society* (Spanish Town, Jamaica, 1844), p. II.

63. King, *State and Prospects of Jamaica*, p. 227.

64. Pares, *Yankees and Creoles* p. 3. See also Richard B. Sheridan, "The British Sugar Planters and the Atlantic World, 1763–1775," in *Eighteenth Century Florida and the Caribbean*, edited by Samuel Proctor (Gainesville: University of Florida, 1976), pp. 5–6; and see Eric Williams, *Capitalism and Slavery* (London: Andre Deutsch, 1964), p. 112.

65. Albury, *Story of the Bahamas*, p. 220.

66. For example, see W. Husbands, "The Genesis of Tourism in Barbados," *Caribbean Geography* 1 (1982): 107–120.

67. See chapter 6.

68. Phillippo, *Climate of Jamaica*, pp. 33–34.

69. Johnston, *Jamaica*, p. 7.

70. Nothing as such was new about this recommendation. In the past, medical doctors had time and again advised that the best time for newcomers to arrive in the Caribbean was during the months of the dry season. Benjamin Moseley, for example, advised in a 1789 publication, "the time for the greatest rains, and the greatest heat, on the continent, as well as in the islands is between the months of April and November: and the greatest degree of dryness and coolness is during the months of December, January, February, and March. This is the season

when people, who can choose their opportunity, should arrive in the West Indies; and this is the season when military operations should be carried on there; and also when ships of war, or troops, should be sent out to relieve, or supply, any station or garrison, that the men might be seasoned to the climate, before the time of the greatest heat advancing, and the setting in of the rains, and unhealthy season." Another advantage of these months, Moseley pointed out, is that they are outside the hurricane season. Benjamin Moseley, *A Treatise on Tropical Diseases; on Military Operations; and on the Climate of the West Indies*, 2d ed. (London, 1789), pp. 8–9.

71. Quoted in Charles Rampini, *Letters from Jamaica, the Land of Streams and Woods* (Edinburgh, 1873), p. 160. Of Barbados, for example, around the mid-seventeenth century, Starkey stated: "Mosquitoes, flies, ants, and cockroaches were prevalent pests. Furniture was set in water-filled containers to keep crawling insects off the bed and tables; shelves were hung by tarred ropes; sugar was put on one side of the room or table to attract ants and flies from the occupied portions." Starkey, *Economic Geography of Barbados*, p. 60.

72. *Colonial Standard and Jamaica Despatch*, 16 April 1895.

73. Ibid.

74. Sydney Olivier, "The Land of Rest," in *The Book of Jamaica*, edited by Francis Dodsworth (Kingston: Sollas and Cocking, 1904), p. 17.

75. "Jamaica as a Health Resort," *Lancet*, 7 December 1907.

76. Ibid.

77. *Lancet*, 16 November 1907.

78. Ibid.

79. Prout, "Malaria."

80. Ibid., pp. 492–93.

81. For example, Bessie Pullen-Burry, *Jamaica As It Is, 1903* (London: Unwin, 1903), p. 39; and Dodsworth, ed., *Book of Jamaica*, p. 105.

82. See chap. 6 in particular.

83. *Jamaica Times*, 27 July 1912.

Chapter 3. God's Agents in Paradise

1. James Stark, *Stark's Jamaica Guide (Illustrated): Containing A Description of Everything Relating to Jamaica of Which the Visitor or Resident May Desire Information* (London, 1898), p. 42.

2. Ibid.

3. Ella Wheeler Wilcox, *Sailing Sunny Seas* (Chicago: Conkey, 1909); also, Johnston, *Jamaica*.

4. On the Jamaican economy after Emancipation, see Hall, *Free Jamaica;* also, Eisner, *Jamaica;* and Philip Curtin, *Two Jamaicas: The Role of Ideas in a Tropical Colony, 1830–1865* (New York: Atheneum, 1975).

5. On this concept consult Sidney W. Mintz, *Caribbean Transformations* (Chicago: Aldine, 1974), pp. 151–52. Also see S. W. Mintz and Douglas Hall, "The Origins of the Jamaican Internal Marketing System," Yale University Publications in Anthropology 57 (1960).

6. W. K. Marshall, "Notes on Peasant Development in the West Indies since 1838," *Social and Economic Studies* 17 (1968). For details specific to the development

of the fruit culture in Jamaica, consult *United States Consular Reports: Fruit Culture in Several Countries. Reports from the Consuls of the United States, in Answer to a Circular from the Department of State, on the Cultivation of Oranges, Lemons, Olives, Figs and Raisins in Their Several Districts,* no. 41½ (Washington, June 1884), pp. 789–801.

7. Olivier, *Jamaica,* p. 379.

8. Sewell, *Ordeal of Free Labor* pp. 223–24, emphasis added.

9. N. W. Simmonds, *Bananas,* 2d ed. (London: Longmans, Green, 1966), p. 313.

10. Douglas Hall, *Ideas and Illustrations in Economic History* (New York: Holt, Rinehart, and Winston, 1964), p. 56.

11. Ibid., chaps. 4 and 5.

12. Ibid. See, as well, Simmonds, *Bananas,* p. 313 ff. In particular see C. F. Batchelder and W. D. Bradstreet, "Tropic Gold: The Story of the Banana Pioneer Captain Lorenzo Dow Baker" (mimeo inscribed "For the West Indian Reference Library of the Institute of Jamaica . . . ," 1951).

13. C. A. Wilson, *Men of Vision: A Series of Biographical Sketches of Men Who Have Made Their Mark upon Our Time* (Kingston: Gleaner, 1923), p. 46.

14. For general insights on the impact of such developments, see R. D. McKenzie, "The Concept of Dominance and World Organization," *American Journal of Sociology* 33, no. 1 (July 1927).

15. Olivier, *Jamaica,* p. 379.

16. Ibid.

17. Batchelder and Bradstreet, "Tropic Gold," pp. 49, 74.

18. Ibid., p. 56.

19. For example, see Simmonds, *Bananas,* p. 317.

20. Stacy May and Galo Plaza, *The United Fruit Company in Latin America* (New York: National Planning Association, 1958), p. 6.

21. Olivier, *Jamaica,* chap. 31. On the domination of the United Fruit Company generally, see May and Plaza, *United Fruit Company;* see also, Charles Kepner and Jay Soothill, *The Banana Empire: A Case Study of Economic Imperialism* (New York: Russell and Russell, 1967); and Charles Wilson, *Empire in Green and Gold: The Story of the American Banana Trade* (New York: Holt, 1947).

22. *Colonial Standard and Jamaica Despatch,* 12 February 1892.

23. A. C. Sinclair and Laurence R. Fyfe, comp., *Handbook of Jamaica for 1889–90* (Kingston, 1889), p. 264.

24. Ansell Hart, "The Banana in Jamaica's Export Trade," *Social and Economic Studies* 3, no. 2 (September 1954).

25. Stephen Hill, comp., *Who's Who in Jamaica, 1916: A Biennial Biographical Record Containing Careers of Principal Public Men and Women of Jamaica* (Kingston: Gleaner, 1916), p. 214.

26. Batchelder and Bradstreet, "Tropic Gold," pp. 69–70.

27. Johnston, *Jamaica,* pp. 19–20.

28. Batchelder and Bradstreet, "Tropic Gold," p. 70.

29. See for example, Rampini, *Letters from Jamaica,* pp. 52–54; also see John Amphlett, *Under a Tropical Sky: A Journal of First Impressions of the West Indies* (London, 1873), p. 143. For more details, see chap. 5, this volume.

30. Batchelder and Bradstreet, "Tropic Gold," p. 87.

31. Ibid., pp. 76–77.

32. Johnston, *Jamaica*, p. 11.
33. Ibid.
34. Sydney Olivier, "Recent Developments in Jamaica: Internal and External," *Journal of the Royal Society of Arts* 64, no. 3,291 (17 December 1915): 82.
35. Olivier, *Jamaica*, p. 83.
36. *Telegraph and Guardian*, 21 August 1911.
37. On Jones's problems in the banana business, see Olivier, "Recent Developments," p. 83; also, Olivier, *Jamaica*, pp. 381–86.
38. Olivier, *Jamaica*, pp. 381–86.
39. Frank Thistlewaithe, *The Great Experiment: An Introduction to the History of the American People* (London: Cambridge University Press, 1961), p. 214.
40. Harold Faulkner, *American Economic History*, 8th ed. (New York: Harper, 1960), p. 392. On economic growth in the United States, consult Samuel Hays, *The Response to Industrialism 1885–1914* (Chicago: University of Chicago Press, 1957), pp. 6–15.
41. Young, *Tourism: Blessing or Blight?* p. 24.
42. *Jamaica Post*, 7 May 1890.
43. *Jamaica Post*, 28 December 1892.
44. Letter from "Hope" to *Jamaica Post*, 22 May 1891.

Chapter 4. Jamaica Awakens

1. "Memorial from the Inhabitants of the City and Parish of Kingston to His Excellency the Governor, praying for the Revival of Steam Communication between Kingston and New York, with Certain Correspondence relating thereto," in *Minutes of the Legislative Council of Jamaica, in a Session Begun on the 31st Day of December, 1870, (during the Administration of Sir John Peter Grant, K.C.B.) and Prorogued by His Excellency on 23rd June, 1871, Appendix No. IX* (Kingston, 1871).
2. See chap. 3.
3. S. P. Musson and T. Laurence Roxburgh, comp., *Handbook of Jamaica for 1891–92* (Kingston, 1891), p. 570. Also, report of an interview between Sir Henry Blake and a foreign correspondent for the *New York Herald, Jamaica Post*, 17 May 1890.
4. Ibid.
5. C. Washington Eves, "Jamaica and Its Forthcoming Exhibition" (a paper read before the foreign and colonial section of the Society of Arts, 15 May 1890), reported in the *Jamaica Exhibition Bulletin* 1, no. 8 (28 June 1890). For details on the regulations regarding the Jamaica Exhibition of 1891, see "Consular Reports on Commerce, Manufactures, Etc.," *Reports from the Consuls of the United States No. 114, March 1890* (Washington, 1890), pp. 428–33.
6. Ibid.
7. *Jamaica Post*, 10 May 1890.
8. Ibid.
9. This lack of perception of the local resource potential is well brought out by Sewell, though his emphasis is on the failing of the planter class. See Sewell, *Ordeal of Free Labor*, p. 223.
10. *Jamaica Post*, 10 May 1890.
11. Eves, "Jamaica and Its Forthcoming Exhibition," loc. cit.

12. Jamaica's postemancipation history is riddled with yearning for such captains of industry. For example, see Sewell, *Ordeal of Free Labor*, p. 275.

13. Op. cit., p. 576.

14. The gestation of this idea is treated in chapter 6.

15. *Jamaica Post*, 17 May 1890.

16. Sir Henry Blake, "A Letter to the People of Jamaica," Reprinted in A. C. Sinclair and S. P. Musson, comp., *The Handbook of Jamaica for 1890–91* (Jamaica, 1890), p. 549.

17. On the quality of the current hotel accommodation, see Rampini, *Letters from Jamaica*, pp. 52–54. Also see Amphlett, *Under a Tropical Sky*, p. 143.

18. Editorial, *Jamaica Post*, 15 August 1890. Also see E. E. Prichard, letter to the editor, *Jamaica Post*, 13 August 1890.

19. Ibid.

20. *Colonial Standard and Jamaica Despatch*, 25 April 1890. (Hereafter cited as *Colonial Standard*.)

21. For example, the *Tri-Weekly Budget*, 10 May 1890; also, *Colonial Standard*, 27 May 1890.

22. Anon., *The 'Hotels Scheme' Examined . . . Supplemented by Remarks on the Railway* (Jamaica, 1893).

23. *Jamaica Post*, 3 March 1890.

24. *Jamaica Post*, 10 May 1890.

25. This and other popular suspicions were reported in *Jamaica Post*, 2 May 1890, and *Colonial Standard*, 8 April 1890.

26. Blake, "A Letter to the People of Jamaica," *loc. cit.*

27. Ibid.

28. 2 Kings 20:1, *Gall's Newsletter*, 3 January 1890.

29. *Gall's Newsletter*, 13 September 1890.

30. *Tri-Weekly Budget*, 1 January 1891.

31. Report of a sitting of the legislature, *Jamaica Post*, 5 March 1891.

32. *Colonial Standard*, 22 January 1890; also, *Colonial Standard*, 3 March 1890.

33. Ibid.

34. On the inauguration of the exhibition, see Villiers Stuart, *Adventures Amidst the Equatorial Forests and Rivers of South America; Also in the West Indies and the Wilds of Florida. To Which is added Jamaica Revisited.* (London, 1898), app., chap. 2. Also, see Musson and Roxburgh, *Handbook of Jamaica for 1891–92*, p. 577.

35. Musson and Roxburgh, *Handbook of Jamaica for 1891–92*, pp. 578–79.

36. Ibid., p. 578.

37. 4 May 1891. According to the *Colonial Standard*, 2 July 1890, the size of the deficit was £4,548.5.6. Against this could be placed the value of the exhibition building and its appurtenances.

38. Musson and Roxburgh, *Handbook of Jamaica for 1891–92*, p. 580.

39. 4 May 1891.

40. *Colonial Standard*, 15 March 1892.

Chapter 5. "Ho-tel Me Not"

1. Anon., "Old and New Hostels of Jamaica: The Old Fashioned Inn and the Modern Hotel," *Planters' Punch*, no. 3 (1927), p. 3.

2. Anthony Trollope, *The West Indies and the Spanish Main* (New York, 1860), pp. 24–25.

3. Samuel J. Capper, "Trip to the Tropics" (newspaper excerpts dated January to March 1887, at the National Library of Jamaica).

4. "Old and New Hostels of Jamaica," p. 3. Also see Rampini, *Letters from Jamaica*, pp. 52–54.

5. Amphlett, *Under A Tropical Sky*, p. 143.

6. For example, Sewell, *Ordeal of Free Labor*, p. 201.

7. "Old and New Hostels of Jamaica," p. 3.

8. Amphlett, *Under A Tropical Sky*, p. 140, 141.

9. Great Britain, Public Record Office, C. O. 137/468, Advance of money for erection at Kingston of an Hotel on the American principle, Grant to Holland, 15 Nov. 1872.

10. Ibid.

11. Ibid.

12. "Consular Reports on Commerce, Manufactures, Etc." *Reports from the Consuls of the United States No. 113, February 1890* (Washington, 1890), p. 193.

13. *Colonial Standard*, 7 May 1890.

14. *Colonial Standard*, 27 May 1890.

15. Ibid.

16. *Tri-Weekly Budget*, 10 May 1890.

17. For example, Anon., *The 'Hotels Scheme' Examined*.

18. Letter from "Trachanus" to the *Jamaica Post*, 24 March 1893.

19. Musson and Roxburgh, *Handbook of Jamaica for 1891–92*, pp. 495–96.

20. Joseph Ford and Frank Cundall, *The Handbook of Jamaica for 1914* (Jamaica: Government Printing Office, 1914), p. 512.

21. *Jamaica Post*, 1 June 1891.

22. *Colonial Standard*, 17 July 1891.

23. According to Musson and Roxburgh, *Handbook of Jamaica for 1891–92*, pp. 495–96, debentures to the extent of £30 thousand were issued under the terms of the Hotels Law in the instance of the Myrtle Bank Hotel. As regards the Constant Spring, the amount guaranteed was £16,750. The Moneague Hotels Company, on the other hand, issued debentures to the extent of £7 thousand. These figures differ somewhat from those found, for example, in the Hotels Law of 1893 (Law 23 of 1893). Nevertheless, as a proportion of the total amount actually issued in debentures, the combined figure for both the Myrtle Bank and Constant Spring hotels was still about two-thirds.

24. *Colonial Standard*, 25 April 1891.

25. Ibid.

26. S. P. Musson and T. Laurence Roxburgh, *The Handbook of Jamaica for 1895* (Jamaica, 1895), p. 482.

27. S. P. Musson and T. Laurence Roxburgh, comp., *The Handbook of Jamaica for 1897* (Jamaica, 1897), p. 484. Also, Jos. Ford and A. C. Finlay, comp., *The Handbook of Jamaica for 1905* (Jamaica, 1905), p. 469.

28. *Colonial Standard*, 1 February 1892.

29. Ford and Cundall, *Handbook of Jamaica for 1914*, p. 512. The year 1914 is considered to terminate the foundation phase of Jamaican tourism because of the outbreak of World War I. More specifically, however, it was anticipated

that the industry would attain new and greater dimensions following the opening of the Panama Canal. See Dodsworth, *The Book of Jamaica*, p. 105.

30. Advertisement, *Colonial Standard*, 25 January 1890.

31. *Colonial Standard*, 17 July 1891.

32. Anon., *The 'Hotels Scheme' Examined*, pp. 8–9.

33. Ibid.

34. Letter from "An Old Jamaican," *Colonial Standard*, 1 September 1893.

35. Ibid.

36. This is summarily treated in Frank Taylor, "The Birth and Growth of the Jamaica Tourist Association," *Jamaica Journal* no. 4 (November 1987–January 1988): 40–44.

37. *Jamaica Post*, 27 April 1894.

38. *Tri-Weekly Budget*, 21 June 1892.

39. "The Hotel Business in Kingston: A Bad Outlook," *Jamaica Post*, 22 February 1899.

40. Mortimer De Souza, *A Tourists Guide to the Parishes of Jamaica, Together with An Account Descriptive of the Jamaica Exhibition* (Kingston, 1891), p. 9.

41. Anon., *The 'Hotels Scheme' Examined*, pp. 7–8. The old Myrtle Bank Hotel referred to was owned by James Gall of *Gall's News Letter*. It was sold in May 1890 to the Kingston Hotels Company for £3,500. Upon purchase, the building was demolished and a new and commodious structure erected on the site. On Myrtle Bank before 1890, see Anon., "Old and New Hostels of Jamaica." p. 4. The Park Lodge was another old hotel in Kingston.

42. "Scientific Notes," *Gall's News Letter*, 20 November 1895. These criticisms are strikingly reminiscent of Trollope's. See Trollope, *West Indies*, pp. 24–25; also see, *Leader*, 2 January 1904.

43. *Gall's News Letter*, 12 January 1895.

44. "Ruthless Changes at Myrtle Bank," *Jamaica Post*, 13 January 1899. Also see *Gall's News Letter*, 13 January 1899. On the depressed state of the economy at the time, see *West India Royal Commission Report* (London, 1897).

45. *Jamaica Post*, 13 January 1899.

46. See chapter 1. Also see "Our Trade with Jamaica," *New York Times*, 10 November 1896.

47. Olivier, *Jamaica*, p. 382.

48. *Daily Telegraph and Anglo-American Herald*, 10 January 1903 (extracts from an official report on the condition and progress of Jamaica dated 30 September 1902). This, however, is at variance with the figure, put forward by Johnston, of approximately £30 thousand. See Johnston, *Jamaica*, p. 11.

49. *Minutes of the Legislative Council of Jamaica. In a Session Begun on the 4th Day of February, 1902, and Adjourned sine die on the 4th Day of November 1902 (during the Administration of His Excellency Sir A. W. L. Hemming, G.C.M.G.)*, pp. 3–4.

50. *Daily Telegraph and Anglo-American Herald*, 10 January 1903 (extracts from an official report, dated 30 September 1902, on the condition and progress of Jamaica).

51. Ibid. Also, see Collector General's Report, *Supplement to the Jamaica Gazette, from January to December, 1902*, vol. 25, no. 1 (Kingston: Government Printing Office, 1903), p. 58.

52. *Leader*, 19 February 1904.

53. *Leader,* 22 April 1904.

54. "General Revenue and Tourists," *Jamaica Guardian,* 25 January 1909.

55. Johnston, *Jamaica,* p. 20.

56. *Jamaica Times,* 31 October 1908.

57. Joseph C. Ford and Frank Cundall, comp., *The Handbook of Jamaica for 1912* (Jamaica: Government Printing Office, 1912), p. 554.

58. *Daily Gleaner,* 27 January 1905.

59. A. Lopez and J. Petras, eds., *Puerto Rico and Puerto Ricans: Studies in History and Society* (New York, John Wiley, 1974); J. R. Benjamin, *The United States and Cuba: Hegemony and Dependent Development, 1880–1934* (Pittsburgh: University of Pittsburgh Press, 1977), Eric Williams, *From Columbus to Castro: The History of the Caribbean, 1492–1969* (London, Andre Deutsch 1970).

60. T. L. Roxburgh and Jos. C. Ford, comp., *The Handbook of Jamaica for 1901* (Jamaica: Government Printing Office, 1901), p. 518.

61. Advertised in Mortimer De Souza, *Jamaica: The Land of Perpetual Sunshine . . .* (Kingston: Mortimer C. De Souza, 1912–13); H. G. DeLisser, *Twentieth Century Jamaica* (Jamaica: Jamaica Times, 1913), app. p. xxix.

62. *Leader,* 2 January 1904.

63. *Daily Gleaner,* 5 January 1905.

64. Capper, "Trip to the Tropics."

65. Trollope, *West Indies,* pp. 25–26.

66. Frank Bullen, *Back to Sunny Seas* (London: Macmillan, 1905), p. 60.

67. *Gall's News Letter,* 9 February 1895.

68. Bessie Pullen-Burry, *Ethiopia in Exile: Jamaica Revisited* (London: Unwin, 1905), p. 26.

69. R. M. Overend and Walker Overend, *Wintering for Invalids in the West Indies* (London: Spottiswoode, 1910), p. 51.

70. *Gall's News Letter,* 12 January 1895.

71. On these techniques of passive resistance at an earlier era in the history of Jamaica, see Orlando Patterson, *The Sociology of Slavery: An Analysis of the Origins, Development and Structure of Negro Slavery in Jamaica* (London: Granada, 1973), p. 260. Also, consult Melville Herskovits, *The Myth of the Negro Past* (Boston: Beacon, 1958), p. 99 ff.

72. A. W. Farquharson, letter to *Colonial Standard,* 16 December 1892.

73. "Old and New Hostels, of Jamaica," p. 4.

74. Ibid.

75. Infra, chap. 6.

76. "Those who are inclined to undervalue the character of the West Indians tax them with ostentation and self importance. The charge must in part be admitted; but let not these imperfections be exaggerated or too severely reprehended, when the virtues of benevolence and hospitality are so strikingly their concomitants. From the prevalence of the latter virtue, there is not a tolerable inn throughout all the West Indies." Thus claimed Bryan Edwards in *The History Civil and Commercial, of the British Colonies in the West Indies. To Which Is Added an Historical Survey of the French Colony in the Island of St. Domingo. Abridged from the History by Bryan Edwards, Esq.,* (London, 1798), p. 126.

77. Trollope, *West Indies,* p. 28.

78. Frank Tatchell, *The Happy Traveller. A Book for Poor Men* (London: Methuen, 1924), p. 251.

79. Ibid., p. 258.

Chapter 6. The Ratooning of the Plantation

1. Robert Renny, *An History of Jamaica with Observations on the Climate, Scenery, Trade, Productions, Negroes, Slave Trade, Diseases of Europeans, Customs, Manners, and Dispositions of the Inhabitants. To Which Is Added, An Illustration of the Advantages, Which Are Likely to Result from the Abolition of the Slave Trade* (London, 1807), pp. 216–17.

2. Bryan Edwards, *The History, Civil and Commercial of the British Colonies in the West Indies,* 3 vols., 3d ed. (London: 1801), p. 9.

3. Anon., "Old and New Hostels of Jamaica," p. 4.

4. Edward Long, *The History of Jamaica,* vol. 2, pp. 281–82.

5. J. Stewart, *An Account of Jamaica and Its Inhabitants* (London, 1808), p. 153.

6. Quoted in Williams, *Capitalism & Slavery,* p. 83. For a critical analysis of absenteeism, see Douglas Hall, "Absentee Proprietorship in the British West Indies, to about 1850," in *Slaves, Free Men, Citizens: West Indian Perspectives,* edited by Lambros Comitas and David Lowenthal (New York: Anchor, 1973), pp. 105–35.

7. Stewart, *Account of Jamaica,* p. 175.

8. Ibid., pp. 178–79.

9. Ibid., p. 188.

10. Curtin, *Two Jamaicas,* p. 53.

11. Edwards, *History, Civil and Commercial,* vol. 2, p. 10 n.

12. Renny, *History of Jamaica,* pp. 216–17. In particular, Anon., *Marly; or A Planter's Life in Jamaica* (Glasgow, 1828), p. 14.

13. Stewart, *Account of Jamaica,* p. 152.

14. Ragatz, *Fall of the Planter Class,* p. 7 ff. Patterson, *Sociology of Slavery,* p. 50.

15. Anon., *Marly,* p. 215.

16. Patterson, *Sociology of Slavery,* p. 274.

17. Renny, *History of Jamaica,* p. 215.

18. Curtin, *Two Jamaicas,* p. 53.

19. See chapter 3.

20. This the white majority in the legislature sought to do by restricting the number of people eligible for the suffrage and by control of the qualifications required for entry into the legislature. See Curtin, *Two Jamaicas,* chap. 9. According to William Sewell, in 1860 there were fifty thousand freeholders eligible for the vote, but because of the ten-shilling tax that the Jamaica legislature levied on the vote to discourage the participation of the freeholders, the actual number of voters did not exceed three thousand. Sewell, *Ordeal of Free Labor,* p. 258.

21. Bedford Pim, *The Negro and Jamaica. Read before the the Anthropological Society of London, February 1, 1866, at St. James Hall, London* (London, 1866), p. 35.

22. Thomas Milner, *The Present and Future State of Jamaica Considered* (London, 1839), p. 3.

23. Arbuthnot J. G. Knox, "Race Relations in Jamaica, 1833–1958. With Spe-

cial Reference to British Colonial Policy." Ph.D diss., University of Florida, 1962), p. 202.

24. Trollope, *West Indies,* p. 123.

25. Sewell, *Ordeal of Free Labor,* p. 254. Douglas Hall informs that the assembly that was elected in 1863, however, had but ten colored members and thirty-seven whites. Hall, *Free Jamaica,* p. 251.

26. John Henderson, *Jamaica. Painted by A. J. Forrest* (London: Adam and Charles Black, 1906), chap. 14.

27. *Daily Telegraph and Jamaica Guardian,* 30 September 1911.

28. *Jamaica Advocate,* 1 November 1902.

29. On the background of the Montego Bay riots see *Jamaica Advocate,* 12 April 1902. It should be noted that while the rank and file in the police force were black, the officer corps was white. In the police force of the times, no black or colored man could "go beyond the position of Sergeant Major" (*Daily News,* 15 June 1911). A large part of the animosity that existed between the black population and the colonial police might have stemmed from a conviction on the part of the populace that the repressive actions of the police were in response to the dictates of the white power structure. In this context, attention should be paid to words allegedly used by one of the men involved in the Kingston riots of 1912. The same man was convicted of assaulting Governor Olivier with a stone during one of the frays. This rioter allegedly cried out: "White give black authority to shoot and I am going to take two before they kill me" (*Jamaica Times,* 16 March 1912). The attitude of the black Jamaican toward the laws made by the British colonial government is summed up in the early twentieth century by one local author:

> He regards them as something outside and apart from himself. They are something imposed upon him which he is sometimes inclined to think of as oppressive. The laws are "buckra laws," laws made by white men; and though he knows that white as well as black men are supposed to obey them, he is never quite sure that the white men will not be specifically favoured in some way. He doubts the absolute impartiality of the law. (H. G. DeLisser, *In Jamaica and Cuba* (Kingston: Gleaner, 1910), p. 113.

30. Knox, *Race Relations in Jamaica,* pp. 233, 317.

31. Curtin, *Two Jamaicas,* p. 105 ff. "A hundred Anglo-Saxon colonists would benefit Jamaica infinitely more than a thousand coolie immigrants"—see the *Colonial Standard,* 26 March 1895.

32. Ibid.

33. Clinton Black, *History of Jamaica,* 3d ed. (London and Glasgow: Collins Clear-Type Press, 1965), p. 204.

34. See chapter 1, for example.

35. "Our Country Market People" (a paper read at a meeting of the Kingston Ministers Association), reported in *Jamaica Post,* 13 January 1892.

36. Ibid.

37. *Gall's News Letter,* 6 November 1890.

38. Editorial, *Jamaica Post,* 21 March 1898.

39. *Gall's News Letter,* 6 November 1890.

40. Herskovits, *Myth of the Negro Past,* p. 1.

41. Curtin, *Two Jamaicas,* p. 67.

42. Poem by "Tropica" (M. O. Walcott) in *A Rainbow of Rhyme,* compiled by Cecil McIntosh (Kingston: Gleaner, 1918), p. 29.

43. *Guide Issued by the Jamaica Tourist Association (1914/15)* (Kingston: Mortimer C. De Souza, 1914), p. 4.

44. For example, Trollope, *West Indies;* also, Thomas Carlyle, "Occasional Discourse on the Nigger Question," *Fraser's Magazine* 40 (London, December 1849).

45. Extract from *The Field,* reproduced under "What Is Said of Us," *Gall's News Letter,* 26 June 1895.

46. Complaint made by "a distinguished English jurist," for example. See *Daily Gleaner,* 1 February 1913.

47. On migration, see Malcolm Proudfoot, *Population Movements in the Caribbean* (Port of Spain: Caribbean Commission, 1950).

48. "Drifting Whither? The Fool's Paradise in Which We Are Living," *Telegraph and Guardian,* 17 June 1911.

49. Harry Johnston, *The Negro in the New World* (London: Methuen, 1910), p. 279.

50. Wilcox, *Sailing Sunny Seas,* p. 136.

51. Special correspondent, "Through the Land of Streams," *Jamaica Post,* 17 January 1890.

52. Beryl Brown, "A History of Portland," M.A. thesis, University of the West Indies, Jamaica, 1974, p. 166.

53. Ibid.

54. Ibid.

55. Ibid.

56. Ibid.

57. DeLisser, *In Jamaica and Cuba,* p. 97.

58. "News of the Week," *Jamaica Times,* 25 April 1908.

59. *Supplement to the Jamaica Gazette, from January to December 1906,* vol. 29, no. 9 (Kingston: Government Printing Office, 1907), p. 142.

60. E. A. Smith, president, Jamaica Tourist Association (JTA), in a letter to *Daily Gleaner,* 22 May 1913. Also, "JTA Annual Report of 1914," *Jamaica Times,* 24 October 1914.

61. For example, "Advertising Jamaica," the *Daily News,* 2 May 1911.

62. T. D. J. Farmer, "Some Plain Truths. Why Tourists Do Not Come," *Daily Chronicle,* 6 March 1914.

63. *Telegraph and Guardian,* 9 February 1911.

64. Letter, *Daily Chronicle,* 23 March 1914.

65. "What Jeremiah Thinks," *Leader,* 5 February 1904.

Chapter 7. Paradise on the Auction Block

1. *Colonial Standard,* 30 July 1891.

2. *Jamaica Daily Telegraph and Anglo-American Herald,* 18 February 1904. Quoted from correspondence between Mr. A. Smith and the government on the subject of a tourist bureau for Kingston.

3. *Jamaica Daily Telegraph and Anglo-American Herald,* 10 February 1904.

4. *Leader,* 2 January 1904.

5. Norman Rankin, "Jamaica, Past and Present," *Canadian Magazine of Politics, Science, Art and Literature* 11 (1898): 419.

6. Henderson, *Jamaica,* p. 2

7. For example, Pullen-Burry, *Jamaica As It Is,* p. 3, makes it clear that her purpose in writing the book is to present something "which may be of use to people contemplating a visit to Jamaica."

8. Charles K. Needham, "A Comparison of Some Conditions in Jamaica with Those in the United States," *Journal of Race Development* 4, no. 1 (October 1913).

9. Ibid.

10. Ibid., pp. 200–201.

11. Pullen-Burry, *Jamaica As It Is,* p. 27.

12. Ibid., passim. Also see Henderson, *Jamaica.* For like suggestions regarding another West Indian island, see Moxley, *Account of a West Indian Sanitarium,* p. 162.

13. Henderson, *Jamaica,* p. 87.

14. Rampini, *Letters from Jamaica,* p. 164.

15. Henderson, *Jamaica,* p. 86.

16. *Daily Gleaner,* 28 January 1913.

17. *Daily Gleaner,* 29 January 1913.

18. J. W. Graham, letter to *Daily Gleaner,* 1 February 1913.

19. *Jamaica Post,* 16 May 1892. So extensive was begging, in fact, that one visitor even claimed that the black people of Jamaica were socialized as beggars and that as soon as a Jamaican child learned to talk he would supplement his first words with a request to the stranger for a "quattie." Allan Eric (Charles Willis) *Buckra Land. Two Weeks in Jamaica. Details of A Voyage to the West Indies Day by Day, and A Tour of Jamaica, Step by Step* (Boston, 1897), p. 19.

20. *Daily Gleaner,* 1 February 1913.

21. For example, see *Jamaica Times,* 30 May 1914.

22. *Daily Gleaner,* 1 February 1913.

23. *Daily Telegraph and Jamaica Guardian,* 6 February 1912.

24. *Daily Gleaner,* 20 January 1913.

25. *Telegraph and Guardian,* 9 February 1911.

26. Ibid.

27. Ford and Cundall, *Handbook of Jamaica for 1914,* p. 512. Also, *Daily Chronicle,* 18 March 1914.

28. "General Revenue and Tourists," *Jamaica Guardian,* 25 January 1909.

29. For example, *Colonial Standard,* 15 January 1895; *Jamaica Post,* 21 March 1898; and *Daily Gleaner,* 17 January 1913.

30. Plant claimed that in the winter of 1894, for example, he took 50 thousand visitors to Havana. *Gall's News Letter,* 27 March 1895.

31. *Jamaica Post,* 5 February 1898. For a sample of business opinion at the time, see "Shall They Have A Subsidy? The Plant Line of Steamers. Opinions of A Number of Representative Business Men on the Subject," *Jamaica Post,* 5 March 1894.

32. *Royal Jamaica Society of Agriculture & Commerce and Merchants' Exchange,*

Twentieth Annual Report of the Council, for the Year Ending 31st May, 1903. Presented at A General Meeting, Held on Thursday, the 29th September, 1904. (Jamaica: Colonial Publishing, 1904), p. 7.

33. For a full report, consult *Jamaica Daily Telegraph and Anglo-American Herald,* 10 February 1904.

34. For example, *Jamaica Daily Telegraph and Anglo-American Herald,* 2 February 1904.

35. *Jamaica Daily Telegraph and Anglo-American Herald,* 10 February 1904.

36. Ibid. Actually, over a decade earlier quite similar suggestions had been forwarded in a letter from "An Old Jamaican" to *Colonial Standard,* 1 September 1893.

37. *Jamaica Daily Telegraph and Anglo-American Herald,* 16 March 1904.

38. For example, *Telegraph and Guardian,* 17 September 1910.

39. "Local Tourist Association. Appeal for Funds to carry on Work Taken in Hand," *Telegraph and Guardian,* 3 November 1910.

40. *Jamaica Times,* 5 November 1910.

41. *Guide Issued by the Jamaica Tourist Association (1914/15).*

42. Letter from E. Astley Smith to *Telegraph and Guardian,* 18 August 1911.

43. Jamaica Tourist Association Annual Report, 1914, *Jamaica Times,* 24 October 1914. (This journal carries the full text of the president's report.)

44. Jamaica Tourist Association Committee Meeting, *Telegraph and Guardian,* 13 February 1911.

45. Letter from E. Astley Smith (E.A.S.) to *Telegraph and Guardian,* 18 August 1911. Smith was the first president of the association.

46. Jamaica Tourist Association Annual Report, 1914.

47. Jamaica Tourist Association Committee Meeting, *Jamaica Times,* 13 January 1912.

48. Jamaica Tourist Association Annual Report, 1914.

49. Ibid.

50. Jamaica Tourist Association Committee Meeting, *Jamaica Times,* 26 April 1913.

51. Jamaica Tourist Association Annual Report, 1914.

52. *Jamaica Times,* 7 September 1912.

53. Jamaica Tourist Association Annual Report, 1914.

54. *Jamaica Times,* 7 September 1912.

55. Advertisement in *Daily Gleaner and De Cordova's,* 25 February 1901.

56. E. Astley Smith, letter to *Jamaica Daily Telegraph and Anglo-American Herald,* 17 March 1904.

57. *Jamaica Guardian,* 25 January 1909.

58. *Telegraph and Guardian,* 17 September 1910.

59. *Telegraph and Guardian,* 29 April 1911.

60. *Telegraph and Guardian,* 27 April 1911.

61. Ibid.

62. *Daily Telegraph and Jamaica Despatch,* 15 April 1912.

63. For example, examine the lot of the Kinematograph Company, described in chapter 7.

64. *Daily Gleaner,* 22 February 1913. On earlier criticisms, see *Jamaica Daily*

Telegraph and Anglo American Herald, 24 January 1905; also, "Jamaica's Friend," letter to *Daily Gleaner,* 24 February 1905.

65. Sewell, *Ordeal of Free Labor,* p. 174.

Chapter 8. Resurrection and Revival

1. "Getting the Tourists to Come Again," *Daily Gleaner,* 15 February 1923.

2. Shirley Robertson, "Maritime History of Jamaica in the 20th Century," Symposium on Caribbean Economic History, 7–8 November 1986, University of the West Indies, Mona, Jamaica (mimeo). Also see *Herald,* 28 October 1922.

3. *Herald,* 28 October 1922. For data on the United Fruit Company's policy regarding the tourist traffic to Jamaica, see "Jamaica Is at the Mercy of the Great United Fruit Company," *Herald,* 19 May 1923.

4. For the list of requirements for the island's tourist trade development drawn up by William Wilson, chairman of the Tourist Trade Development Board, consult "Special Tourist Trade Supplement," the *Herald,* 18 October 1924.

5. "The Jamaica Tourist Association," *Jamaica Times,* 29 May 1920.

6. "We Might Get That Twenty Million if We Attract Canadian Tourists," *Jamaica Times,* 22 May 1920.

7. *The Canada-West India Magazine* (July 1924), extracts reproduced in "Special Tourist Trade Supplement," the *Herald,* 18 October 1924.

8. Preston Slosson, *The Great Crusade and After, 1914–1928* (New York: Macmillan, 1930), pp. 237–50.

9. Ibid., p. 249. In European countries taken together, American visitors at this time numbered in the region of half a million persons. See Foster Dulles, *America's Rise to World Power, 1898–1954* (New York: Harper and Row, 1963), pp. 141–42.

10. Slosson, *Great Crusade,* p. 249.

11. Tourist Trade Development Board (Jamaica), *Report and Accounts for Financial Year, 1st April, 1923, to 31st March, 1924* (Kingston: Government Printing Office, 1924).

12. Extracts from Tourist Trade Development Board Annual Report to 31 March 1923, in "Special Tourist Trade Supplement," *Herald,* 18 October 1924.

13. W.A. Cover, comp., *The Handbook of Jamaica for 1939,* (Kingston: Government Printing Office, 1939), pp. 594–95.

14. *Herald,* 10 March 1923; and *Daily Gleaner,* 15 February 1923.

15. Philip Olley, "The Tide of Travel Is on the Permanent Increase and Jamaica Should Seek to Get Her Share of the Tourist Traffic," *Jamaica Mail,* 23 September 1926. Olley became secretary of the Tourist Trade Development Board in April 1923 and remained in this post throughout the interwar period.

16. Philip Olley, "The Tourist Trade of Jamaica," *Jamaica Review* 1, no. 3 (October 1925): 17. Also see "Special Tourist Trade Supplement," *Herald,* 18 October 1924.

17. "Special Tourist Trade Supplement."

18. "Our Sun Baths," *Daily Gleaner,* 2 March 1925.

19. *Daily Gleaner,* 3 March 1925.

20. "Special Tourist Trade Supplement."

21. Editorial, *Jamaica Times,* 6 May 1933; also see editorial, *Jamaica Times,* 10 February 1934.

22. By way of comparison, Bermuda's 1924 tourist trade development grants amounted to over £50 thousand—Olley, "Tourist Trade of Jamaica," p. 18. For its part, the government of the sister colony of the Bahamas had pledged itself to expend on tourism development at least £35 thousand per year for a ten-year period, according to *Herald,* 10 March 1923.

23. On this debate, see *Jamaica Times,* 21 March 1931.

24. *Interim Report on post-War Tourist Trade Development in Jamaica* (Kingston's Tourist Trade Development Board, 1944), p. 17.

25. Cover, comp., *The Handbook of Jamaica for 1939,* pp. 594–95.

26. The Jamaica Tourist Trade Development Board and the Tourist Trade Convention Committee, *Survey and Report on the Potentialities of the Tourist Industry of Jamaica, With Recommendations for post-War Development* (Kingston: Government Printer, 1945), p. 2.

27. Ibid.

28. See *Jamaica Times,* 9 September 1933.

29. Tourist Trade Development Board, *Report for the Year Ended 31st December, 1931* (Kingston: Government Printing Office, 1932), p. 4.

30. The following resolution relating to travel within the British Empire was introduced by the Jamaican delegate at the Thirteenth Congress of Chambers of Commerce (London, 1933) and was unanimously adopted by the meeting. It states: "The Congress, impressed with the potentialities of tourist traffic as a means of strengthening friendly relations and establishing business connections; and recognising the economic importance of what is virtually an industry, emphasizes the desirability of British citizens spending their holidays, whenever possible, in British countries, and calls for the general adoption of the slogan 'Travel within the Empire'" (Tourist Trade Development Board, *Report for the Year Ended 31st December, 1933,* [Kingston: Government Printing Office, 1934,] p. 4). For more on Jamaica's role and interest in promoting intra-empire tourist travel, consult *Daily Gleaner,* 22 October 1937.

31. Editorial, *Jamaica Times,* 5 October 1935.

32. Editorial, *Jamaica Times,* 21 December 1935.

33. Eisner, *Jamaica 1830–1930,* pp. 287–88.

34. *The Jamaica Imperial Association Report for the Year 1927* (Kingston: Jamaica Imperial Association, 1928), p. 23.

35. "Special Montego Bay Supplement," *Herald,* 30 May 1925.

36. "The Thing to Do," *Daily Gleaner,* 27 February 1925.

37. "Special Montego Bay Supplement."

38. Ibid. Also see *Daily Gleaner,* 27 February 1925.

39. *The Annual General Report of Jamaica, together with the Departmental Reports for 1937* (Kingston: Government Printing Office, 1939), p. 31.

40. Una Marson, "The Tourist Menace," *Public Opinion,* 16 October 1937.

41. "United Fruit Company in Jamaica: What Island Would Be Without It and Some of Its Drawbacks," reprinted from *Boston Chronicle* in *Herald,* 29 March 1924.

42. W. A. Domingo, "Discrimination on Steamships," *Public Opinion,* 20 November 1937.

43. Ibid.
44. For passing references to this, see *Jamaica Critic*, October 1926. Also see letter, *Daily Gleaner*, 29 August 1923. By way of recollection, see Reverend Sam Reid, "Tourism in Jamaica: Another Point of View," *Daily Gleaner*, 15 May 1971.
45. The apparent reason for this was that "in certain quarters in Jamaica it is not thought polite to speak on the race problem, because in some people's imagination race prejudice is below the dignity of polished, educated ladies and gentlemen." *Herald*, 28 June 1924.
46. *Northern News and Provincial Advertiser*, 6 February 1926 (hereinafter, *Northern News*).
47. *Northern News*, 15 February 1926.
48. *Northern News*, 25 December 1926.
49. *Northern News*, 13 November 1926.
50. *Northern News*, 9 January 1926.
51. *Northern News*, 25 December 1926.
52. *Northern News*, 9 April 1927.
53. *Northern News*, 7 May 1927.
54. See, for example, R. L. M. Kirkwood, "Develop Our Tourist Trade," *Public Opinion*, 7 September 1940.
55. *Daily Gleaner*, 6 April 1929. For some indication of public feeling on the matter, see *Northern News*, 20 April 1929.
56. *Daily Gleaner*, 6 April 1929.
57. Marson, *Tourist Menace*.
58. "The Philosopher Views the Passing Show," *Public Opinion*, 28 May 1938.
59. For instance, letter from K. R. P., *Public Opinion*, 17 April 1937.
60. Olivier, *Jamaica*, p. 11.
61. Letter from K. R. P.
62. Letter, *Daily Gleaner*, 15 March 1938.
63. *Daily Gleaner*, 14 March 1938.
64. *Jamaica Labour Weekly*, 10 September 1938. For similar sentiments, see "The Tourist Evil," extract from *Waters of the West* by Kenneth Pringle, in *Public Opinion*, 27 August 1938.
65. Letter from K. R. P.
66. G. St. C. Scotter, "Buying the Tourist," *Daily Gleaner*, 18 May 1938.
67. Marson, *Tourist Menace*.
68. Ibid.
69. Philip Olley, "Our Roads Are . . . Air Roads," *Jamaica Times*, 28 November 1931.
70. Ibid.
71. "A Connecting Link," editorial, *Jamaica Times*, 28 November 1931.

Chapter 9. The Second Coming

1. *Daily Gleaner*, 19 May 1955.
2. Ibid.
3. Ibid.

4. Ferdie Martin, "Public Relations—A Need of Our Tourist Trade," *Daily Gleaner*, 9 March 1954.

5. "What the Hicks Report Did Not Say about Jamaica's Tourist Industry," *Daily Gleaner*, 6 June 1955.

6. L. F. Bouman, *K.L.M's Caribbean Decade: The Story of the Operations of Royal Dutch Airlines in the West Indies since 1934* (New York: Rogers-Kellog-Stillson, 1944), pp. 67–68.

7. Ibid.

8. Theodore Sealy, "Jamaica's Gold Coast," *Daily Gleaner*, 6 May 1952.

9. "The Economic Development of Jamaica." Report by a mission of the International Bank for Reconstruction and Development (Washington, D.C., September 1952), p. 108. Mimeo.

10. Sealy, "Jamaica's Gold Coast."

11. *Daily Gleaner*, 1 April 1957.

12. *Annual Report of the Jamaica Tourist Board, Year Ended 31st March, 1961* (Kingston, 1962), p. 8.

13. "Economic Development of Jamaica," p. 108.

14. Maxine Feifer, *Tourism in History: From Imperial Rome to the Present* (New York: Stein and Day, 1985), chap. 8; Louis Turner, "The International Division of Leisure: Tourism and the Third World," *World Development* 4, no. 3, (March 1976): 254. On the Caribbean, see John Bryden, *Tourism and Development: A Case Study of the Commonwealth Caribbean* (London: Cambridge University Press, 1973), pts. 2 and 3.

15. For example, while stay-over visitors to Jamaica numbered 122,149 in 1955, the figures for Trinidad and Barbados were 22,083 and 23,243. While tourist revenue amounted to nearly £7 million for Jamaica in 1955, it was £1,041,666 for Barbados. See *Financial Times*, 8 June 1956.

16. *Jamaica Tourist Board Annual Report 1964–65* (Kingston: Government Printing Office, 1965), p. 4.

17. *Jamaica Tourist Board Annual Report 1965–66* (Kingston: Government Printing Office, 1966), p. 5; *Jamaica Chamber of Commerce Journal* (April 1970): 20; *Daily Gleaner*, 20 January 1966.

18. *Daily Gleaner*, 23 July 1963; Owen Jefferson, *The Post-War Economic Development of Jamaica* (Kingston: Institute of Social and Economic Research, University of the West Indies, 1972), p. 173.

19. "Economic Development of Jamaica," p. 110. "What the Hicks Report Did Not Say."

20. "Independence Supplement—2," *Daily Gleaner*, 21 July 1962.

21. Ibid.

22. "What the Hicks Report Did Not Say." Also see "Independence Supplement—2."

23. Ross Pearson, "The Geography of Recreation on A Tropical Island: Jamaica," *Journal of Geography* 56 (January 1957): 15–16.

24. Ibid., p. 16.

25. *Daily Gleaner*, 4 March 1959.

26. "Economic Development of Jamaica," p. 110.

27. The Jamaica Tourist Board and the Jamaica Information Service, *Our Tourist Industry: Facts on Jamaica*, series no. 30 October 1972, p. 4.

28. *Daily Gleaner*, 1 April 1957.

29. Caribbean Commission, *Caribbean Tourist Trade—A Regional Approach* (Port of Spain, Trinidad, 1945).

30. Ibid., p. 109. Also see Robert Voyles, *The Tourist Industry in the Caribbean Islands* Area Development Series No. 6 (Miami: Bureau of Business and Economic Research, University of Miami, 1956), pp. 29–30.

31. *Daily Gleaner*, 2 September 1958.

32. Feifer, *Tourism in History*, p. 219 ff. Also see *Daily Gleaner*, 28 April 1966.

33. Tom Barry, Beth Wood, and Deb Preusch, *Other Side of Paradise*, pp. 77–78.

34. Mary Vaughan, "Tourism in Puerto Rico," in *Puerto Rico and Puerto Ricans*, edited by A. Lopez and J. Petras, p. 273.

35. Ibid.

36. On this issue, see Barry, Wood, and Preusch, *Other Side of Paradise*, p. 75 ff; Jefferson, *Post-War Economic Development*, p. 178; Iserdeo Jainarain, *Trade and Underdevelopment: A Study of the Small Caribbean Countries and Large Multinational Corporations* (Guyana: Institute of Development Studies, 1976), p. 307.

37. For example, *Daily Gleaner*, 18 January 1957.

38. *Jamaica Tourist Board Annual Report 1964–1965*, p. 4.

39. Jamaica Tourist Board and the Jamaica Information Service, *Our Tourist Industry*, p. 5.

40. *Jamaica Tourist Board Annual Report 1968–69* (Kingston: Government Printing Office, 1969), p. 2. Also see, Jamaica Tourist Board and the Jamaica Information Service, *Our Tourist Industry*, p. 5.

41. Jamaica Tourist Board and the Jamaica Information Service, *Our Tourist Industry*, p. 5.

42. Niger Cooley, "Of This and That," *Daily Gleaner*, 5 May 1965.

43. A. W. Maldonado, "Tourism in Jamaica: Dollar Bonanza," *El Mundo* (Puerto Rico), 28 December 1966. Translated and reproduced in Jamaica Tourist Board, "From Jamaica" (n. d.), p. 9. Mimeo.

44. Anthony Ashley, "Renewed Antipathy Towards Tourism," *Daily Gleaner*, 16 November 1969.

45. *Daily Gleaner*, 25 June 1964.

46. Edwin Chapman, "Problems of Tourism in Jamaica," in *Tourism in the Caribbean: Essays on Problems in Connection with Its Promotion* (Netherlands: Royal Van Gorcum, 1963), p. 128.

47. Ibid.

48. Sam Reid, "Tourism in Jamaica: Another Point of View," *Daily Gleaner*, 15 May 1971.

49. Alvin Wint, "Don't Block Out the Sea," *Daily Gleaner*, 7 April 1959.

50. Cleveland Amory, "Jamaica's Old Boy with the New Ideas," *Saturday Review*, 10 October 1964, p. 57.

51. Turner and Ash, *The Golden Hordes*, p. 15.

52. Ibid., p. 193. Also see Jay Munroe, "The Milking Shed," *Sunday Gleaner*, 21 October 1962.

53. Quoted in Herbert Hiller, "Escapism, Penetration, and Response: In-

dustrial Tourism and the Caribbean," *Caribbean Studies* 16, no. 2 (July 1976): 101–02.

54. Mary Carley, *Jamaica: The Old and the New* (New York: Praeger, 1963), p. 104.

55. Susan Lewis, "Tourism and the Village Boys," *Daily Gleaner,* 27 September 1955.

56. Ibid.

57. *Daily Gleaner,* 7 April 1971.

58. Chapman, "Problems of Tourism," p. 129. Also see editorial, *Daily Gleaner,* 29 July 1961.

59. Ibid.

60. Peter Abrahams, *Jamaica: An Island Mosaic* (London: Her Majesty's Stationery Office, 1957), pp. 228–29. Also see Chapman, "Problems of Tourism," p. 126.

61. Maldonado, "Tourism in Jamaica," p. 9.

62. *Jamaica Hansard. Proceedings of the House of Representatives of Jamaica. (Published by Authority.) Session, 1968–1969,* vol. 1, no. 1, p. 139.

63. *Daily Gleaner,* 13 November 1970.

64. *Jamaica Tourist Board Annual Report 1968/69,* p. 1.

65. "Homemaking Guide," *Jamaica Daily News,* 21 November 1973.

66. For example, see the statement of the deputy prime minister and minister of finance, Donald Sangster, to the JHTA convention, as reported in *Daily Gleaner,* 26 June 1964.

67. Tourism Supplement, *Daily Gleaner,* 5 July 1970, p. LI.

68. Ibid., p. XXXI.

69. Agency for Public Information, Jamaica, *Jamaica: Tourism in A Nutshell* (Kingston: Agency for Public Information, 1980), p. 4.

70. See *Daily Gleaner,* 22 January 1970.

71. Agency for Public Information, Jamaica, *Jamaica: Tourism in A Nutshell,* p. 4.

72. Jefferson, *Post-War Economic Development,* p. 178.

Chapter 10. Conclusion

1. See, for example, Jean Holder, comp., *Caribbean Tourism: Policies and Impacts. Selected Speeches* (Barbados: Caribbean Tourism Research Center [CTRC], 1979).

2. Speech delivered to the Montego Bay Community, on 12 August 1972, by Minister of Industry and Tourism P. J. Patterson. Reproduced in two parts in *Daily Gleaner:* pt. 1, *Daily Gleaner,* 17 August 1972; pt. 2, *Daily Gleaner,* 18 August 1972. A digest of this speech as well as the minister's speech two weeks later at Ocho Rios can be found in P. J. Patterson, *Tourism An Essential Plank of Our Development* (Jamaica Tourist Board, n.d.).

3. *Daily Gleaner,* 17 August 1972.

4. Patterson, *Tourism An Essential Plank of Our Development.*

5. *Daily News,* 14 July 1974. Also see *Daily News,* 27 November 1975.

6. *Sunday Gleaner,* 28 December 1975.

7. Ibid.

8. "People Must Become Involved in Tourism says P. J. Patterson," *Daily Gleaner*, 5 December 1975.

9. *Sunday Gleaner*, 28 December 1975.

10. *Daily Gleaner*, 18 August 1972.

11. Ibid. Also see, *Daily Gleaner*, 17 August 1972. According to Tourist Director, Eric Abrahams, the opportunity cost of crime was an average of $30 million per year in the early 1970s. *Daily Gleaner*, 18 May 1974.

12. *Daily Gleaner*, 11 February 1979.

13. Eric Abrahams, "Tourism in Jamaica," *Sunday Gleaner*, 22 April 1973.

14. Ibid. For statistics on room occupancy, see Jamaica Tourist Board and the Jamaica Information Service, *Our Tourist Industry*, p. 6.

15. *Daily Gleaner*, 3 July 1971.

16. Kempe Hope, *Economic Development in the Caribbean* (New York: Praeger, 1986), p. 45.

17. Dermot Dusey, "Discover Jamaica—Now," *Jamaica Daily News* Holiday Guide, 14 July 1974. Adrian Robinson. "We Offer More," *Jamaica Daily News*, 7 November 1975.

18. "Tourism: Foreign Policy Fatality," *Daily Gleaner*, 16 September 1976. On the events of the era, consult Michael Kaufman, *Jamaica Under Manley: Dilemmas of Socialism and Democracy* (London: Zed, 1985); and Clive Thomas, *The Poor and the Powerless* (New York: Monthly Review, 1989).

19. Michael Manley, *Jamaica: Struggle in the Periphery* (London: Third World Media, n.d.), p. 94.

20. Ben Henry, "The State of Domestic Tourism," *Daily Gleaner*, 9 August 1985.

21. Ibid. Also see Butch Stewart, "On Hotel Prices," *Daily Gleaner*, 13 September 1985.

22. Ministry of Mining, Energy and Tourism, *Annual Travel Statistics 1987*, p. 6; Ministry of Tourism, *Travel Statistics—Jamaica 1980*, p. 4; Ministry of Tourism, *Annual Travel Statistics 1990*, p. 7.

23. Jan Rogozinski, *A Brief History of the Caribbean: From the Arawak and the Carib to the Present* (New York: Facts on File, 1992), p. 254.

24. See *Jamaica Record*, 15 November 1988.

25. *Daily Gleaner*, 15 August 1987, carries a report on this.

26. *Daily Gleaner*, 25 August 1987. Also see Margaret Morris, "Nudism Is Big Business!" *Sunday Gleaner*, 30 August 1987.

27. *Jamaica Record*, 26 November 1989.

28. Carl Stone, "A Socio-Economic Study of the Tourism Industry in Jamaica," *Caribbean Affairs* 4, no. 1 (January–March 1991): 11.

29. Ibid., pp. 7, 8.

30. Ibid., p. 16.

31. Brian Hudson, "The End of Paradise: What Kind of Development for Negril," *Caribbean Review* 8, no. 3 (summer 1979): 32.

Selected Bibliography

MANUSCRIPT SOURCES

Batchelder, C. F., and Bradstreet, W. D. "Tropic Gold: The Story of the Banana Pioneer, Captain Lorenzo Dow Baker." (Inscribed, "For the West India Reference Library of the Institute of Jamaica.") 1951.

Brown, Beryl. "A History of Portland." M.A. dissertation, University of the West Indies, Jamaica, 1974.

Colonial Office Correspondence. C.O. 137/468. "Advance of Money for Erection at Kingston of an Hotel on the American Principle, Grant to Holland, 15 November 1872." Public Record Office, London.

Jones, John. "Tourism as a Tool for Economic Development with Specific Reference to the Countries of Jamaica, Trinidad and Guyana." Ph.D. dissertation, University of Florida, 1970.

Knox, Arbuthnot J. G. "Race Relations in Jamaica, 1833–1958. With Special Reference to British Colonial Policy." Ph.D. dissertation, University of Florida, 1962.

Ohiorhenuan, John. "The Social and Economic Implications of Technology Transfer in Jamaican Tourism." Trade and Development Board, Committee on Transfer of Technology, UNCTAD, November 1979.

Randle, George. "Attitudes to Race and Class in a Tourist Community: Ocho Rios." Paper presented at the Bellevue Seminar, 21–23 April 1972. Department of Government, U.W.I. Jamaica.

OFFICIAL PUBLICATIONS

Agency for Public Information, Jamaica. *Jamaica: Tourism in a Nutshell.* Kingston, 1980.

International Bank for Reconstruction and Development. *The Economic Development of Jamaica.* Washington, D.C., September 1952.

Jamaica Tourist Board. *Annual Report of the Jamaica Tourist Board.* Kingston: Government Printing, Office, 1958–1968/69.

Jamaica Tourist Board and Jamaica Information Service. *Our Tourist Industry: Facts on Jamaica.* Series no. 30. Kingston, October 1972.

Laws of Jamaica. (Specifically, Law 27 of 1890; Law 23 of 1893; Law 3 of

1899; Law 15 of 1904; Law 10 of 1907; Law 37 of 1909; Law 36 of 1910; Law 15 of 1922; Law 16 of 1935; Law 10 of 1936; Law 55 of 1944.) Kingston: Government Printing Office, 1890–1944.

Ministry of Tourism. *"Travel Statistics—Jamaica."* Mimeograph. Kingston, 1980–90.

Minutes of the Legislative Council of Jamaica. Kingston: Government Printing Office, 1870–72, 1889–1900.

Report by the Central Board of Health. Presented to the Legislature under the Provisions of the 14th Vic. Chap. 60, and Printed by Order of the Assembly. Spanish Town, 1852.

Reports from the Consuls of the United States. Washington, D.C.: Government Printing Office, 1880–93.

Scott, James (Commissioner of Health). *Papers Relating to the Present Sanitary State of Kingston.* Kingston, 1874.

Supplement to the Jamaica Gazette. Kingston: Government Printing Office, 1903–11.

Tourist Trade Development Board. *Report and Accounts for Financial Year.* Kingston: Government Printing Office, 1922–39.

————. *Interim Report on Post-War Tourist Trade Development in Jamaica.* Kingston, 1944.

Tourist Trade Development Board and the Tourist Trade Convention Committee. *Survey and Report on the Potentialities of the Tourist Industry in Jamaica, With Recommendations for Post-War Development.* Kingston: Government Printer, 1945.

NEWSPAPERS, 1890–1914

Colonial Standard and Jamaica Despatch, January 1889–June 1895.

Daily Chronicle, June 1913–March 1914.

Daily Gleaner and De Cordova's, January–June 1901.

Daily Gleaner, January–June 1905, January–June 1913.

Daily News, December 1910–June 1911.

Daily Telegraph and Jamaica Guardian, September 1911–June 1912.

Gall's News Letter, January 1889–March 1899.

Jamaica Advocate, January 1900–December 1905.

Jamaica Daily Telegraph and Anglo-American Herald, January 1903–March 1909.

Jamaica Guardian, January–December 1909.

Jamaica Post, January 1890–April 1899.

Jamaica Times, November 1898–December 1914.

Leader, January–July 1904.

Telegraph and Guardian, January 1910–September 1911.

Tri-weekly Budget, March 1890–December, 1892.

NEWSPAPERS, 1919–1990

Daily Gleaner, January 1919–December 1990 (scattered issues).

Herald, September 1922–June 1928.

Jamaica Daily News. November 1973–January 1983 (scattered issues).

Jamaica Labour Weekly, September 1938.

Jamaica Mail, September 1926.

Jamaica Times, May 1920–December 1935.

Northern News and Provincial Advertiser, January 1926–June 1929.

Public Opinion, April 1937–September 1940.

TRAVEL LITERATURE AND DESCRIPTIVE WORKS

Abrahams, Peter, *Jamaica: An Island Mosaic.* London: Her Majesty's Stationery Office, 1957.

Amphlett, John. *Under a Tropical Sky: A Journal of First Impressions of the West Indies.* London, 1873.

Anderson, William Wemyss. *A Description and History of the Island of Jamaica, Comprising an Account of Its Soil, Climate, and Productions, Showing Its Value and Importance as an Agricultural Country, and a Desirable Place of Residence for Certain Classes of Settlers, Reprinted (It is Believed for the First Time), from the Great Work, "An Account of America, or the New World," by John Ogilby, Esq., Master of Revels in Ireland: First Published in the Year 1671, with Preliminary Chapter and Notes, to Connect the Work with Our Times.* London and New York, 1851.

———. *Jamaica and the Americans.* New York, 1851.

Bacon, Edgar Mayhew, and Aaron, Eugene Murray. *The New Jamaica: Describing the Island, Explaining Its Conditions of Life and Growth and Discussing Its Mercantile Relations and Potential Importance: Adding Somewhat in Relation to Those Matters Which Directly Interest the Tourist and the Health Seeker.* New York, 1890.

Baird, Robert. *Impressions and Experiences of the West Indies and North America in 1849.* London, 1850.

Bellows, W. *In Fair Jamaica.* Kingston: Educational Supply, 1907.

Bradford, Mary F. *Side Trips in Jamaica.* Boston and New York: Sherwood Publishing, 1902.

Bullen, Frank T. *Back to Sunny Seas.* London: Macmillan, 1905.

Butcher, T. B. *A Peep at Jamaica and Its People.* London: Charles H. Kelly, n.d. [1902?].

Caffin, Mabel Blanche. *A Jamaica Outing.* Boston, 1899.

Caine, W. R. H. *The Cruise of the Port Kingston.* London: Collier, 1908.

Chapman, Esther, ed. *Pleasure Island: The Book of Jamaica.* Jamaica: Arawak Press, 1958.

Cornish, Vaughan. *The Travels of Ellen Cornish: Being the Memoir of a Pilgrim of Science.* London: W. J. Ham-Smith, 1913.

Cundall, Frank, ed. *Jamaica in 1895, a Handbook of Information for Intending Settlers and Others.* Kingston, 1895.

DeLisser, Herbert George. *In Jamaica and Cuba.* Kingston: Gleaner, 1910.

———. *Twentieth Century Jamaica.* Kingston: the Jamaica Times, 1913.

Dennys, N. B., *An Account of the Cruise of the St. George on the North American and West Indian Station, During the Years 1861–62.* London, 1862.

De Souza, Mortimer C. *A Tourists Guide to the Parishes of Jamaica. Together with an Account Descriptive of the Jamaica Exhibition.* Kingston, 1891.

———. *Jamaica: The Land of Perpetual Sunshine . . . .* Kingston: De Souza, 1912–1913.

Dodsworth, Francis, ed. *The Book of Jamaica.* Kingston: Sollas and Cocking, 1904.

Eric, Allan. (Charles W. Willis.) *Buckra Land, Two Weeks in Jamaica. Details of a Voyage to the West Indies, Day by Day, and a Tour of Jamaica, Step by Step.* Boston, 1897.

Hale, W. H. *The Island of Jamaica: An Illustrated Lecture* (cover title: *Jamaica: An Illustrated Tour of the Island.*) Boston: United Fruit, 1914.

Henderson, John. *Jamaica: Painted by A. S. Forrest.* London: Adam and Charles Black, 1906.

Hotel Rio Cobre, Spanish Town, Jamaica. Jamaica: Aston W. Gardner, 1893.

Howe, E. W. *The Trip to the West Indies.* Topeka, Kan.: Crane, 1910.

Jamaica Times. The Jamaica Times Tourist Guide: The Island of Jamaica. Kingston: Times Printery, 1909.

Jamaica Tourist Association. *Guide Issued by the Jamaica Tourist Association.* (Issues 1911–1915 consulted. Title varies slightly in some years.)

James, Winnifred. *The Mulberry Tree.* London: Chapman and Hall, 1913.

Johnston, Harry. *The Negro in the New World.* London: Methuen, 1910.

Johnston, Jas [James]. *Jamaica, the New Riviera: A Pictorial Description of the Island and Its Attractions.* London: Cassel, 1903.

Leader, Alfred. *Through Jamaica with a Kodak.* London: Simpkin Marshall, 1907.

Marly: Or, a Planter's Life in Jamaica. Glasgow, 1828.

Matthewan, L. "Summering in Winter." *The Era: A Monthly Magazine of Literature* 10, no. 6 (December 1902).

Mills, I. P., ed. *Jamaica Tourist and Motor Guide: A Complete Guide to the Island of Jamaica, with Maps Showing Motor Routes, Illustrations, History, Points of Interest, Descriptions of Towns, Hotels, Methods of Travel, etc.* Boston: Ainslie and Grabow, 1908.

Needham, Charles K. "A Comparison of Some Conditions in Jamaica with Those in the United States." *Journal of Race Relations* 4, no. 1 (October 1913).

Olley, P., ed. *Guide to Jamaica.* Kingston: Tourist Trade Development Board, 1937.

Overend, R. M., and Overend, Walker. *Wintering for Invalids in the West Indies.* London: Spottiswoode, 1910.

Pullen-Burry, Bessie. *Jamaica As It Is, 1903.* London: Unwin, 1903.

———. *Ethiopia in Exile: Jamaica Revisited.* London: Unwin, 1905.

Rampini, J. G. *Letters from Jamaica, the Land of Streams and Woods.* Edinburgh: 1873.

Reinhardt, Charles. "Jamaica for Health and Pleasure." *Health Resort* (November 1903). (Photocopy at the Jamaica Public Library.)

Robertson, F. H. *Tourism, Facts and Other Information on the Tourist Industry in Jamaica and Other Countries.* Kingston, 1943.

Scott, Sibbald David. *To Jamaica and Back.* London, 1876.

Sewell, William G. *The Ordeal of Free Labor in the British West Indies.* London: Frank Cass, 1968. (A new impression of the 1862 second edition.)

[Stewart, J.] *An Account of Jamaica and Its Inhabitants, by a Gentleman Long Resident in the West Indies.* London, 1808.

Symmonett, Ethel Maud. *Jamaica: Queen of the Carib Sea.* Jamaica: De Souza, 1895.

Tatchell, Frank. *The Happy Traveller: A Book for Poor Men.* 4th ed. London: Methuen, 1924.

Trollope, Anthony. *The West Indies and the Spanish Main.* London, 1860.

Vaquero (pseudonym). *Life and Adventure in the West Indies. A Sequel to Adventures in Search of a Living in Spanish-America.* London: John Bale, Sons and Danielsson, 1914.

Villiers-Stuart, H. *Adventures Amidst the Equatorial Forest and Rivers of South America; also in the West Indies and the Wilds of Florida. To Which is added "Jamaica Revisited."* London, 1891.

Wilcox, Ella Wheeler. *Sailing Sunny Seas.* Chicago: Conkey, 1909.

A Winter in the West Indies and Florida: Containing General Observations upon Modes of Travelling, Manners and Customs, Climates and Productions, with a Particular Description of St. Croix, Trinidad de Cuba, Key West, and St. Augustine as Places of Resort by Northern Invalids. New York, 1839.

WORKS ON
EARLY PUBLIC HEALTH

Anderson, Izett. *Yellow Fever in the West Indies.* London, 1898.

Bancroft, Edward Nathaniel. *An Essay on the Disease Called Yellow Fever, with Observations Concerning Febrile Contagion, Typhus Fever, Dysentery, and the Plague, Partly Delivered as the Gulstonian Lectures before the College of Physicians in the Years 1806 and 1807.* London, 1811.

———. *A Sequel to an Essay on the Yellow Fever; Principally Intended to Prove, by Incontestable Facts and Important Documents that the Fever called Bulam, or Pestilential, has no Existence as a Distinct or Contagious Disease.* London, 1817.

Bone, George Frederick. *Inaugural Dissertation on Yellow Fever and on the Treatment of That Disease by Saline Medicines. With an Appendix (by Hugh Bone, M.D.) on the Principles to be Observed in Providing Barracks and Hospitals for Troops in the West Indies.* London, 1846.

Boyce, Sir Rupert William. *Health Progress and Administration in the West Indies.* London: Murray, 1910.

———. *Mosquito or Man? The Conquest of the Tropical World.* 3d ed. London: Murray, 1910.

Epitomes or Extracts of Letters in Answer to the Circular of the Society for Promoting Sanitary, Educational, Moral and Social Remedial Measures, Soliciting Information on the Sanitary State of the Island, Especially the Country Districts, and Remedial Suggestions. With introductory and explanatory notes by Bayly Kingdon. N.p., 1859 (?).

Hunter, John. *Observations on the Diseases of the Army in Jamaica: and on the Best Means of Preserving the Health of Europeans, in That Climate.* London, 1788.

King, Reverend David. *The State and Prospects of Jamaica: With Appended*

Remarks on Its Advantages for the Cure of Pulmonary Diseases, and Suggestions to Invalids and Others Going to That Colony. London, 1850.

Lempriere, William. *Practical Observations on the Diseases of the Army in Jamaica, as They Occurred between the Years 1792 and 1797; on the Situation, Climate, and Diseases of That Island; and on the Most Probable Means of Lessening Mortality among the Troops, and among the Europeans in Tropical Climates.* 2 vols. London, 1799.

Maunsell, S. E. *Contribution to the Medico-Military History of Jamaica: A "Retrospect," (An Expansion of a Paper Read before the Jamaica Branch of the British Medical Association, Kingston).* Jamaica, 1891.

The Memorial of the Society for Promoting Educational, Sanitary, Social and Moral Remedial Measures, Presented to His Excellency the Governor of Jamaica . . . on Friday November 27th, 1857, and Published by His Excellency's Permission.

Phillippo, James. *The Climate of Jamaica.* London, 1876.

Prout, W. T. "Malaria." *Annals of Tropical Medicine and Parasitology,* series T.M., vol. 3, no. 4 (17 November 1909).

Scott, H. Harold. *A History of Tropical Medicine. Based on the Fitzpatrick Lectures Delivered before the Royal College of Physicians of London 1937–38.* 2 vols. London: Edward Arnold, 1939.

Thomas, Elizabeth. "Quarantine in Old Jamaica." *Caribbean Studies* 4, no. 4 (January 1965).

OTHER WORKS

Barry, Tom, Wood, Beth, and Preusch, Deb. *The Other Side of Paradise: Foreign Control in the Caribbean.* New York: Grove, 1984.

Bouman, L. F. *K.L.M.'s Caribbean Decade: The Story of the Operations of Royal Dutch Airlines in the West Indies since 1934.* New York: Rogers-Kellogg-Stillson, 1944.

Bryden, John. *Tourism and Development: A Case Study of the Commonwealth Caribbean.* London: Cambridge University Press, 1973.

Burkart, A., and Medlick, S. *Tourism: Past, Present and Future.* London: Heinemann, 1974.

Caribbean Commission. *Caribbean Tourist Trade—A Regional Approach.* Port of Spain, Trinidad, 1945.

Chen-Young, Paul. "Tourism in the Economic Development of Small Economies: Jamaica's Experience." In *Problems and Policies in Small Economies,* edited by B. Jalan. New York: St. Martin's 1982.

Cumper, George. "Tourist Expenditure in Jamaica, 1959." *Social and Economic Studies* 8, no. 3 (September 1959).

Eisner, Gisela. *Jamaica, 1830-1930: A Study in Economic Growth.* London: Manchester University Press, 1961.

Floyd, Barry. "The Two Faces of Jamaica: Dual Standards in A Subtropical Tourist Mecca." *Geographical Magazine* 46, no. 8, (May 1974).

Hall, Douglas. *Ideas and Illustrations in Economic History.* New York: Holt, Rinehart and Winston, 1964.

————. "The Colonial Legacy in Jamaica." *New World Quarterly* 4, no. 3 (High Season 1968).

The Handbook of Jamaica . . . Comprising Historical, Statistical and General Information Concerning the Island. Compiled from Official and Other Reliable Records. Kingston: Government Printing Office, 1890–1940.

Hart, Ansell. "The Banana in Jamaica's Export Trade." *Social and Economic Studies* 3, no. 2 (September 1954).

Hawkins, Irene. *The Changing Face of the Caribbean.* Barbados: Cedar, 1976.

Hiller, Herbert. "Escapism, Penetration and Response: Industrial Tourism and the Caribbean." *Caribbean Studies* 16, no. 2 (July 1976).

Holder, Jean, comp. *Caribbean Tourism: Policies and Impacts. Selected Speeches and Papers.* Barbados: Caribbean Tourism Research Center, May 1979.

The "Hotels Scheme" Examined . . . Supplemented by Remarks on the Railway. Kingston, 1893.

Hudson, Brian. "The End of Paradise. What Kind of Development for Negril?" *Caribbean Review* 8, no. 3 (Summer 1979).

Jamaica Exhibition Bulletin 1, no. 8 (28 June 1890).

Jefferson, Owen. *The Post-War Economic Development of Jamaica.* Kingston: Institute of Social and Economic Studies, University of the West Indies, 1972.

Kaufman, Michael. *Jamaica Under Manley: Dilemmas of Socialism and Democracy.* London: Zed, 1985.

Long, Edward. *The History of Jamaica, Or General Survey of the Ancient and Modern State of That Island: With Reflections on Its Situation, Settlement, Inhabitants, Climate, Products, Commerce, Laws and Government.* 3 vols. London, 1774.

Lowenthal, David. *West Indian Societies.* London: Oxford University Press, 1972.

McKay, Lesley. "Tourism and Changing Attitudes to Land in Negril, Jamaica." In *Land and Development in the Caribbean,* edited by Jean

Besson and Janet Momsen. Warwick University Caribbean Studies, 1987.

Manley, Michael. *Jamaica: Struggle in the Periphery.* London: Third World Media, n.d.

Meikle, Louis S. *Confederation of the British West Indies versus Annexation to the United States of America: A Political Discourse on the West Indies.* London: Sampson, Low, Marston, 1912.

Olivier, Sydney. *Jamaica, the Blessed Island.* London: Faber and Faber, 1936.

————. "Recent Developments in Jamaica. Internal and External." *Journal of the Royal Society of Arts* 64, no. 3,291 (17 December 1915).

Olley, Philip. "The Tourist Trade of Jamaica: Why It Should Be Developed." *Jamaica Review* 1, nos. 1–3 (August–October 1925).

Pearson, Ross. "The Geography of Recreation on a Tropical Island: Jamaica." *Journal of Geography* 56 (January 1957).

Pim, Bedford. *The Negro and Jamaica. Read before the Anthropological Society of London, February 1, 1866, at St. James Hall, London.* London, 1866.

Prize Essays Containing Suggestions as to the Opening Up and Development of Trade between Bristol and Jamaica. Liverpool: Philip, Son and Nephew, n.d. [1900?].

Rankin, Norman S. "Jamaica, Past and Present." *Canadian Magazine of Politics, Science, Art and Literature* 11 (1898).

Stone, Carl. "A Socio-Economic Study of the Tourism Industry in Jamaica." *Caribbean Affairs* 4, no. 1 (January–March 1991).

Tourism in the Caribbean: Essays on Problems in Connection with Its Promotion. Netherlands: Royal Van Gorcum, 1963.

Turner Louis. "The International Division of Leisure: Tourism and the Third World." *World Development* 4, no. 3 (March 1976).

Turner, Louis, and Ash, John. *The Golden Hordes: International Tourism and the Pleasure Periphery.* New York: St. Martin's, 1976.

Voyles, Robert. *The Tourist Industry in the Caribbean Islands.* Area Development Series no. 6. Miami: Bureau of Business and Economic Research, University of Miami, 1956.

Williams, Eric. *Capitalism and Slavery.* London: Andre Deutsch, 1964.

Wilson, Reverend C. A. *Men with Backbone, and Other Pleas for Progress.* Kingston: Educational Supply, 1913.

Index

Advertising, for tourism: campaign of, after 1870s, 55; censorship of, 117–18; cost of, 142; debate over public funding for, 142–43; erotic messages of, 172, 174; foundation of bureau for, 113–15, 123; government indifference toward, 113–15, 122, 124; government support for, 121, 126, 142–43; importance of, 81; by Jamaica Tourist Association, 126–33; by Jamaica Tourist Board, 140, 164, 166–67, 174, 177, 180; and promotion of Jamaica as health spa, 13, 20, 27, 29, 31–35; racist sterotypes in, 174–75; regulation of, 117–18; slow beginnings of, 81, 113–15, 124–33
Air travel, 154–59, 162–63, 166
American Airlines, 167
American Hotel and Motel Association, 177
American Hotels Company, 75
Amphlett, John, 69
Anderson, William, 27, 29–31
Anglo-American Caribbean Commission, 165
Arab-Israeli war (1973), 183
Avensa, 158
Avianca, 158

Bahamas, 4, 29–30, 72–73, 120
Baird, Robert, 20
Baker, Eugene, 61
Baker, Lorenzo D., 40, 42–43, 46, 48, 50–51, 53–54, 109
Banana export industry: attempt to extend to Great Britain, 84; cultivation of, 37–39; and government encouragement of white property ownership, 104; and hurricane of 1903, 122; Jones's failure in, 130;

monopolistic practices of, 41–42, 48; as origin of Jamaican tourism, 37–38, 46, 48, 50–51; risks of, 41–42; seasonality of, 52; and U.S. market, 6–7, 39–40, 109
Barbados, 4, 29–30, 112, 120, 160
Barker, Herbert, 14
Beach Control Authority, 170
Beaches, 140–41, 169–71, 180, 187
Beauperthy, Louis Daniel, 24
Begging, 107–08, 118–19, 153
Bermuda, 112, 120
Blacks: advertised as "primitives," 116; alleged docility of, 115–16; alleged poor manners of, 108; alleged sexual harmlessness of, 115; beaches closed to, 148–52; as beggars, 107–08, 118–19; discriminated against as steamship passengers, 147; emigration of, 107; growing political power of, 99–104; hostility toward hotel service among, 69, 89–93, 175; inadequate housing for, 104–05, 107; as innkeepers, before 1890, 69; poverty among, 107; as proportion of population in colonial times, 98–99; racist stereotypes of, 105–07, 115–18, 174–75; and resentment of U.S. racism, 7–9, 36, 69, 110; self-sufficiency of, 38–39; as victims of hotel industry, 112. See also Emancipation; Race relations; Racism; Slavery; Whites
Blake, Henry, 55, 59, 62, 73, 81, 121
Blue Mountains, 86
BOAC. See British Overseas Airways Corporation
Bone, George, 17, 19
Boston Fruit Co., 37
Bowden Hotel, 89
Bowlan, Charles, 110

233